Also by Bill Neal
Bill Neal's Southern Cooking

BISCUITS · SPOONBREAD · AND · SWEET · POTATO · PIE

BISCUITS · SPOONBREAD · AND · SWEET · POTATO · PIE

by Bill Neal

Alfred A. Knopf • New York • 1991

Library of Congress Cataloging-in-Publication Data

Neal, Bill.
    Biscuits, spoonbread, and sweet potato pie
    by Bill Neal. — 1st ed.
        p.   cm.
    Includes index.
    ISBN 0-394-55941-X
    1. Baking.   2. Confectionery.   3. Cookery,
American — Southern style.   1. Title.
TX763.N33   1990
641.7'1 — dc20   *89-33148 CIP*

Manufactured in the United States of America
Published June 27, 1990
Reprinted Twice
Fourth Printing, December 1991

This book is for Maxine Mills and Matthew Neal

CONTENTS

INTRODUCTION

This book of recipes is about the breads and sweets that have been the pride of Southern cooks for over three hundred years. It is for those cooks today, both Southern and non-Southern, who love the yeasty smell of rising dough, the on hands relationship with the foods they eat, the joy of finding the season's best produce in the market. It is a Southern trait to have a story for every occasion, and almost every recipe in this book has a little preface or explanation about how that dish is part of my life or part of the life of the region. When I cook, I am constantly telling my children something like "This is your grandmother's biscuit." I mean it isn't just something to fill up their stomachs; it's part of the way crafts, traditions, and cultures have been perpetuated for thousands of years — one generation teaching the next. Almost everyone has a special recipe from a grandmother or an aunt that means more than how it tastes. All the recipes of this book belong to that kind of heritage. They will belong to the future as we cook them and share them with those we love.

I grew up eating the foods that an independent Southern farmer would have eaten one or even two hundred years ago: home-baked breads mostly of cornmeal, beans, and squashes of all sorts; lots of pork, both fresh and cured; fresh milk and butter. It was wonderful food — seasonal, plentiful, and mostly produced at home. We grew vegetables almost year-round, and even in the dead of winter there were spicy wild field cresses for a pot of greens. My grandparents kept livestock — pigs, milk cows, mules for plowing, and chickens that scratched the earth, ate corn, and gave eggs with yolks as brilliant as a setting sun. It seemed as if our whole world was about food: growing, gathering, and preparing it. Almost everything that went onto our table had the input of three generations' work and care. I am amazed today when I think of the array of fruits and berries that we picked as children. Blackberries from neglected pastures; wild plums, persimmons, and muscadines from the woods; cherries, peaches, and apples from our small orchard and pears from the neighbors'; and figs from the tree that grew behind the smokehouse. It was a staggering harvest that didn't seem to daunt my mother or grandmothers. They turned out pies, cakes, cobblers, and ice creams almost daily from what we brought in. And the intense aromas of fruits reducing for jams and jellies were the perfume of the kitchen. It was a life as idyllic for children as it was tenuous and exhausting for adults.

By the time I was six or so, that way of life began to disappear. My father turned to manufacturing for his income. We still kept a garden but no longer raised so much of our food. When I was about four, I earned my first quarter for hoeing my father's cotton. By the time I was twelve, much of that cotton field was under the asphalt of an interstate highway, and the rest of the field was the site of a factory producing synthetic fibers. Such changes have eroded the traditional rural life of the South for over one hundred years. Eudora Welty poignantly expressed this sense of loss in *The Wanderers* (1949).

> Later, back in the parlor, she cried. They said, "She used to set out yonder and sell muscadines, see out there? There's where she got rid of all her plums, the early and late, blackberries and dewberries, and the little peanuts you boil. Now the road goes the wrong way." Though that was like a sad song, it was not true: the road still went the same, from Morgana to McLain, from Morgana to Vicksburg and Jackson, of course. Only now the wrong people went by on it. They were all riding trucks, very fast or heavily loaded, and carrying blades and chains, to chop and haul the trees to mill. They were not eaters of muscadines, and did not stop to pass words on the season and what grew. And the vines had dried. She wept because they could not tell it right, and they didn't press for her reasons.

The sad theme of loss runs through all of Southern culture from way back. The black spirituals and blues are its musical expression. But its countertheme is endurance. Today, Southerners are more and more aware of their traditional foods as the rest of their culture blends into that of the nation as a whole. Certain dishes give identity to entire communities. Yearly, thousands of people flock to small towns all over the South for festivals in honor of such lowly foodstuffs as chitlins, ramps, and collards. A few years ago, most Southerners wouldn't admit to still eating these foods. Now we see bumper stickers directing us to "Eat more possum." It isn't just a joke. We know we are Southerners because we do eat possum and grits and okra. When we no longer eat these foods, we no longer will be Southerners. Our diet reflects the history of the region and its people: Native Americans, Europeans, and Africans. Our food tells us where we came from and who we have become.

All Southerners, Indian and black and white, have shared the basic diet of beans and corn. It is the original diet of this hemisphere, the core of Southern as well as Caribbean and Central American cooking. When outsiders ask "What is Southern cooking?" I think they don't look far south enough for the answers. Our style is more similar to Mexican than to European cooking. I can't imagine a Southern kitchen without cornmeal, and our breads begin with it.

Many of our dishes are European. Some passed directly into the tradition with little or no change. Wine jellies, trifles, and fruitcakes are scarcely distinguishable from their eighteenth-century British ancestors. Other European techniques are adapted to native ingredients: French tortes made with the native pecans, crumpets made with grits, custard pies thickened with cornmeal. This hybrid cooking is the most intriguing to me; it reveals the ingenuity and creativity of the Southern cook combining Old World practices and New World foods.

The third major, and most exotic, influence is African. Our sweet potato biscuits, for example, are in the African tradition of using starchy tubers rather than milled cereal grains to make bread. The peoples of the West Indies and the South prepared their breads not only from yams, but from cassava, manioc, tanyah, and arrowroot. And they brought from their homelands techniques for working with sugar in a hot, humid climate which influenced the way we make candies and confections.

The first published recipes that are recognizably Southern, incorporating these three cultural influences, come to us from three nineteenth-century books: *The Virginia House-wife, The Kentucky Housewife,* and *The Carolina Housewife.* Mary Randolph, who was of a distinguished family and a relation by marriage of Thomas Jefferson, published *The Virginia House-wife* in 1824. In her mid-forties, after losing a secure income, she opened a boarding house in Richmond, which was celebrated for its splendid meals. Mrs. Randolph's taste ran much to the Continental; her collection of recipes sometimes reminds me of Patrick Henry's remark about Mr. Jefferson: "[he] came home from France so Frenchified that he abjured his native victuals." Mrs. Lettice Bryan's *The Kentucky Housewife* (1839) is more down to earth. She knows the frontier and has practical instructions on open-fire cooking, as well as offering detailed descriptions for formal entertaining. Sarah Rutledge, sophisticated and rich, compiled the most important collection of Southern recipes we have, *The Carolina Housewife* (1847). Her recipes reflect the cooking of all levels of society, from the plantation foods to those directly from the African tradition. Many of her dishes have long since disappeared from the home kitchen, as is true of those of Mrs. Randolph's and Mrs. Bryan's, but without these three "housewives," a reconstruction of the historical cooking of the South would be sadly incomplete. When I don't have recipes drawn from my own experience, the three housewives provide a source and inspiration for recreating the cooking of yesterday.

All this background may seem rather abstruse stuff if we forget that the origins of Southern cooking were dynamic, extemporaneous, and creative. One aspect of cooking—and an impetus to it I've not yet mentioned—is the force of hospitality in the South; here it is a moral obligation of the host to feed the guest. The tradition is ancient and echoes Homer in *The Odyssey* when Eumaios welcomes the unknown and shipwrecked Odysseus: "Strangers and beggars come from Zeus: a small gift, then, is friendly. Give our new guest some food and drink. . . . " How much more do we owe those we love and who gather together at our table daily? I invite you to cook these recipes in that spirit and in the spirit in which they were first created, foods to nourish the heart and soul as well as the body.

ACKNOWLEDGMENTS

❦ My thanks are due to

Barbara Tolley

Gene Hamer

Seymour Zimmerman

Martha Collett

Frank Mellon

Tom Kenan

Patricia Owens

Lee Smith

Daphne Athas

Molly Renda

William Warner

Hoppin' John Taylor

My gratitude to Caulie Gunnells cannot be measured.

Also, Mr. John White of the Southern Historical Collection, Mr. Jerry Cotten of the North Carolina Collection, both at Wilson Library, the University of North Carolina at Chapel Hill; and Mr. Roger Jones of the North Carolina Department of Cultural Resources, Raleigh.

• • • • • • • • • • •

Finally, I have cooked for four people especially during the course of making this book. They are my severest critics, the ones I value most, and the best reasons I know to cook for:

Madeline Neal

Elliott Neal

Amanda Bryan

Taylor Bryan

THE · GIFT · OF · CORN
BREADS, DUMPLINGS, PANCAKES, AND FRITTERS

Hushpuppies
Delta Dogs
Corn Crisp
Sweet Potato Crisp
Sweet Potato Corn Cake
Red Pepper Corn Cake
Corn Light Bread
Light Corn Bread
St. Charles Indian Bread
Appalachian Corn Bread
Company Corn Bread
Souffléed Corn Bread
Mexican Corn Bread
Green Corn Bread
Blueberry Corn Cake
Awendaw

Plain Cooked Grits

Mush Bread

Virginia Spoonbread

Farm-Style Spoonbread

American Bean Bread

Bean Cakes

CORN

Their Provision which grows in the Field is chiefly Indian Corn, which produces a vast Increase, yearly, yielding Two plentiful Harvests, of which they make wholesome Bread, and good Bisket, which gives a strong, sound, and nourishing Diet; with Milk I have eaten it dress'd various ways: Of the Juice of the Corn, when green, the Spaniards with Chocolet, aromatiz'd with Spices, make a rare Drink of an excellent Delicacy. I have seen the English amongst the Caribbes roast the green Ear on the Coals, and eat it with a great deal of Pleasure. The Indians in Carolina parch the ripe Corn, then pound it to a Powder, putting it in a leathern Bag: When they use it, they take a little quantity of the Powder in the Palms of their Hands, mixing it with Water, and sup it off: with this they will travel several days. In short, it's a Grain of General Use to Man and Beast, many thousands of both kinds in the West Indies having from it the greater part of their Subsistence. The American Physicians observe that it breeds good Blood, removes and opens Oppellations and Obstructions. At Carolina they have lately invented a way of makeing with it good sound Beer; but it's strong and heady: By Maceration, when duly fermented, a strong Spirit like Brandy may be drawn off from it, by the help of an Alembrick.
—Thomas Ashe, *Carolina, or a Description of the Present State of that Country*, 1682

For thousands of years, corn was the staff of life in the western hemisphere, and today, its prevalence is the most recognizable feature of Southern cooking. Unlike the baking of the rest of the country, which is based on wheat flour, our breads start with cornmeal: ashcakes, hoecakes, dodgers, hushpuppies, spoonbread. The list goes on and on, as do our memories of them. All these breads are homemade, cooked for the family. Commercial bakeries have never much figured in the foodways of the South. We all grew up with the aroma of baking breads in the kitchen. And with the sound: When my grandmother made corn bread, she first rendered a bit of pork fat in a cast-iron skillet and then poured the batter in. Such a sizzle! And I learned early on that the sound of good cooking was almost as important as the smell and taste. What I learned later was that corn and corn breads can tell in large part the history of our region, both before and after any member of my family came to these shores.

By the time the English attempted settlement on the Eastern seaboard, corn was well known in Europe. Columbus's sailors had found both corn and tobacco on the same day in 1492 in the West Indies. Though Columbus seems to have taken little notice of the grain, he evidently spoke of it to Peter Martyr, an Italian scholar at the Spanish court who published one of the first accounts of the New World. In 1511, Martyr unmistakably described corn for the first time to Europeans; in 1516, he created a Latin name for it — *maizium.* Maize, as most of the world knows corn, probably comes from a West Indian word, *mahiz;* the Aztecs called the grain *tlaolli;* the Incas, *sara* or *zara;* southeast coastal natives, *pegatowr.* All these native names connote the idea of a universal mother goddess or a life-sustaining force. A force it was — in agriculture, as well as in medicine and religion. The native economy revolved around the value of the crop; it could be passed as currency anywhere in the hemisphere. Later Spanish, Portuguese, and French explorers gave unusually full reports of the importance of the grain in the American southeast. By the time of the first English account of corn and its culture — in 1586 — corn literature was almost one hundred years old. Despite the early attempts by the Spanish court to limit knowledge of their New World discoveries, news of corn had spread throughout Europe.

So the English settlers could have known a great deal about corn even before they set sail westward. When they arrived, the earliest colonists of Carolina and Virginia found corn along with beans and squashes the basis of the native diet. The coastal Indians lived in established villages with adjacent fields cleared for crops. These settlements were sometimes sold outright to the European newcomers. In Maryland, the Calvert community was one such beneficiary, when it bought an entire town with its cultivated land from the natives. Many native uses of corn were adopted, too. Corn was consumed green as a vegetable, dried as a boiled grain, and ground as a flour for breads, dumplings, and tortillas. Sugar from the sap of certain corn varieties was extracted for a sweet. The Cherokees made a fermented drink they later wrote as Gv-No-He-Nv. Sharing the drink was the central ritual of their hospitality. Corn silks were medicinal, as were ashes from the cobs, which were used for fuel. Houses were built from the stalks; in 1983, in the remote highlands of Mexico, I saw entire villages built primarily of cornstalks. That construction had gone on in the southeast, too, practiced by blacks and whites as well as natives. A popular nineteenth-century song went

On Tom-Big-Bee River
so bright I was born,

in a hut made of husks
ob de tall yaller corn.

The link between man and corn is more than economical — and even more than historical. It is mysterious. Corn has been cultivated for almost six thousand documented years, perhaps far, far longer. Yet no wild corn exists today and no fossil evidence for a wild form has been found. All corn is dependent on man's cultivation, and most scientists agree that it would take only three generations of neglect for it to become extinct. At the same time, man in this hemisphere could not have survived without corn. This bond is expressed repeatedly in religion. In Mexico today, women take the corn seed to the priest for blessing on May fifteenth, the feast day of San Isidro. Mexican men engage in their own rituals when they plant. While making the sign of the cross, they drop seeds and chant prayers such as, "God bless you. I bury you and if you return while I still live the satisfaction will be mine; if not, then my descendants." The promise of the Christian resurrection has been completely incorporated into the traditional planting rituals. In North America, the early English settlers linked the corn crop to their religion as well. As a result, we celebrate the harvest of corn at Thanksgiving.

In 1796, the first cookbook written by an American was published, Amelia Simmon's *American Cookery*. She gave the earliest recipes calling for Indian meal, as cornmeal was then known. The first published Southern recipes, which appeared in Mary Randolph's *The Virginia House-wife* of 1824, for polenta and mush along with a hominy johnnycake, a cornmeal bread, and a couple of Indian puddings are a meager contribution to cornmeal cooking. Mrs. Lettice Bryan in *The Kentucky Housewife* (1839) offered a much expanded slate with recipes for muffins, batter cakes, yeast-raised loaves, and even yeast itself, all made from the native grain. But it is Sarah Rutledge's *The Carolina Housewife* of 1847 that is the first Southern cookbook to reflect accurately the importance of the native grain in bread preparation. Her observations form one of the most important statements on Southern cooking. She calls for corn products in forty bread recipes of all types, from spoonbreads to waffles.

All these early Southern cooks were using whole-grain corn, stoneground. The relatively high moisture and oil content of the flour necessitated quick consumption before it turned rancid. Whole-grain milling still takes place in the traditional mountain communities of the South. A family may grind one or two bushels of corn at a time for home use. The mills are usually gasoline or diesel powered these days, and are operated rather erratically for neighbors and friends. A few water-powered grist mills, which are often tourist attractions or an indulgence on the part of the miller, are in operation throughout the South. The products of these mills are almost without exception superb and meant, as in the early days, for immediate use. The grind is usually irregular and slow to absorb liquid. Thus many old recipes call for meal that has been partially cooked before assembling the complete batter, or they instruct you to beat the batter very hard for a long time. Mrs. Bryan, particularly, advocates the violent route.

We drive seventy miles to get cornmeal and grits, which have been ground continuously for two hundred years at the Old Mill of Guilford. Mr. and Mrs. Charles Parnell, the millers, ship their fine traditional products all over the globe. (Their address is 1340 N.C. 68 North, Oak Ridge, North Carolina 27310.) But whole-grain, stone-ground cornmeal is superior only as long as it is fresh. Otherwise, any grocery store brand may do. Because all brands of cornmeal vary significantly and all batches of stone-ground meal vary one from the other, you will have to experiment a little to correct the grind for each recipe. Southerners generally prefer white cornmeal but yellow is interchangeable.

Another versatile corn product is hominy, which is whole-grain, dried corn, traditionally soaked in a lye solution made from wood ashes to rid it of its outer husk. The kernels may be prepared as a starchy vegetable. Canned hominy is found in grocery stores all over the South, as well as in northern cities with large black populations. Pozole (whole-grain dried hominy) can be bought in cities with Latin American markets. Grits are ground dried corn or hominy, and they must be cooked slowly for a long time. Instant and quick grits are inferior and do not belong in any discerning cook's pantry. If you have any of the excellent Low Country Carolina recipe collections, always remember that what is hominy there is cooked grits to the rest of us Southerners.

INDIAN CORN

Corn grows majestically in the highland valleys of western North Carolina where the Cherokees preserve their ancient traditions. A Cherokee woman
pounds the dried grain in a hollowed-out tree stump with a marvelously balanced
and heavily weighted pestle. She sifts the meal by hand, the finest for breads,
coarser meal for cereals and stews. A family portrait includes the traditional
hand-hewn wooden bread trays that are passed from one generation to the next
and are still much used and prized throughout the South.

Cornmeal Dumplings

Cornmeal dumplings are about as close as we get to native cooking in our kitchens. The earliest English settlers of coastal Virginia and North Carolina learned to make them from the Indians, and the technique has persevered in Southern cooking for almost four hundred years. Dumplings cook quickly in liquid and are used to complete stews and soups, one-pot meals similar to the native dishes once simmered in pottery over open fires.

Nowadays, the dumplings most often go into a pot of greens — mustard, turnip, collards, kale — well seasoned with pork side meat (fatty cuts such as jowl, pork belly, or streak-of-lean). They also go into vegetable soups. In early spring I cook them in rich chicken broth, then throw in a great handful of thinly sliced scallions and radishes.

1 c. cornmeal
½ tsp. salt
1 Tb. melted bacon fat or lard

½ c. plus 1 Tb. boiling water (or more)

Combine the ingredients in a bowl and work hard with the back of a spoon until the dough comes together. Work in a little more water if it doesn't. Pinch off pieces of about ½ ounce. Form into a checker-size disc, thinner in the middle (⅛ inch) than at the edge (¼ inch) to facilitate even cooking. Drop into a simmering liquid to cook, covered, for 7–10 minutes. ✗ *20 dumplings*

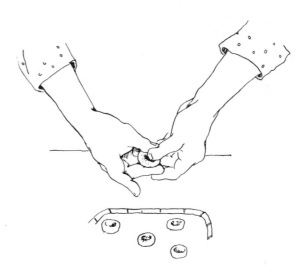

Chestnut Dumplings

The native population made a chestnut version of the dumpling and shared it with mountain settlers until a blight in the early twentieth century wiped out the native American chestnut in the Southern forests. Chestnuts were shelled, peeled, then boiled until tender, and mashed in the cooking water. Cornmeal was beaten in until stiff. The dough was shaped into little cakes, wrapped in corn, hickory, or oak leaves and simmered or steamed much like tamales.

Indian Mush

Like many other of our receipts, the process of making mush is quite plain and simple, yet is often badly prepared, and to the inexperienced some instructions are necessary. Sift some fine Indian meal, make a smooth batter of it by stirring in a sufficiency of cold water. Having ready a pot of boiling water, throw in a handful of salt, and stir in your batter till it is like very thick soup. Boil it till of the proper consistence, and stir it frequently to prevent its being lumpy, and to keep it from burning at the bottom. Mush, made in this manner, will never fail to be thoroughly done and clear of lumps, which are two common failures. Cold mush may be sliced and fried brown in butter. They are very good for breakfast.
— Lettice Bryan, The Kentucky Housewife, 1839

Cornmeal mush, a basic native dish, is found throughout the South. Mary Randolph, whose affections were often more European than American, published a recipe for it in *The Virginia House-wife* in 1824 under its Italian name, polenta.

To Make Polenta. Put a large spoonful of butter in a quart of water, wet your corn meal with cold water in bowl, add some salt, and make it quite smooth, then put it in the buttered water when it is hot, let it boil, stirring it continually till done; as soon as you can handle it, make it into a ball and let it stand till quite cold, then cut it in thin slices, lay them in the bottom of a deep dish so as to cover it, put on it slices of cheese, and on that a few bits of butter, then mush, cheese, and butter, until the dish is full, put on the top thin slices of cheese, put the dish in a quick oven; twenty or thirty minutes will bake it.

The humble dish of mush has been taken quite seriously throughout the years of Southern cooking. At the beginning of the twentieth century, the process was described explicitly in *The Picayune Creole Cook Book* (1901):

🦋 *Add the fresh, sweet white cornmeal, putting a handful at a time into the water, and stirring with a spoon, or a pudding stick, round and round, as the meal falls lightly from the hand. When one handful is exhausted, refill it, and continue stirring and letting the meal fall by degrees, until the pudding stick will stand in it. This is the test.*

Today, its popularity has waned in much of the region, replaced by grits. I suspect this is an indication of the decline in quality of the cornmeal. Mush made from the degerminated grain of most large millers is rather insipid; whole-grain, water-ground cornmeal has a life of its own that is highlighted in simple dishes such as mush and pancakes. Coush-coush is the Cajun version of mush and today is found more often than its suaver cousin. Use the batter for cornmeal mush, but pour it into a hot cast-iron skillet. Let a light crust form. Stir it up and let a crust form again. Repeat and repeat. Serve with cane syrup, sausages, bacon, ham. Though coush-coush is considered thoroughly Cajun by the rest of the country, local Louisiana recipes still often note, "This is an Indian dish."

Cornmeal Mush

☞ Double boiler

• • • • • • • •

⅔ c. cornmeal
⅔ c. cold water

6 Tb. uncooked grits
1½ tsp. salt
4½ c. boiling water
4 Tb. butter

Combine the cornmeal and cold water, stir well and let sit 10 minutes. Beat in the grits, salt, and slowly add the boiling water. Transfer to the top of a double boiler and cook over simmering water for 45–50 minutes, stirring from time to time. Beat in the butter and serve as a savoury accompaniment to meats, especially those with gravies. Sweetened, with milk, it can be served to young children, but not to adults, who should take it more seriously. ✖ *6 servings*

Fried Mush

Fried mush is more in the line of starchy foils such as hushpuppies, grits croquettes, griddle cakes — cereal preparations that take the place of baked breads at lunch, dinner, or supper.

Prepare Cornmeal Mush (opposite). When done, beat in 4–6 ounces grated sharp cheddar cheese, if desired. A little Tabasco sauce is also optional. Pour onto a cold plate, smoothly spread, and chill. Cut into rounds, squares, whatever, and fry in a small amount of appropriate fat: lard or bacon fat for pork dishes, chicken fat for robust chicken dishes, butter for delicate dishes, and so forth. These little pancakes are more delicate than regular fried grits and often go to the table with fried chicken in Maryland.

Cornmeal Pancakes

☞ Griddle

• • • • • • • •

1 c. cornmeal
½ c. flour
½ tsp. salt
2 Tb. sugar

2 tsp. baking powder
½ tsp. baking soda
2 eggs
1¼ c. buttermilk
2 Tb. melted butter

Sift the dry ingredients together. Beat the eggs, add the buttermilk and melted butter. Add to the meal and beat to make a smooth batter. Let stand 10 minutes, then drop by the large tablespoon onto a lightly greased, medium-hot griddle. Cook until brown on each side, turning once, and serve with butter, jam, fruit sauce, honey, the whole breakfast run of condiments. ✖ *18 pancakes*

Green Onion Cakes

Southern food mixes the sweet and savoury as eclectically as any cuisine. Cakes that are slightly sweet, such as this one is, would not be surprising on any table south of the Mason-Dixon line, especially when served as a contrast to our very salty country hams. I find a teaspoon or so of sugar enough to accent the flavor of corn in most recipes without overwhelming it.

½–⅔ c. finely chopped green
    onions
1 recipe Cornmeal Pancakes
    (p. 13) with sugar to taste, a
    tsp. or more

Ham or bacon fat

Fold the onions into the batter, drop by the large tablespoon into ⅛-inch hot fat, ham or bacon preferably, and fry until brown and crisp, turning once. Serve the hot, crisp cakes with a meat dish; this is a popular side for fried chicken with gravy. ✖ *18 pancakes*

Uncle Henry's Seafood Fritters

Uncle Henry is an almost legendary waterman of New Hanover County, North Carolina. His family prepares the traditional Carolina oyster roast over hardwood coals and under steaming burlap only for those with the instincts of a homing pigeon who can trace their way through sand pits and under moss-filled live oaks to a ramshackle building by the water. All the seafood — shrimp, clams, and oysters — is harvested by the men in the family; they can tell the diner exactly which creek or bend any oyster or shrimp came from. The seafood fritters are chunky pancakes that accompany roasted oysters, steamed shrimp, hushpuppies, and tart coleslaw.

⅓ c. finely chopped onion
1 Tb. chopped fresh parsley
1 c. chopped cooked shrimp,
    crab, or clams
Dash of cayenne

1 recipe Cornmeal Pancakes
    (p. 13) with about 1 tsp. sugar
    or to taste
Ham or bacon fat

Stir the onion, parsley, seafood, and cayenne into the cornmeal batter. Drop by the large tablespoon into hot fat, preferably ham or bacon, and fry till brown and crisp, turning once. ✖ *18–24 fritters*

Corn Crêpes

Corn crêpes are a delicious hybrid of native and French cooking. Richer and more robust than the traditional crêpe, they are more delicate and more complex than the tortilla because the corn flour used is very finely milled. I like to serve the crêpes topped with fried shellfish, especially oysters, garnished with tartare sauce. All together, this makes a very polished first course for a formal dinner; at the coast, we have it for breakfast, with bacon and fried tomatoes. Corn flour is available at health food stores.

☞ 5-inch crêpe or frying pan

. . . .

¼ c. cornmeal
¼ c. corn flour
1–2 Tb. flour
½ tsp. salt

Pinch of sugar
1 egg
½ c. buttermilk
2–3 Tb. cold water
1 Tb. melted butter

Sift the cornmeal, corn flour, 1 tablespoon flour, salt, and sugar together. Beat the egg with the buttermilk, 1 tablespoon water, and the melted butter. Add to the meal and stir all together until smooth. Set aside at room temperature for 20 minutes. Check the consistency of the batter; thin with water if need be.

Cook as very thin pancakes in a medium-hot, buttered pan. Drop about 1½ tablespoons batter into the pan. Rotate and tilt the pan so the batter spreads quickly, evenly, and thinly to make the crêpe. Consider the first crêpe or two an experiment. Thin the batter with water if the crêpes are too thick or coarse. Add a little flour if too thin. The higher the heat, the lacier and crisper the crêpes will be. Lower heat makes for a more delicate and custardlike consistency. ✖ *12 crêpes*

Oyster Crêpes Tartare

16 plump oysters

Flour

1 egg, beaten with 2 Tb. water

Fine bread crumbs seasoned with
    salt and white pepper

Clarified butter

4 Corn Crêpes (p. 15)

Tartare sauce

Lemon wedges

Drain the oysters and pat them dry. Sprinkle lightly on both sides with flour, then dip into the egg beaten with the water. Toss into the bread crumbs seasoned with salt and pepper. Let oysters rest a minute or so before frying in hot clarified butter.

To serve, put a warm corn crêpe on a warm plate. Arrange 4 oysters on each crêpe, centered around a dollop of tartare sauce. Garnish with lemon and serve immediately. ✕ *4 servings*

Tartare Sauce

Estelle Wilcox in *The New Dixie Cook-Book* of 1889 says, "This is called the perfection of sauces for fried fish." It is a staple of seafood restaurants and fish camps, though usually served niggardly in tiny, fluted paper cups with every plate of fried fish. Naturally, a homemade version swamps its rivals.

½ c. homemade mayonnaise

5 tsp. minced sweet pickle relish

1 Tb. minced onion

1 Tb. minced celery

1 Tb. minced green olives

2 Tb. chopped fresh parsley

½ – 1 tsp. chopped fresh tarragon,
    to taste

Pinch of whole celery seed

1½ tsp. Dijon mustard

1 tsp. lemon juice

Cayenne or Tabasco, to taste, but
    enough to taste

Combine the ingredients, mixing well, tasting. Let marry 1 hour before serving. ✕ *⅔ cup sauce*

Hushpuppies

Hushpuppies are deep-fried cornmeal fritters and the classic accompaniment to outdoor fish fries and barbecues. Some are little more than the fried dough of the cornmeal dumpling variety, but most are enriched these days with eggs, butter, milk, and onion. Almost every corn milling operation in the South puts out a hushpuppy mix and few cooks make hushpuppies from scratch; one popular North Carolina mix is Blue Ribbon, made from stone-ground cornmeal. It may be ordered from Isler Davis Mill Site, Blue Ribbon Company, Seven Springs, North Carolina 28578. For hushpuppies from scratch, here is a typical recipe.

☞ Electric deep fryer with thermostat

* * * * * * * *

2 c. cornmeal
1 tsp. baking powder
½ tsp. baking soda
⅔ tsp. salt
2 tsp. sugar

⅛ tsp. black pepper
¾ c. grated onion
1 egg
1 c. buttermilk
Fat for deep frying: shortening, lard, vegetable oil, or a combination

Sift together the dry ingredients. Beat the onion, egg, and buttermilk together; add to the meal mixture. Beat well and let stand at room temperature for about 15 minutes. Cook a test hushpuppy — drop by the large teaspoon into 350° F. deep fat. Test after it has browned, in 2–3 minutes; if the hushpuppy is not cooked through, add a little more cornmeal to the batter. If the outside is very rough and the inside too heavy, add a little buttermilk. Proceed, cooking the puppies about 2–3 minutes until golden brown. Drain on brown paper and serve immediately. ✄ *36 hushpuppies*

Delta Dogs

These Mississippi hushpuppies aren't traditional at all. They are hotter than blazes and absolutely delicious. You will need a lot of cold beer. Unlike most hushpuppies, these are served as an hors d'oeuvre fritter or snack.

☞ Electric deep fryer with
    thermostat

• • • • • • • •

2 Tb. chopped green or red sweet
    pepper
1 c. grated onion
1 c. grated sharp cheddar
1 c. cornmeal

¾ tsp. salt
1 tsp. black pepper
1 tsp. cayenne
¾ c. boiling water
Fat for deep frying: shortening,
    lard, vegetable oil, or a
    combination

Toss the sweet pepper, onion, cheese, cornmeal, and seasonings together. Pour the boiling water over and beat well. Drop by the teaspoon into 350° F. fat and fry until golden brown. Drain on brown paper; serve immediately. ✗ *24 hushpuppies*

CORN CRISP

In cold weather we often cook in the fireplace. The hearth was built about 20 inches above floor level for easy access. We roast oysters, chickens, and even bake cupcakes by the open fire. The children love it and are always eager to help. The main rule for this kind of cooking is to have a good bed of coals. Little or no open flame is desirable. Most baking is exceedingly difficult in the fireplace, but rough pioneer foodstuffs such as the corn crisp are better this way than oven baked. You can follow Sarah Rutledge's recipe; the board she refers to is hardwood. Oak slabs are traditional in the South for cooking a variety of foods before an open flame. Spring shad and fall mullet roasted this way are seasonal hallmarks along the coastal rivers. Not everyone appreciates this pioneer bread, witness Mrs. Bryan in *The Kentucky Housewife* (1839): "Indian water cakes, when made of stiff dough, and baked with a hard crust, of all cakes are the most disgusting . . ."

Corn Crisp. *One pint of meal, a table-spoonful of lard, a little salt; and if the scalding of the meal should not make the mixture soft enough, add a little water. Make it into a cake about half an inch thick, and lay it upon your board; put it before the fire, and when sufficiently browned, pass a coarse thread under it, and turn it upon another board. When baked on that side, take it up, split the cake, and scrape out the inside; then put the crusts on the gridiron, and brown and crisp them.*
—*Sarah Rutledge, The Carolina Housewife, 1847*

Baking sheet, greased

2 c. cornmeal
1 tsp. salt

1⅛ c. water
2 Tb. lard or butter, plus additional butter

Sift the meal and salt. Bring the water to a boil with the fat and beat thoroughly into the meal. Turn the dough out onto a lightly greased baking sheet and form into a rectangle about ⅛-inch thick, approximately 6 × 9 inches.

Using the side of the hand, pat longways across the dough to make 12 slight, parallel furrows on top.

Bake about 40 minutes in an oven preheated to 325° F. Turn carefully and bake for 25 more minutes, until golden brown and crisp throughout. Turn back over. Dot top of cake heavily with butter. Run under a broiler until toasted and butter is bubbling in the furrows.

1 corn crisp

Sweet Potato Crisp

Add ⅔–1 cup of mashed sweet potato to the Corn Crisp recipe (p. 19). Form and bake in the same manner.

Sweet Potato Corn Cake

To the recipe for Corn Crisp (p. 19), add ⅔–1 cup mashed sweet potato, 1 egg beaten with 1¼ cups buttermilk, and ⅔ cup flour sifted with 2½ teaspoons baking powder and 1 teaspoon baking soda. Bake in a buttered 9-inch tin, in an oven preheated to 375° F., 30 minutes or until golden brown on top. This is delicious split and buttered with honey or molasses. ✖ *6 servings*

Red Pepper Corn Cake

Another variation: Add red pepper flakes to the Sweet Potato Corn Cake (above) to your taste, at least a teaspoon; good with fried fish, chicken, pork, greens, just about anything Southern.

Corn Light Bread

Corn Light Bread begins with a breeding ground for wild yeast that works overnight, is made into a batter, rises again, and comes out somewhere between the primitive plank breads and the modern soda-rising corn breads. It is the equivalent of a salt-rising bread. Like all spontaneously fermented breads, Corn Light Bread is subject to the vagaries of chance, to the lighting of the proper host of air-borne yeasts upon the corn mush slurry. This bread is mostly of the western part of the South — the Appalachians and beyond. Mrs. Bryan in *The Kentucky Housewife* of 1839 gives this recipe.

❧ Corn Light Bread. *Having ready a pot of boiling water, throw in a small handful of fine salt, and make it into a common bread dough, with sifted Indian meal. Stir it very hard with a wooden paddle, till well mixed; sprinkle on the top a handful of dry meal, cover it and set it in a warm place to rise. In a few hours it will look very light and crack on the top; then heat your oven as for other Indian bread, grease it with a little lard, rub it with a handful of dry Indian meal, and bake your bread with common heat. It will keep moist for several days, and will be found quite convenient, being always in readiness.*

The keeping quality of this bread is often mentioned. Recipes will sometimes direct the cook to leave the bread for 24 hours before serving. Most modern recipes also command the use of water-ground cornmeal asserting that the degerminated ordinary cornmeal will not work. Though recipes for Corn Light Bread are found in modern collections, they are usually entitled "Grandma's . . ." or "Aunt Beady's Corn Light Bread," indicating this technique is identified with an older generation. I doubt this bread will be practiced much longer in the South. Finally, the "light" refers to the yeast fermentation, not to the texture or color of these poncs, as in Mrs. Lettice Bryan's instructions on a batter: "let it stand till it gets sweet, but not till it becomes light."

☙ 10-inch cast-iron skillet	1 Tb. bacon fat
	⅓ c. sugar
4 c. cornmeal (water-ground only)	¼ c. molasses
4 c. boiling water	2 tsp. salt
1 c. cold water	1 Tb. fat: lard, bacon fat, or shortening

Add 1 cup of the cornmeal slowly to the boiling water stirring all the while and continue to stir and cook over medium-low heat about 10 minutes. Let cool some, and in the meanwhile, stir the cold water and 1 cup of the remaining cornmeal together and let sit about 10 minutes.

Combine the cooked and uncooked mushes with the bacon fat, beat well, and cover loosely. Put in a very warm place and let sit overnight or until the mush is bubbly and obviously fermenting. Add the remaining cornmeal and the rest of the ingredients except for the fat; beat well. Cover again and return to the warm place until the batter just shows some sign of fermenting. Melt a spoonful of fat in a heavy cast-iron skillet over medium heat and preheat oven to 350° F. When the skillet is hot, carefully pour the batter into it, give it a shake or two to level the cake and bake for about 40 minutes, until lightly browned.

✖ *6–8 good servings*

Light Corn Bread

This very moist bread can also be prepared as crumpets, cooked in rings on a griddle.

☞ 9-inch cake pan, buttered;
    thermometer

♦ ♦ ♦ ♦ ♦ ♦ ♦ ♦

1 c. milk
2 c. water
1 c. cornmeal

1½ c. flour
1 tsp. salt
1 Tb. sugar
2 Tb. butter
1½ tsp. dry yeast
2 eggs

Bring the milk and water to a boil and carefully sift in the meal, stirring constantly. Reduce heat, stir occasionally to prevent sticking, and cook until thickened. Remove from heat and let cool to about 100° F. Beat in flour, salt, sugar, butter, and yeast. Cover and let ferment about 1½ hours. Before baking, beat in the eggs. Pour the batter into a buttered 9-inch cake pan and let rise 15 minutes or so. Bake in an oven preheated to 375° F. for about 35 minutes or until lightly browned. Serve immediately, cut into wedges, split, and butter well. This bread is very moist and delicate, much like a spoonbread.

✖ *4–6 servings*

St. Charles Indian Bread

The celebrated Indian bread, prepared at the St. Charles Hotel, New Orleans, is made as follows: Beat two eggs very light, mix alternately with them one pint of sour milk or buttermilk and one pint of fine Indian meal; melt one tablespoonful of butter and add to the mixture; dissolve one tablespoonful of soda or saleratus, etc., in a small portion of the milk and add to the mixture the last thing, beat very hard and bake in a pan in a quick oven.
— *The Rural Carolinian*, December 1869

Appalachian Corn Bread

Appalachian Corn Bread is a no-frills remnant of a pioneer cuisine, straightforward, hearty, and nourishing. The only grain is corn, the only luxury an egg (and many recipes of this type omit that). It is nonetheless delicious on a cold night and keeps well. With all its ancient origins, this bread is still commonly prepared in the mountain regions of Georgia, Tennessee, the Carolinas, and the Virginias as a home or family bread.

9-inch cast-iron skillet or heavy cake pan

2 Tb. bacon fat or lard
2 c. white cornmeal

1 tsp. baking soda
1 tsp. salt
1 egg
1¼ c. buttermilk

Put the skillet or pan over a low heat and melt the fat in it.

Sift the dry ingredients together into a bowl. Beat the egg and buttermilk together and stir into the meal until smooth. Pour into the preheated skillet, smooth out, and bake in an oven preheated to 375° F. for about 35 minutes. When cooked, the top will look rather dry and crackled, but the sides of the cake will pull away from the pan. Serve hot with lots of butter.

To serve cold, crumble this bread into a glass and cover with cold buttermilk. With thick slices of fresh tomatoes, thinly sliced sweet peppers and cucumbers, and whole, tender scallions, that's a summer supper on the farm. *4–6 servings*

Company Corn Bread

A world of difference exists between the Appalachian and the Company Corn Breads. Here we no longer experience the world of subsistence farming, but find some showing off going on. Luxuries such as flour, sugar, additional eggs, and butter turn the old plain loaf common to all the Native Americans and the settlers into a new, distinctly creole staple fit for the finest guests.

☞ 9-inch cast-iron skillet or heavy cake pan

- - - - - - - -

1½ c. white cornmeal
½ c. all-purpose flour
2 tsp. baking powder
1 tsp. baking soda
1 tsp. salt
1–2 Tb. sugar, to taste
2 eggs
1½ c. buttermilk
3 Tb. butter

Heat the skillet or cake pan over low heat.

Sift the dry ingredients together into a bowl. Beat the eggs well. Add the buttermilk to the eggs and beat well again. Melt the butter in the skillet, then pour into the egg-milk mixture beating vigorously. Quickly mix liquid and dry ingredients and pour into the hot pan.

Pop into an oven preheated to 425° F. and bake approximately 30 minutes, until the top is light brown. ✗ *4–6 servings*

Souffléed Corn Bread

In the summer, fresh green corn is cut from the cob and added directly to a corn bread batter. Later, in the fall, a "gritted" corn bread is made. Fully mature corn, almost dried but still chewy, is grated from the cob using special metal scrapers called gritters — made from tin buckets opened out and flattened, then punched over all with a nail and attached to a board. The gritted cornmeal is used alone or added to regular cornmeal for breads, both oven and pancake types. In the Appalachian region and west through Kentucky and Tennessee, the late summer/early fall season is marked by the appearance of these distinctive seasonal breads. But at any time, Southerners like whole kernel texture in their corn breads. Without fresh or gritted corn, cooks turn to the cabinet and canned corn. Most frequently used is the cream-style corn, slightly sweet, sticky, and rich. It may be added to the Company Corn Bread (opposite) as follows:

Sift the cornmeal, flour, baking powder, soda, and salt together. Omit the sugar. Separate the eggs, beating the yolks and adding to the buttermilk.

Add ¾ cup cream-style canned corn to the liquid, and turn all the liquid into the dry ingredients. Stir about. Beat the whites until stiff, fold in, and proceed to cook according to the recipe. ✕ *4–6 servings*

Mexican Corn Bread

Mexican Corn Bread is actually Texan as are most "Mexican" foods in the southeast. It is very popular and is often the only corn bread regularly prepared by cooks who have dropped the more traditional corn breads from their repertoire. Though it has been around for decades, Mexican Corn Bread is still considered rather novel and special enough for parties.

To make Mexican Corn Bread, add to any of the preceding three recipes: 1 cup grated cheddar cheese and about 3 finely chopped jalapeño or cayenne peppers (seeds discarded). I suspect most Mexicans would find this a bit too rich, if not downright decadent, but there is no mistaking the often ignored common heritage of the native southeastern and South of the Border cuisines. ✕ *4–6 servings*

Green Corn Bread

In the South, green corn is the sweet, fresh corn usually prepared as a vegetable, as for corn-on-the-cob.

☞ 9-inch cast-iron skillet, greased
   and preheated on low heat

• • • • • • •

1½ c. white cornmeal
¾ c. all-purpose flour
1½ tsp. baking powder
¾ tsp. baking soda

¾ tsp. salt
1 tsp. sugar
2 c. buttermilk
¼ c. water
1 egg, separated
3 ears corn, grated, to yield 1¼ c.
   grated kernels

Sift the dry ingredients together into a large bowl. Beat the buttermilk, water, and egg yolk together lightly. Stir in the grated corn kernels. Beat the egg white until stiff, and fold all ingredients together lightly. Turn into the preheated skillet and pop into an oven preheated to 450° F. Immediately reduce oven temperature to 375° F. Bake 25 minutes or until light brown and the sides pull away from the edges of the pan. ✕ *6–8 servings*

Blueberry Corn Cake

My family's farm was on a high plain of the Piedmont that ran up to the slopes of Mt. Whittaker, the last of a dramatic, though not very tall, range of hills, the most famous of which, King's Mountain, 6 miles away, was the site of the important victory of the Carolina frontiersmen against the British forces. In my grandmother's time, there were berrying parties to harvest the tiny, intensely sweet huckleberries that grew wild in the hills and to catch the cooler breezes of the slopes in August.

☞ 9-inch cast-iron skillet, greased
    and preheated on low heat

• • • • • • • •

⅜ c. cornmeal
¾ c. flour
2 Tb. sugar
1 tsp. baking powder

½ tsp. salt
½ tsp. baking soda
⅞ c. buttermilk
1 egg, separated
⅔ c. grated fresh corn, from
    about 1 ear corn
1 c. blueberries

Sift the dry ingredients together into a large bowl. Beat together lightly the buttermilk, egg yolk, and grated corn. Add liquid to dry ingredients and stir to mix well. Beat the egg white until stiff and fold into the batter along with the blueberries.

Turn into the preheated skillet and bake in an oven preheated to 375° F. about 25 minutes or until top browns and sides pull away slightly. ✖ *6 servings*

SPOONBREAD

BISCUITS, SPOONBREAD, AND SWEET POTATO PIE

John Mariani, in *The Dictionary of American Food and Drink,* tells us that the term spoonbread is first mentioned in print in 1906. The dish existed long before it was in print. It is a soft often soufflélike starchy pudding made of cornmeal. One traditional Carolina Low Country version is Awendaw (or Owendaw), named for an Indian settlement outside of Charleston and assuredly of the native cuisine. Sarah Rutledge published the first recipe for it in her 1847 collection. She also gave directions for a "Corn Spoonbread," but the spoon refers to the technique: "Bake on a griddle, or grease a pan and drop in spoonfuls." Before this century, the dish was often published as mush bread or batter bread, though the service was explicit: "serve with a spoon."

Spoonbread is considered the most elegant preparation of cornmeal in all of Southern cooking, and it is known throughout the entire region. It accompanies all sorts of roasts and game at formal dinners (dinners are 2 or 3 o'clock afternoon meals in the South). Except for Awendaw, spoonbread is the universally recognized name today.

🐾 Owendaw Corn Bread. *Take about two tea-cups of hommony, and while hot mix with it a very large spoonful of butter (good lard will do); beat four eggs very light, and stir them into the hommony; next add about a pint of milk, gradually stirred in; and lastly, half pint of corn meal. The batter should be of the consistency of a rich boiled custard; if thicker, add a little more milk. Bake with a good deal of heat at the bottom of the oven, and not too much at the top, so as to allow it to rise. The pan in which it is baked ought to be a deep one, to allow space for rising. It has the appearance, when cooked, of a baked batter pudding, and when rich, and well mixed, it has almost the delicacy of a baked custard.*
—*Sarah Rutledge,* The Carolina Housewife, *1847*

Awendaw

Awendaw is one of the most delicious legacies of the native cuisine. The following recipe is slightly enriched by a little extra butter and egg — and gussied up just a bit by beating the egg whites separately — but otherwise it is the real McCoy. A completely nontraditional springtime variation is delicious: fold in about 1 cup of chopped, blanched fresh asparagus with the egg whites. Serve as a luncheon dish or a separate dinner course with a fresh tomato sauce.

☞ 9-inch cake pan, greased

• • • • • • • •

1 c. cold, Plain Cooked Grits (below)
2 Tb. butter

¾ c. milk
¾ c. white cornmeal
¾ tsp. salt
3 eggs, separated

Combine the cooked grits, butter, and milk in a heavy-bottomed saucepan and slowly bring to the boiling point, stirring constantly. Add the cornmeal all at once, remove from the heat, and beat well. Reserve until lukewarm. Beat in the salt and the 3 egg yolks.

Beat the egg whites until stiff and fold into the batter. Pour into a greased 9-inch pan and bake in a preheated oven at 375° F. about 20 minutes, until puffed and just brown. Serve hot with butter.

This spoonbread may be cut into wedges with a little extra care.

✖ *4 servings*

Plain Cooked Grits

The longer grits cook over low heat the better. Cooking in a double boiler is preferred by many for a creamy texture. Grits should never appear to be bits of hard starch in a watery compound. Long, slow cooking is the remedy. "Instant" grits aren't instant, just undercooked. Some stone-ground grits may need "washing," as old cookbooks direct. This is to remove the chaff. Pour the grits into a large amount of cold water. Stir gently and skim off the chaff that floats to the surface. The grits will sink to the bottom. Drain and cook as directed.

4 c. water

1 c. uncooked grits

Bring the water to the boil and sift in the grits, stirring constantly. Reduce heat and cook slowly, stirring frequently for 30–40 minutes. ✖ *4 cups cooked grits*

Mush Bread

Sprinkle slowly half a pint of white cornmeal into a pint of hot milk. Cook until it is a smooth mush. Take from the fire; add the yolks of four eggs and then fold in the well-beaten whites. Turn into a baking-dish and bake in a quick oven for thirty minutes.
—*Woman's Club Cook-Book of Southern Recipes*, Charlotte, N.C., 1908

Virginia Spoonbread

☞ 8 × 8 × 2-inch pan, buttered

1 c. cornmeal
¼ c. uncooked grits
2½ c. water

4 Tb. butter, plus extra
1 c. heavy cream
1 tsp. salt
3 eggs, separated

Stir the cornmeal and grits into the water and cook very slowly over low heat until the mixture is quite thick and smooth. Stir frequently — it will take about 30 minutes.

Beat in the butter, cream, and salt, and then the egg yolks, beaten. Whip the whites until soft peaks form and fold into the mush. Pour into a lightly buttered pan and bake in a preheated oven at 375° F. for about 30 minutes, until puffed and lightly browned. Serve immediately with much butter. ✗ *4–6 servings*

Farm-Style Spoonbread

☞ 9-inch cake pan, greased

2 c. water
4 Tb. bacon fat
1 c. cornmeal

2 eggs, separated
½ c. cold water
⅞ c. flour
1 tsp. salt
2 tsp. baking powder

Bring the water and the bacon fat to a boil. Slowly pour over the cornmeal, stirring vigorously all the while. Set aside until cool.

Beat the egg yolks with the cold water and stir into the cooled mush. Sift the dry ingredients together and add to the mush. Beat the egg whites until stiff and fold into the batter. Turn into a greased 9-inch cake pan and bake in an oven preheated to 375° F. for about 30 minutes, until lightly browned, puffed, and just set in the middle. ✗ *4 servings*

American Bean Bread

Beans provide the complementary nutrients for corn, making the two, when eaten together, a perfect protein. Corn and beans are paired throughout Southern cooking, from native breads as below, to vegetable side dishes such as succotash, to major preparations such as Brunswick stew. The combination is the basis of the Native American cooking as well as later soul and white-trash cooking.

Bean breads are still prepared in Native American communities in the southeast, especially at cultural festivals. A stiff bean dough may be shaped by hand and wrapped in leaves — corn, hickory, oak, pumpkin, fig — to be baked in the ashes or dropped tamale-wise into hot liquid. An oven-baked bean bread is obviously a later development; it is shared by both native and black populations.

☞ 8 × 5 × 2¾-inch loaf pan, greased

• • • • • • • •

1⅔ c. cooked, sieved pinto beans *or* one 15-oz. can pinto beans with liquid, sieved

1½ c. cornmeal
2 eggs, beaten
¾ c. buttermilk
Salt to taste, about ½ tsp.
1 tsp. baking soda

Combine all the ingredients, beating just enough to make a smooth batter. Turn into a greased loaf pan and bake 45–50 minutes in an oven preheated to 375° F. When top browns and sides pull away from the pan, turn out and cool on a rack. Delicious warm with butter.
✗ *1 small loaf*

Bean Cakes

Make one half of the batter for American Bean Bread (above). Drop by the large tablespoon into ¼-inch hot fat, preferably lard. Cook well, turning once, until nicely brown, crisp, and puffed. Very good with pork, game, and hearty stews, but in the South, these are often served as a replacement for meat at a meal with lots of other prepared and raw vegetables. Since sausage in the South is often fried as small patties, these cakes, seasoned like pork with cayenne and sage, are also known as pea or bean sausage cakes and are served at breakfast.
✗ *4 servings*

THE · PRIDE ·
OF · THE · SOUTH
HOT BISCUITS

Basic Beaten Biscuits

Fancy Beaten Biscuits

Zephyrinas

Sweet Milk Biscuits

Buttermilk Biscuits

Cheese Biscuits

Sweet Potato Biscuits

Louise's Sweet Potato
Biscuits

Sweet Potato Crackers

Angel Biscuits

Worms

Another Worm

Hominy Ham Biscuits

Hot Hominy Ham
Crackers

Black Pepper Dumplings

Green Bean Dumplings

Corncob Dumplings

Fried Biscuits

Cheese Straws No. 1

Cheese Straw Dough
No. 2

Cocktail Olives

Ham and Sauerkraut Pie

Roasted Pecans

Martha's Breast of
Chicken

HARVEST

Family, friends, neighbors, and workers all gather to complete the harvest tasks at a cornshucking on the farm of Mr. Fred Wilkins in Granville County, North Carolina, on November 16, 1939.

The photographer noted that the food was prepared by Mrs. Wilkins and her four sisters-in-law and one Negro woman (their tenant's wife).

The meal included "stew" (also referred to as soup) that was a mixture of chicken, beef, and vegetables; potato salad, cole slaw, cabbage, turnips, pickles, biscuits, chicken cooked with dressing, sweet potato pudding, iced tea, chocolate and caramel cake. Only the cake had been cooked on the preceding day.

*After the meal, work resumed: women in the kitchen, men at the shucking.
It was day's end before rest, harvest done.*

BEATEN BISCUITS

Beaten biscuits are, like grits, very much of a mystery to the unini-
tiated. They may be the forerunner of the modern raised biscuit, but these
chewy, unleavened morsels resemble more the hard tack produced by early
European bakers for armies and navies than anything else served up in the
modern South. Pilot bread and sea biscuit are terms for similar breads that
reflect their practical use.

Country ham has for some time wedded the beaten biscuit in Southern
cuisine. At the most traditional fancy parties and weddings, biscuits no
bigger than a quarter are invariably served up with baked, cured ham sliced
as thin as imaginable sandwiched inside and spiked with mustard. Otherwise, beaten biscuits are rarely seen anymore.

They sound harder to make than they are. People who won't knead
their own bread should skip on to some other recipe, but those who enjoy a
physical relationship with their doughs should be in heaven here. There is
no getting around the activity. Fifteen minutes of heavy, consistent abuse is
the minimum. You can use a rolling pin, a hammer, the side of an axe;
whatever, it must be heavy. A little sawed-off broom stick will not do.
And, understandably, you must work on a very heavy, sturdy surface.
Remove to a safe distance all fragile objects that may vibrate into oblivion.
In the old days, the dough was beaten on a tree stump in the yard. When
properly beaten, the dough will blister at each blow. It will develop a
strange plastic quality and be smoother than any other bread dough you
have ever seen. If you have ever made pasta dough, imagine it pushed
beyond endurance. While beating, constantly fold the dough back on itself,
turn it over, around, and so forth, so that all parts of the dough receive
equal stress.

The biscuits, when done, will be dry throughout, yet soft in the middle. A wet center, however, will be undigestible and lead to quick spoilage.
They should barely color — light brown on the bottom, cream on top.

Basic Beaten Biscuits

Here is a no-frills, delicious, long-lasting biscuit made with the traditional fat, lard.

4 c. all-purpose flour	3 Tb. lard
1 tsp. salt	1 c. water

Sift the flour and salt together into a bowl, and rub the lard in with the fingertips. Add the water and stir until the dough coalesces.

Turn out onto a lightly floured surface, procure a heavy rolling pin, axe, Indian club, what have you, and commence beating. Fold the dough back on itself frequently as it flattens. You cannot be too vigorous or too physical. Keep at it for 15 minutes, no less. If you stop to rest, add that time onto the total. If you feel a little weak today, make up for it by punishing the dough a few more minutes. There are no shortcuts and no appliances to help you here. Arm power, not electricity, will transform these raw ingredients into an unbelievably smooth and plastic dough.

Pinch off small balls of dough weighing ½ ounce each, about the size of a Ping-Pong ball. Roll in the palms to smooth and place on an ungreased baking sheet. Flatten with a three-pronged fork, and press again crosswise.

Bake in an oven preheated to 400° F. for about 30 minutes, until only lightly colored but dry in the middle. ✖ *50 biscuits*

Fancy Beaten Biscuits

Fancier, richer, but no more sophisticated than the preceding recipe.

4 c. all-purpose flour	7 Tb. butter
1 tsp. salt	1 c. milk or water
1 tsp. sugar	

Prepare according to preceding directions. This dough will be softer, slightly stickier, and slower to develop, so beat a little longer.
✖ *50 biscuits*

Zephyrinas

Zephyrinas are an old Charleston biscuit, what we now call a cracker, versatile for soup, cheese, pâtés, and so forth. The delightful name from Zephyros, the Greek god of the west wind, describes the fragile puff that emerges from a hot oven. They make impressive presents (and are an intense labor of love). Be sure to give them only to friends with a proven aptitude for gratitude. Most will respond, "I didn't know crackers could be made at home." Indeed, they rarely are today, which is all the more reason to persevere and reclaim a stolen delight.

You can use either of the preceding beaten biscuit recipes. If you plan to use the entire batch for crackers, it is not necessary to work the dough as much as described for beaten biscuits, but it must be very smooth. Scraps of beaten biscuit dough are well used as zephyrinas.

Roll out the dough very thin on a lightly floured surface. Cut with a 2-inch round. Remove the dough scraps first, then with a thin metal spatula, carefully transfer the crackers to an ungreased sheet. If you handle the cut dough with your hands, you will most likely stretch or tear it. Prick 2 or 3 times with a fork and bake in an oven preheated to 400° F. quickly, about 5–7 minutes or until the crackers puff and brown lightly and erratically. Do not overcook or they will be bitter. Cool on a rack and store airtight.

R A I S E D   B I S C U I T S

🐦 Everything I cook is a favorite to me cause if it weren't, I wouldn't cook it. But everybody goes hog wild about my biscuits. I take a sifter of flour, to make say nine biscuits. Then I take about 5 spoonsful of lard or Crisco, put it in there, take a cup of buttermilk, work it up.
— Azilee Edwards, Cabbagetown Families, Cabbagetown Food, 1976

In 1986 I got a phone call from an exasperated lady in Pennsylvania who, with no introduction whatsoever, demanded, "What's wrong with my biscuits?" after an article on Crook's Corner, where I was chef, appeared in the Philadelphia *Inquirer.* It is a common plaint, and one that is not easily answered. For one, recipes for biscuits vary widely in the ratio of fat to flour. One old Kentucky recipe I have calls for 3 tablespoons lard to 2 cups flour while another popularly printed recipe has 8 tablespoons fat for the same amount of flour. When one searches through the local church and community cookbooks of the South, one frequently encounters a disheartening disclaimer such as this one from Lafayette, Louisiana's *Talk About Good II:* "This recipe comes from North Georgia from my great grandmother who of course never measured a thing." Biscuits, like all baking but more so, are in the hands, not the head.

A few pointers, though, can help a new cook through most biscuit recipes. First, the flour is extraordinarily important, as much if not more so than in making pasta. I believe the absolutely best flour for biscuits is White Lily. It is fascinating to make two batches of biscuits side-by-side, identical but for flour. I guarantee your surprise and pleasure with the special soft-flour qualities of White Lily. If White Lily is unavailable, other excellent low-gluten flours from the South exist and should be used before resorting to hard Northern flour. You can try reducing gluten content by substituting in part some cake flour for non-Southern brands, but since the folks at White Lily are so easy to work with, go ahead and write them for shipping information at White Lily Kitchens, P.O.B. 871, Knoxville, Tennessee 37901.

After flour, the next most important ingredient is fat, and for biscuits it comes in three varieties: lard, shortening, and butter. Lard renders the best layers, long and distinct (vegetarians are out of luck). Vegetable shortening produces a tender and fluffy biscuit, lacking somewhat the taste and texture that comes from lard. Butter gives the best flavor and weakest structure. I often mix the fats, using some of each for its own properties. A biscuit without some little bit of lard will never taste truly Southern to me, but I must admit that shortening will be easiest for cooks new to biscuits to handle. Veteran biscuit makers will have their own ideas and ignore anything I suggest, anyway.

42

Combining these two ingredients — flour and fat — is the next consideration. It is much like making pie dough — though less short — and to the same end: Each individual milled iota of flour must be enrobed by fat so that no liquid can activate the gluten upon stirring. Complete incorporation of fat and flour is essential for tenderness and flakiness. If any naked flour is grabbed up by the recipe's liquid, the gluten will develop too much, and the result is a heavy, doughy biscuit. The other side of the coin: If you overwork the mixture at this point, the fat will melt, and you'll have a greasy product. Try chilling the fat. In the summer, I keep the flour in the refrigerator and chill the bowl as well. Work lightly, quickly, and thoroughly.

Exercising the dough after the liquid is added is the most difficult part of the process to convey in writing. English simply does not have cooking terms with the fine shadings of meaning required here. To say knead will almost guarantee the novice will overwork the dough, but better that it is slightly overworked to start with than to end up with a crumbled mess lacking internal structure. Turn the dough out on a floured surface; push it out gently, then pull it back on itself about 10 times. Use the motion of kneading, but omit the vigor.

The final caveats go to cutting the biscuits. Avoid dull, bent, dented cutters. Do not use a glass or a jar or anything that does not allow air to escape while cutting. The air pressure will obviously compress your biscuit, and anything other than the sharpest edge will pinch your biscuit top to bottom. Do not twist the cutter side to side. Remove all dough from the cutting edge as you go along; however if you have a sharp edge, dip the cutter into flour each time, and cut straight from top to bottom, no dough will stick to your cutter anyway.

Remembering these procedures, you should be able to personalize your own biscuit recipe quickly. Biscuits are great fun — the variety is endless, the rewards great, especially on cold mornings. (I'm rather daffy in the early a.m., so I combine all ingredients except the liquid the night before, refrigerate, and manage to have a hot breakfast for the children while still possessing a completely empty mind.) Southern biscuits are never cut in half with a knife, but always split or pulled apart by hand to preserve the natural, delicate interior structure.

Sweet Milk Biscuits

2 c. low-gluten all-purpose flour,
  White Lily preferred
Heaping ½ tsp. salt
3¼ tsp. baking powder

1 tsp. sugar, if desired
5 Tb. chilled shortening, lard, or
  butter, or a combination
⅞ c. whole milk

Sift the dry ingredients together into a large bowl. Add the cold shortening and work the fat through the flour with the fingertips. Every bit of flour should be combined with a bit of fat. Add the milk and stir vigorously until the dough forms a ball.

Turn the dough out onto a lightly floured surface. Knead lightly about 10 strokes. Stop just as soon as the dough begins to look smooth.

Pat the dough out to approximately an 8 × 7 × ¾-inch rectangle. Cut into 2-inch rounds. Scraps may be gently pushed together, lightly patted, and recut. They will rise more and be more tender if the dough is worked as little as possible. Place on an ungreased sheet in an oven preheated to 500° F. and bake about 8 minutes, until browned. Serve immediately. ✖ *12 biscuits*

Buttermilk Biscuits

Opposites not only attract, they marry, and expand. This is the simple notion behind the reliable risings produced by baking powder and baking soda. For most normal baking the proportion of the opposites—acid and base—is satisfied by commercial baking powder, which is composed of 3 parts cream of tartar (or tartaric *acid*) and 2 parts bicarbonate of soda. The liquid of the recipe sets the two at each other to produce carbon dioxide. The batter traps the rising gas, and the heat of the oven sets the starch and proteins so the dough doesn't fall. The acceptance and availability of reliable commercial baking powders has become the general principle of Southern home baking, overshadowing yeast, eggs, and general arm power.

In the American South before refrigeration, a sweet whole milk was not always available. Further, Southerners have a real penchant for the sour, often preferring buttermilk and clabber to sweet milk. Incorporating this acid source, via the milk, into standard recipes requires adjustment in the acid-base ratio. The standard safe substitution is 1 teaspoon base (baking soda) for every cup of sour liquid. However, I have found that ½ teaspoon per cup of liquid is sufficient unless you are using yogurt as the acid substitute—then use the full teaspoon.

With this knowledge you should move easily back and forth in adapting recipes to what you have in the kitchen. You can always make

44

tender pancakes and biscuits from yogurt even if there is no cream or milk in the refrigerator for your coffee. One substitution I don't like is souring sweet milk with lemon juice or vinegar. I prefer adapting the recipe chemically over introducing the alien flavors that are inherent in this souring method.

The only reason I am presenting the buttermilk biscuit *after* the sweet milk biscuit is so that you can easily compare the simple chemical corrections. But in the South, sour milk breads would almost always take first place over sweet milk because the sweet-sour flavors and the resulting finer crumb are widely appreciated.

2 c. all-purpose flour	½ tsp. baking soda
Heaping ½ tsp. salt	5 Tb. chilled shortening, lard, or
3 ¼ tsp. baking powder	butter, or a combination
1 tsp. sugar, if desired	⅞ c. buttermilk

Sift the dry ingredients together into a large bowl. Add the cold shortening and work all through the flour with the fingertips. Every bit of flour should be combined with a bit of the fat. Add the buttermilk and stir vigorously until the dough forms a ball.

Turn the dough out onto a lightly floured surface. Knead lightly for 10 strokes. Stop just as soon as the dough begins to look smooth.

Pat the dough out to approximately an 8 × 7 × ¾-inch rectangle. Cut into 2-inch rounds. Place on an ungreased sheet and bake in an oven preheated to 500° F. for 8 minutes, until lightly browned. Serve hot with lots of butter. ✖ *12 biscuits*

Cheese Biscuits

A delicious short dough is made by adding 4 ounces grated sharp cheddar cheese to either the Sweet Milk Biscuits (p. 44) or Buttermilk Biscuits (p. 44) recipes. After working in the fat, vigorously stir in the cheese. Then proceed according to the recipe. Since the cheese increases the proportion of fat, roll the biscuits somewhat thinner, but not crackerlike. They should still rise and split beautifully. Also, except on the most well-seasoned baking sheet, there may be a problem with sticking so just rub the sheet very lightly with fat first as a precaution. Do not overgrease the pan or the biscuit bottoms will fry.

Southerners generally find that cayenne and cheese go hand in hand in baking. A pinch of cayenne is a nice pick-up, but I prefer fresh coarsely ground black pepper, around ¼ teaspoon per recipe. With country ham and hot mustard, these biscuits are delectable and always served hot — except when picnicking.

Sweet Potato Biscuits

A sweet potato biscuit tradition exists in the South and reflects the Caribbean heritage, which was heavily influenced by African cooking. In the tropical zones, cereals fare poorly, but breads are often made from the starchy preparations of other foodstuffs: cassava or manioc, tanyah or elephant ear, breadfruit. The results are rich, rather chewy, pully biscuits and rolls. Almost all of these breads have a nutritional advantage over wheat products; the sweet potato is notably rich in vitamin A.

Again, use one of the two basic recipes for Sweet Milk Biscuits (p. 44) or Buttermilk Biscuits (p. 44). Add 4 ounces (½ cup) thoroughly mashed, riced, or pureed cold, cooked sweet potato to the liquid, beat well, and proceed as directed. These biscuits will be a little more moist and heavier so roll them out no more than ½-inch thick. They're a lovely apricot color.

Louise's Sweet Potato Biscuits

Scraps from this dough are leaden when re-rolled — even more so than for regular biscuits. But rolled very thin, sprinkled with sesame, coarse salt, and cayenne, the leftover dough makes African-style Sweet Potato Crackers.

1 c. all-purpose flour
2½ tsp. baking powder
Heaping ½ tsp. salt
3 Tb. lard
8 oz. cooked sweet potatoes, about 1 c.
⅓–½ c. milk

Sift the dry ingredients together into a large bowl. Add the lard and work all through the flour with the fingertips. Every bit of flour should be combined with a bit of fat.

Puree the sweet potato with just enough milk to make a smooth mixture. Beat into the flour, stirring vigorously.

Turn the dough out onto a lightly floured surface. Knead well, more than for regular biscuits, about 30 turns. Pat or roll out to ⅜ inch. Cut into 2-inch rounds and bake on an ungreased sheet for about 12–15 minutes in an oven preheated to 450° F., until tops and bottoms are golden. Delicious with game and pork or alone with butter, honey, or molasses. *15 biscuits*

Sweet Potato Crackers

Make a delicious cracker for soups or snacking by rolling Sweet Potato Biscuits (p. 46) or Louise's Sweet Potato Biscuits (p. 47) dough very thin. Cut into rounds or squares or whatever you fancy. Sprinkle with coarse salt, hulled sesame seeds, a very little cayenne, if desired. Bake on an ungreased sheet at 350° F. for 10 minutes, until the bottoms are lightly browned. Flip them over, bake about 3–4 more minutes. Let cool on a rack and store airtight. Serving them warm is a treat and will restore crispness, if necessary. A very good holiday gift.

Angel Biscuits

Angel biscuits are a sort of mule bread, a curious hybrid crossed from baking powder and yeast. Since they are often called Bride's biscuits, I believe that the double leavening was originally an insurance policy for inexperienced cooks. At any rate, the result is a very light roll with a nice crusty bottom.

2¾ c. all-purpose flour
2½ tsp. baking powder
½ tsp. baking soda
½ Tb. salt
1 Tb. sugar

6 Tb. lard
¾ c. buttermilk
½ c. Potato Yeast starter (p. 78), at room temperature*

Sift the flour, baking powder, soda, salt, and sugar together into a large bowl. Add the lard and work all through the flour with the fingertips. Stir in the buttermilk and the yeast. Beat well. The dough will be soft.

Turn the dough out onto a floured surface. Knead gently for a few turns and pat out about ½-inch thick. Cut into rounds and place on an ungreased sheet.

Cover and let rise in a warm place until puffed but not doubled. Bake in an oven preheated to 400° F., 15–20 minutes, until tops are lightly and bottoms are well browned. ✖ *20 biscuits*

* *To substitute dry yeast, see p. 74.*

BISCUITS, SPOONBREAD, AND SWEET POTATO PIE

Worms

Biscuit dough scraps are a vexatious dilemma for every Southern cook. Reworked, no matter how gently, and cut, the dough never yields biscuits as tall and tender as their elder brothers. Cutting the dough into squares eliminates the scraps but poses another baking problem — uneven distances from the center to the edges. Biscuits are small and round so the heat reaches the center of the circle quickly and evenly for effective, even rising. Now, back to scraps.

My grandmother Inez had a different viewpoint. A fine cook, she disdained compromise and had no use for second-rate breads. She gathered the dough up, thinly rolled it, grated fresh apple all over, loaded it down with brown sugar and cinnamon, and made her scraps a hallmark sweet that she christened "worms." She'd do the same with pie dough scraps; practically any scrap of raw dough could be turned into a worm with whatever filling might be at hand. We never got these without being told they were my mother's favorite as a child.

The shape made the worm. After thinly rolling and filling the dough she rolled it up jelly-roll fashion and sliced it about ½-inch thick. Then she placed the dough cut side down, either far apart or close together on a greased sheet or in a greased cake tin. The spiral pastry is the worm.

Recipes learned at an early age (this was the first complete cooking process I observed, understood, and could duplicate) resist codification. Worms are such a funny, whimsical, impromptu pastry that even if you read further, please close the book before you make your own. For worms to work, the cook must be tickled at the joke about to be played and be able to say deadpan to some unsuspecting adult, preferably in the presence of some knowledgeable children, "Would you care for some hot worms?"

This recipe is for worms from scratch, which really don't exist. Worms should be spontaneously generated from scraps.

☞ 9 × 12-inch sheet or 9-inch cake
 tin, greased

♦ ♦ ♦ ♦ ♦ ♦ ♦ ♦

1 recipe Sweet Milk or
 Buttermilk Biscuits
 (p. 44)

3 large cooking apples, peeled
 and grated to yield 2 c.
1 c. light brown sugar
6 Tb. butter
Cinnamon and/or nutmeg to taste

Divide the dough into 2 portions. On a floured surface, thinly roll 1 portion into approximately a 12 × 9-inch rectangle. Leaving about a 1-inch clear margin all around, spread 1 cup of grated apples evenly in the center. Sprinkle with about half of the light brown sugar. Dot with 3 tablespoons butter and add spices to your taste. Roll up jelly-roll fashion, tucking the ends in. Slice into 10 pieces and place on a greased sheet or in a 9-inch cake tin. Bake in a preheated oven at 400° F. for approximately 20 minutes or until golden. Repeat the process for the remaining dough and ingredients. *20 hot worms*

Another Worm

You can make more small worms or even a large caterpillar (this large shape actually works better) from sweet potato dough.

Use the Sweet Potato Biscuits (p. 46) recipe. Roll out the scraps from the biscuit cutting or about half the whole recipe to approximately a 12 × 9-inch rectangle. Leaving a margin around the edges, spread the center with orange marmalade. Spread 1 mashed, cooked sweet potato over (or use 1 grated, raw sweet potato). Sprinkle heavily with light brown sugar. Add a few chopped pecans or black walnuts. Dot with butter, sprinkle with cinnamon. Roll up jelly-roll fashion, tucking the ends in. Slice for worms, or transfer the whole roll to a greased baking sheet. Brush lightly with melted butter and bake in a preheated 375° F. oven for about 30–35 minutes, if whole; 20 minutes, if sliced.

The roll makes a delectable dessert, sophisticated enough for a formal Southern dinner in the fall or winter. Add a little bourbon or rum to the sweet potato and serve thinly sliced with very lightly sweetened whipped cream. Without such adornment, it's delicious at breakfast or tea time.

Hominy Ham Biscuits

Hominy Ham Biscuits may be an ingenious solution to leftover bits of breakfast cooking, but they are delicious enough to start from scratch. It is common in Southern breads to work in bits of cooked cereal — grits, cornmeal, rice. Such creative additions, like mashed potatoes, improve the keeping qualities of the breads.

1 c. all-purpose flour	6 Tb. milk
½ tsp. salt	½ c. cold, Plain Cooked Grits
2½ tsp. baking powder	(p. 29)
¼ tsp. sugar	¼ c. diced cooked country ham
2 Tb. lard	

Sift the flour, salt, baking powder, and sugar together into a bowl. Add the lard and work all through the flour with the fingertips. Stir in the milk. Beat in the grits and ham until well mixed.

Turn the dough out on a lightly floured surface. Knead briefly, about 10 strokes, and roll to a ⅜-inch thickness. Cut into 2-inch rounds. Bake in an oven preheated to 400° F. on an ungreased sheet for about 10 minutes. Check the bottoms; they will brown more quickly than the tops. ✕ *24 biscuits*

Hot Hominy Ham Crackers

Add a little cayenne and freshly ground black pepper to the scraps left after cutting. Knead 10–12 strokes and roll very thin. Cut into 1-inch squares. Bake 8–10 minutes in an oven preheated to 375° F. or until very lightly browned. Do not overcook. Cool on a rack and store airtight. Delicious with cold beer.

Black Pepper Dumplings

Rolled dumplings are poached biscuits. Cooked with chicken in a rich stock, they are part of one of the great sentimental dishes of the South, chicken and dumplings. Some call it chicken and pastry, and in part of eastern North Carolina the dish goes by "chicken slick." It is one dish that is almost always good, even in otherwise hopeless restaurants. It can be rather elaborate with the carved meat carefully garnished with the dumplings and served with a sauce enriched with fresh cream, herbs, and mushrooms. That's a Sunday dinner with salad courses and the good china. More often it's a one-dish meal prepared thusly: Bring a pot of water to the boil with onion, celery, carrot, thyme, bay, and peppercorns. Add a good-size chicken — at least 4 pounds — and cook until tender. Remove the bird and bone it when cool. Chop the meat, not too fine. Boil to reduce the stock by almost half. Strain. Add one chopped onion and 2 or 3 sliced carrots to the stock. Cook until tender. Add chicken, season with salt and pepper. Bring to a boil, drop in dumplings. Throw in a handful of finely sliced scallions. Cover, reduce heat, and simmer about 5 minutes. Thicken sauce, if necessary or desired, with butter and flour mashed to a paste; start with 2 tablespoons each and add more cautiously.

2 c. all-purpose flour	½ tsp. coarsely ground black
1 tsp. salt	pepper
3 tsp. baking powder	4 Tb. lard
1½ tsp. sugar	⅔ c. plus about 1 Tb. milk

Sift the dry ingredients together. Add the lard and work into the flour with the fingertips. Stir in the milk carefully. The dough should be stiffer than for regular biscuits. Beat well, turn out onto a well-floured surface and roll to a thickness of ⅛ inch. Cut into approximately 1 × 1½-inch rectangles. Drop into boiling stew or soup liquid, reduce heat, cover, and simmer for about 5 minutes. Even better reheated.

✖ *4–6 servings*

Green Bean Dumplings

Dumplings show up even when there's no chicken in the pot:

🍃 *Now you take a green bean. A green bean is supposed to be cooked at least three hours anyway if you want to make them taste good.*

For your green bean dumplings — cook your green beans and just when they start to get dry, before they get dry down to the pot, covered with about 2 inches of water, roll you a crust as big as the boiler the beans were in and put it over those beans while they are still in the pot. Cover it up and let it stay covered three minutes. Then take you an egg turner and turn the dumpling over and cook it three more minutes. Take a plate as big as your dumpling and grease it with butter, put your dumpling on it.
— *Azilee Edwards, <u>Cabbagetown Families</u>, <u>Cabbagetown Food</u>, 1976*

Corncob Dumplings

🍃 *Take six ears of corn, cut the corn off, put your cobs in the boiler and boil them till they get tender. Take them out of that boiler and scrape them. Put your scrapings back in where you boiled your cobs. Put you some salt and black pepper to taste. Put you a stick of butter [in the water]. Then roll you some dumplings and put in there and you've got a dish. You don't need anything else to go with it.*
— *Azilee Edwards, <u>Cabbagetown Families</u>, <u>Cabbagetown Food</u>, 1976*

Fried Biscuits

Almost all biscuit doughs can be fried — which must have been serendipitous for lazy housewives, foolish bachelors, and any Southern cook in the summer heat. Here was fresh bread for those who forgot to light, didn't even possess, or simply dreaded the heat from a wood-fired oven.

Fried biscuits are not at all common in the modern South. When they are made, the result is sometimes rather greasy. If you knead the dough more vigorously than usual for biscuits and roll it a little thinner, the biscuits will absorb less grease while cooking. Be sure the frying fat is hot (360° F.) and is less than one half the way up the biscuit. Turn only once, when browned, after about 4 minutes. In Kentucky, fried biscuits survive as a country classic with fried chicken, dropped into the hot fat when the chicken is removed. Serve with milk gravy made from the pan.

CHEESE STRAWS

Cheese Straws are made by every good cook throughout the Southern states. They are a staple of the cocktail table, which Southerners, unlike other serious imbibers, pay special attention to, and they are superb morsels to nibble upon with bourbon and sherry.

With an uncharacteristic single-mindedness, Southern cooks who will bake, fry, and boil biscuit dough rarely exploit the potential of this dough. It will fit nicely in a pie pan for a savoury pie and will wrap conveniently around a chicken breast for an *en croûte* appearance. As is to be expected, tearing may occur (the dough has no liquid). Never mind, it patches as easily as it tears.

The straw originally referred to the shape — long and narrow. Most Cheese Straws in the South are now round like little biscuits. Cheese Straws came from England and, despite the superb true cheddar, often were made solely from Parmesan, which has been imported into England for centuries. Samuel Pepys buried his Parmesan to protect it from London's Great Fire in 1666.

Cheese Straws No. 1

These Cheese Straws are often topped with a pecan half before baking. Finely chopped pecans can be mixed into the dough. Sometimes modern cooks will blend in a cereal like Rice Krispies as an economical substitution for the nuts with good results.

8 Tb. butter
6 oz. grated cheddar cheese, about 1⅔ c.
2 oz. freshly grated Parmesan, about ⅔ c.

1½ c. all-purpose flour
¼ tsp. salt
⅜ tsp. cayenne

Beat the butter until light. Add the cheeses and beat well. Stir in the flour, salt, and pepper until smooth and well mixed. Roll into small balls, about ¼ ounce each or the size of a strawberry. Place on an ungreased sheet and flatten with the tines of a fork. Bake in an oven preheated to 325° F. for about 15 minutes or until bottoms are browned. Do not overcook or the wafers will be tough like fried cheese.
✕ *60 wafers*

Cheese Straw Dough No. 2

This dough is more flexible than No. 1 and can be used for pie crusts and wrapping.

1 recipe Cheese Straws No. 1 (opposite)
1 egg
2 Tb. cold water

Prepare Cheese Straws dough. Beat the egg and water together and add to the dough. Mix just until incorporated. Chill for 20–30 minutes before using in the following recipes.

Cocktail Olives

Cocktail olives are not at all olives and therein lies the charm of a surprise. Anything vaguely olive size and olive shape can be used to fill the dough. The mushroom filling is one of the most delicious though a little difficult to handle.

Cheese Straw Dough No. 2 (above)
Olives, Spanish-style, pimiento stuffed, rinsed under cold water and patted dry
Country (bulk) sausage filling, which must be precooked: Make into little olive shapes and bake at 325° F. until done through, about 15 minutes. Chill before wrapping.
Mushroom filling for Martha's Breast of Chicken (p. 58), chilled or dropped by spoonfuls and frozen
Cheese, cut into small pieces
Roasted pecans (p. 57) or almonds

For all fillings, flatten out a ¼-ounce disk of dough (about the size of a large strawberry). Place filling on dough, pinch together, then repair cracks or breaks. Bake at 350° F. for about 15 minutes. Serve with hot drinks. *50 olives*

Ham and Sauerkraut Pie

Sauerkraut is usually "kraut" to Southerners, especially to those who still make it themselves. When I opened my first restaurant, La Résidence, then in the midst of Chatham County farmland, my housekeeper, Lima McNeil, kept us in kraut all winter from her stoneware kegs. Another friend made kraut for her country restaurant up until 1985. Then the state stepped in and insisted on stainless steel vats for preparation. Without the thick, cool walls of stoneware, the kraut never cured properly, and another Southern tradition was lost to modern bureaucracy.

Use the best kraut you can find. Most stores do carry a glass or plastic packaged version; these are usually superior to the tinned variety. Rinsing the kraut well and cooking it gently are the keys to taming what too many consider a wild beast. With the zesty cheese crust in this pie, the sauerkraut and ham combination is a far cry from the street vendors' dog and kraut. This is an excellent buffet item and belongs, in my mind, to winter suppers, football, and beer.

Everyone likes to dress up, though, and this tart may well show up as a first course of a formal dinner with a spicy gewürztraminer at her side.

Pastry Shell
8 oz. Cheese Straw Dough No. 2
    (p. 55), about ½ recipe
1–2 Tb. Dijon mustard
Filling
1 c. sauerkraut
1 c. sliced onion
2 Tb. bacon fat
Pinch of sugar
¼ tsp. thyme
A few caraway seeds

3 eggs
¾ c. milk
¾ c. heavy cream
½ tsp. salt
Pinch of white pepper
Pinch of fresh grated nutmeg
4 oz. thinly sliced, chopped,
    cooked country ham *or* smoked
    boiled ham
2 Tb. chopped fresh parsley

Roll the dough out to fit a 9-inch pie pan. Chill at least 20 minutes. Bake, filled with beans or rice on foil, for 10 minutes in an oven preheated to 350° F. Remove the weights carefully, prick bottom and sides with a fork, and bake 10 more minutes. Repair any holes or breaks with scraps of raw dough. Brush interior of shell lightly with mustard.

Rinse the sauerkraut under running cold water. Drain well and gently press out excess liquid. Sauté the onion in the bacon fat slowly until tender. Add the sauerkraut, sugar, thyme, and caraway. Cover and cook gently about 15 minutes.

Beat the eggs first, then add the milk, cream, salt, pepper, and nutmeg.

To assemble the pie, strew the sauerkraut/onion mix over the bottom of the prepared pastry shell. Spread the ham all about and sprinkle with the parsley. Pour the prepared custard into the shell and bake in a preheated 325° F. oven for about 45 minutes or until the pie is set.

Let rest a few minutes before slicing. ✂ *6–8 servings*

Roasted Pecans

2 Tb. butter
⅛ tsp. cayenne
½ tsp. sugar (optional)
1 Tb. dry sherry

8 oz. pecan halves
¼ tsp. coarse salt, plus
    additional, if desired

Melt the butter with the cayenne and sugar. Stir in the sherry off heat. Toss the pecans with the butter mixture and scatter over a baking sheet. Sprinkle with coarse salt and bake in a preheated oven at 325° F. for about 20 minutes, stirring about frequently. Do not overbrown or the nuts will be bitter. When done sprinkle with the additional salt if desired. Let cool and store airtight. Serve at room temperature or rewarm slightly. ✂ *About 3 cups*

Martha's Breast of Chicken

Chicken
4 pieces boneless breast, about
   3½–4 oz. each
Salt
Black pepper
2 Tb. butter

Mushroom Filling (about ¾ c.)
1 c. chopped mushrooms
¼ c. chopped scallions
1 Tb. dry sherry
2 tsp. instant flour, such as
   Wondra

½ c. heavy cream
1½ tsp. chopped fresh tarragon
1 tsp. chopped fresh parsley
Salt
White pepper
Nutmeg
½ oz. cooked ham finely diced
   (about 2 Tb.), optional

Pastry
12 oz. chilled Cheese Straw
   Dough No. 2 (p. 55), about ¾
   recipe

Rub the chicken breasts all over with salt and pepper. Sauté lightly but thoroughly, about 4 minutes on each side, in the hot butter. Reserve and chill.

In the same pan, sauté the mushrooms for about 10 minutes or until the liquid is completely evaporated. Add the scallions, stir about for a minute. Pour in the sherry and rapidly boil off the liquid.

Stir the instant flour in and add the cream. Again, boil down, until quite thick. Season highly with fresh herbs, and salt, pepper, and nutmeg to taste. Add ham, if desired.

Refrigerate until well chilled.

To assemble: the chicken, mushroom filling, and cheese dough must be cold.

Slice each chicken breast rather thin on a broad diagonal into four wide slices. Put a bit of mushroom filling between each slice and reassemble each breast.

Thinly roll out one fourth of the dough into a rectangle large enough to wrap a chicken breast. Put a dab of mushroom filling on the pastry, place a reassembled chicken breast on top, dab again with mushroom. Fold the dough over; seal with a little cold water and finger pressure. Trim up and repair any tears or breaks. Repeat for the remaining breasts. Refrigerate, if desired, or bake immediately in a preheated 325° F. oven for about 30 minutes. ✕ *4 servings*

MOSTLY· BREAKFAST· CAKES

Alice's Batter Cakes

Blueberry Pancakes

Overnight Cakes

German Waffles

Blueberry Buttermilk
Waffles

Hominy Waffles

Hominy Cheese Waffles

Cornmeal Waffles

The Lightest Waffles

Farm-Style Waffles

Fancy Pudding

Pain Perdu

Alice's Batter Cakes

These are rich pancakes from a Mississippi recipe. Adjust flour to your taste; the full amount makes thicker, taller pancakes.

☞ Griddle

½ tsp. salt
5 tsp. sugar
2¼ tsp. baking powder

1–1¼ c. all-purpose flour
2 eggs, separated
1 c. milk
2 Tb. melted butter

Sift salt, sugar, baking powder, and flour together. Beat the egg yolks well, then beat in the milk and butter. Stir into dry ingredients just until smooth. Beat the egg whites until quite frothy but not stiff and fold in.

Drop by the tablespoon onto a heated, lightly greased griddle. Turn when brown. Serve with butter, honey, preserves, and/or a fresh fruit sauce. ✖ *24 small pancakes*

Blueberry Pancakes

Use the larger amount of flour called for in Alice's Batter Cakes (above). Add ¼ teaspoon cinnamon, or to your taste. Stir in 1 cup fresh blueberries (or other fruit) before folding in the egg whites. Cherries, raspberries, blackberries, or peaches will all make delicious pancakes.

Overnight Cakes

All griddle-cakes are much nicer mixed and kept overnight, to allow the flour to swell, stirring in the whites of eggs and soda or baking powder, when used, just before baking.
— Estelle Wilcox, The New Dixie Cook-Book, 1889

Many nineteenth-century pan- or griddle-cake recipes call for an overnight rest. Eliza Leslie, in *Miss Leslie's New Cooking Book* (1847), is explicit about where to place her cornmeal batter: "Cover the pan and set it on the dresser till morning." Cakes from whole grains as below benefit even more from a good rest than those of white flour, the coarser grinds absorbing the liquid slowly and erratically. The premixing also makes for short cuts, all the more welcome early in the day.

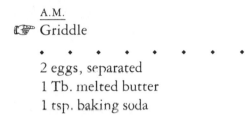

P.M.
1/3 c. whole wheat or
   buckwheat flour
1 c. all-purpose flour
1/2 tsp. salt
1 Tb. sugar
1 c. plus 1 Tb. buttermilk

A.M.
☞ Griddle

2 eggs, separated
1 Tb. melted butter
1 tsp. baking soda

Put the dry ingredients in a large bowl and slowly stir in the buttermilk until smooth. Cover and refrigerate overnight.

Beat the egg yolks with the melted butter and stir into the flour batter with the soda. Stiffly beat the egg whites, gently fold into the batter and cook on a lightly greased griddle over medium low heat, turning once. ✗ *30 small pancakes*

. . . .*Oats and Apples Variation.* To the above p.m. preparation add 1/4 cup rolled oatmeal flakes and increase buttermilk to 1 1/4 cups.

To the a.m. preparation add about 1/2 cup grated fresh apple and 1/2 teaspoon cinnamon along with the egg yolks.

WAFFLES

Waffles are favored for all their fine crisp pockets which trap melting butter, cream, syrups, or gravies. They look like the product of a beehive; the name waffle is derived from the Old High Germanic *waba,* which means honeycomb. The cake itself was frequently identified with the German and Dutch communities in the Southern colonies. Early descriptions are often subtitled "A German Recipe." Eliza Leslie in *Miss Leslie's New Cooking Book* (1847) says, "We are indebted to the Germans for this cake . . ."

Both Sarah Rutledge in *The Carolina Housewife* (1847) and Mrs. Lettice Bryan in *The Kentucky Housewife* (1839) published waffle recipes but Mary Randolph in *The Virginia House-wife* (1824) slighted them, to my surprise. Thomas Jefferson, who was father-in-law to Mary's brother, bought his waffle iron in Paris and returned to Virginia with it. At any rate, by the end of the eighteenth century, waffles were almost a national craze, with social parties devoted to their consumption.

Waffles get more esteem in Southern states than in the rest of the country. One well-traveled bon vivant I know claims the best dish he ever ate is a sauté of sweetbreads, Smithfield ham, and fresh morels on a corn-meal waffle in Virginia. Waffles made with the traditional Southern cereals such as corn and rice are excellent; the low protein and high starch content of our grains make for fine, thin, and crisp crusts. Southern cooks who once saw this cake as foreign have now claimed it as their own. In *Charleston Receipts* (1950) the hominy or grits waffle is a symbol of the antebellum world: "These crisp waffles of the days before the War delighted the people of 'Look Back to Glory.' "

Mrs. Bryan describes the old procedure for waffle making. First, build your fire. Then,

> *Heat your waffle irons moderately, by holding them in the fire; clean them neatly, and grease them well with fresh lard or butter; then put in your batter, filling them quite full, close the irons, confine them at the end with a ring, that is to one side of the irons, and lay them level in the fire, on a bed of clear coals, that the under side may get done as soon as the upper. Take them out, and open them occasionally, to see how the waffle is progressing, and as soon as it is of a light brown on both sides, take it from the irons by running a knife under it.*

The electric irons with nonstick surfaces make our waffling much easier —quicker for me than even pancakes or biscuits—and it isn't necessary to grease them. Of course, grocery stores offer a frozen waffle for the toaster. I prefer the following recipe.

German Waffles

☞ Waffle iron

• • • • • • • •

2 c. all-purpose flour
2 tsp. baking powder
⅔ tsp. salt

2 Tb. sugar
3 eggs, separated
1¾ c. milk
5 Tb. melted butter

Sift the flour, baking powder, salt, and sugar together. Beat the yolks with the milk and stir into the dry ingredients. Add the melted butter, beat the egg whites until stiff, and fold in. A waffle approximately 4-inches square will use a good ¼ cup batter.
✖ *20 waffles*

Blueberry Buttermilk Waffles

Replace milk in the German Waffles recipe (above) with buttermilk. Add 1 teaspoon baking soda to dry ingredients. Fold in 1 cup whole fresh blueberries just before adding the egg whites.
✖ *24 waffles*

Hominy Waffles

☞ Waffle iron

• • • • • • • •

1½ c. all-purpose flour
1½ tsp. baking powder
½ tsp. salt
1 tsp. sugar

1 egg, separated
½ c. Plain Cooked Grits
  (p. 29)
½ c. milk
½ c. water
2 Tb. butter, melted

Sift the flour, baking powder, salt, and sugar together. Beat the egg yolk with the grits and add the milk and water, beating well. Pour through a sieve, and rub all the grits through, back into the liquid. Stir into the dry ingredients along with the melted butter. Last, beat the egg white to soft, firm peaks and fold in. Bake in a waffle iron. ✖ *12 waffles*

Hominy Cheese Waffles

These are awfully good as a savoury base for brunch or supper dishes — anything from scrambled eggs to shrimp and scallops in a Tabasco-spiced hollandaise sauce.

☞ Waffle iron

• • • • • • • •

1 recipe Hominy Waffles
  (p. 63), omitting the sugar if
  desired

3 Tb. freshly grated Parmesan
Good dash of cayenne

Follow the directions for Hominy Waffles, but add the Parmesan and cayenne to the dry ingredients just before the liquid is stirred in. ✗ *12 waffles*

Cornmeal Waffles

☞ Waffle iron

• • • • • • • •

1 c. all-purpose flour
1 c. cornmeal
2 tsp. baking powder
½ tsp. baking soda

1 Tb. sugar
½ tsp. salt
2 eggs, separated
Buttermilk (about 1½ c.)
4 Tb. melted butter

Sift all the dry ingredients together. Beat the egg yolks and add enough buttermilk to make 2 cups liquid total. Stir into the dry ingredients with the melted butter. Beat the egg whites until stiff and fold into the batter. ✗ *16 waffles*

The Lightest Waffles

Follow the recipe for Ashley Rice Bread (p. 118) but omit the cooked rice. Cook in the waffle iron until well browned. This makes the lightest, crispest waffle I have ever eaten. It is especially good as a base for savoury dishes. ✖ *24 waffles*

Farm-Style Waffles

The batter for Farm-Style Spoonbread (p. 30) makes a light waffle with a thin, crisp crust. These are very good as a savoury base. For a sweet or fruit accompaniment, you may want to substitute butter for the bacon fat, but the original bacon flavor with honey, syrup, or fruit would not be odd to Southerners. Reduce the salt to ½ teaspoon. ✖ *24 waffles*

PAIN PERDU

The *Picayune Creole Cook Book* (1901) gives Pain Perdu, or Lost Bread (what we call French Toast outside of New Orleans), a very aromatic treatment: "5 eggs, 2 tablespoons of Orange Flower Water. ½ cup sugar. Slices of Stale Bread. The Finely Grated Zest of a Lemon. 3 Tablespoons of Brandy (if Desired)." That's very eggy and sweet as well. The *Picayune Creole Cook Book* calls a lighter version using milk Spanish Toast. It's what is made today, though the spices seem exorbitant: "½ Ounce Each of Powdered Nutmeg and Cinnamon." One half ounce cinnamon is close to 3 tablespoons, and that's for "6 Slices of Stale Bread"!

The term Spanish Toast has disappeared, but contemporary Cajun and creole cookbooks call the dish French Toast, Pain Perdue, and Lost Bread all on the same page.

French Toast can never be better than the bread you start with. Buy a good, nonsweet French-style baguette. I almost always end up cutting fresh bread, even though the dish is supposed to be a thrifty little mop-up of leftovers. In the spring and summer, my children, Elliott and Madeline, and I start the bread soaking, walk to the Farmers' Market for fresh strawberries, raspberries, the best fruit of the morning — and local honey — and rush home to fry up the toast and top it with whipped cream and our purchases.

Fancy Pudding

Sarah Rutledge knew French Toast under another name.

🦋 Fancy Pudding. *A loaf of French bread sliced, half a pint of milk, poured over it; the other half pint mix with four well beaten eggs; add sugar and cinnamon to your taste; dip each slice of bread in the mixture, and fry it in lard or butter. It is to be eaten with a sauce of sugar, wine and nutmeg.*

And, also, under the most exotic name of all.

🦋 Queen Esther's Bread. *Cut some slices of bread, and lay them in milk for some hours. Then beat two eggs; dip the slices in the egg, and fry them. When of a nice brown, pour over them any syrup you please, and serve up.*
— *The Carolina Housewife*, 1847

Pain Perdu

Twelve 1-inch slices good French
   bread
2 eggs
1¼ c. milk

4 tsp. sugar
¼ tsp. cinnamon
1 tsp. brandy

    Slice the bread the night before and leave on a rack to dry. In the
morning beat the eggs with the milk. Mix the cinnamon and sugar and
stir in with the brandy. Pour into a shallow pan and soak the bread
in the liquid, turning once, until the milk is absorbed and the bread is
saturated, at least 15 minutes. Fry in butter over medium heat about
4 minutes each side, until golden brown. ✖ *3 servings*

YEAST-RISEN· BREADS

Salt-Rising Bread

Potato Yeast

A Good White Loaf

Big Mama's
Everlasting Rolls

Scuppernong Wine
Christmas Loaf

Cinnamon Rolls

Pineapple Rolls

Persimmon Rolls

Moravian Cake

Moravian Sugar Bread

Sweet Potato Yeast Bread

Patent Yeast

Fig Leaf Yeast

CAVEATS ON
BREAD MAKING

Bread making with yeast is one of the most reckless operations in my kitchen. I experiment randomly and wildly and hardly ever follow a recipe or duplicate a loaf I know to be successful. But over the years I have arrived at four basic checkpoints that serve to correct my aberrations.

1) Excess flour. The most common fault in home bread making is too much flour in the dough. Learn to handle doughs that seem soft and sticky at first. Some flours, especially whole-grain or stone-ground, are reluctant to absorb liquid, and you must give them a little time. Moving the dough around a lot while kneading is helpful. Any dough left resting for a time on any surface will adhere. Don't hesitate to do a great deal of kneading and tossing around of the dough in the air.

2) Insufficient kneading. Any good yeast-raised dough must be worked to elasticity. Properly kneaded dough, no matter how soft or stiff, will stretch out to a tissue, like gum blown to a bubble. If the dough tears raggedly, work it more. This is as true of the softest, handbeaten doughs such as Sally Lunn as it is of free-form whole-grain loaves.

3) Surface drying. Once bread is shaped and set to rise, the surfaces must remain moist and soft. If the crust dries before baking, the loaf or roll will be hindered in its final oven rising, moisture will be trapped making a doughy interior, and the surface will crack and pull apart unattractively. Sprinkle the formed breads lightly with water; if baking is free form on a sheet, sprinkle the baking sheet with water as well. Plastic wrap is efficient for creating a moisture-retentive barrier, but every time I use plastic, I think of its lasting a thousand years, so I loosely wrap wax paper over the bread and tuck it under the edges of the pan. If doughs are soft, sprinkle a little extra flour, seeds, oatmeal, cornmeal over the top of the loaves to prevent the cover from sticking. These little additions can add a lot of character to the breads.

4) Slashing the bread. Give full vent to the interior rising of the doughs by slashing the top of the bread just before baking. Use a very sharp knife or single-edged razor blade. Dip the blade in flour for each slash so the cut is clean and doesn't pull or deflate the rising dough. Heat affects bread from the outside. If the crust is set before heat penetrates the interior, the bread steams on the inside and is wet and dense upon slicing. Slashing allows moisture to escape and results in additional volume. It also makes attractive designs and variations in crust development.

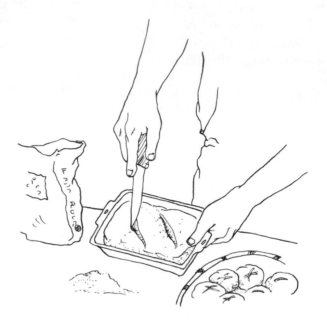

YEAST

Yeast is a one-celled funguslike, ravenous, and ubiquitous plant. Its function, in the kitchen, is to eat — to eat starches and sugars producing carbon dioxide and alcohol. When directed or controlled, yeast gives us two of our most basic and splendid products: bread and wine. Given a free rein, yeast yields corruption and disease. The role of the cook (or winemaker) is to manipulate the natural growth processes of yeast and stop them at their most beneficial stage.

There are many species of yeast in the air around us all the time. The one we cultivate and use commercially for baking is *Saccharomyces cerevisiae.* The famous San Francisco sourdough yeast, according to Harold McGee in *On Food and Cooking,* "is not the usual baker's yeast, . . . but rather *Saccharomyces exiquus* (*exiquus* means small or scanty; *cerevisiae* means "of beer"), which thrives in very acidic environments. . . ."

Many of the other wild yeasts can start doughs rising. Salt-rising loaves begin as unleavened batters just waiting to trap any of the airborne yeasts that are always present. If conditions — mostly temperature — are right and held, the yeasts will multiply rapidly and perform the same functions as store-bought yeast.

Collecting and maintaining the growth of airborne yeasts is difficult, but fascinating. My children love to inspect the starter, eager for the first bubbles of fermentation. In my old, drafty kitchen, the biggest problem is maintaining a constant temperature. In winter, I usually bank the bowl containing the starter with ashes at the edge of the hearth overnight. This is also a good method for Corn Light Bread (see pp. 21–2), but it is not a process that will fit neatly into a schedule. Sometimes it takes a few hours, sometimes a day or more for the starter to develop. The slight, constant heat of a gas pilot light may be more predictable. During the summer, capturing, controlling, and maintaining a healthy yeast culture is just as difficult. The heat and humidity abet rapid growth, and the sourdough-type starters often go too sour or die in their own alcohol.

The simplest, most reliable homemade yeast I've found is the liquid Potato Yeast, a recipe for which follows. Once started, keep it going by reserving a portion each time you use it and then returning bits of raw raised dough to it. Potato Yeast is not for long keeping without frequent use and renewal. I don't follow any exact formula, and I've never had any problem, but any starter that looks gray with acrid as opposed to yeasty smelling liquid separating out of the dough has gone too far. For a more stable, longer-lasting leavener, Southern cooks make yeast cakes, adding hops as a precaution against the yeast's souring. Short-term yeasts such as the Potato Yeast have no need for hops. Any of these yeasts can be frozen for a short while, up to a month.

All homemade yeasts lend a distinctive flavor to baked breads. The cultures invariably collect wild yeasts from the air and become more and more complex in time. The flavor is, to varying degrees, wild, sour, and gamey. The differences between baker's yeast and wild yeast can be compared to the difference between farm-raised and wild game meat. Obviously, the flavor may not be to everyone's immediate palate, but I find it haunting. I also believe the texture of bread is affected by the action of homemade yeast. These breads are strong and glutinous, and not gummy.

Be creative about the use of homemade yeast cultures. I give two basic recipes, one for a loaf, one for classic Southern rolls and variations. You can use commercial yeast instead in any of my recipes or, alternatively, you can use homemade yeast where I call for the store-bought variety. I think that the more you bake, the more you'll want to do it with homemade yeast, but the important thing is: bake!

To substitute dry yeast for 1 cup Potato Yeast, dissolve 1 package dry yeast in ¼ cup warm water. Then add about ½ cup more warm water and stir in ⅓ cup flour until smooth. Set aside in a warm place until very light and bubbly.

SORGHUM

Sorghum was the poor man's sugar cane, the source of molasses for much of the South, but it was known on every table, rich or poor. These photographs were taken on the farm of Mr. Wes Chris, a successful, independent black farmer in Orange County, North Carolina, on September 28, 1939.

From the photographer's notes:

"One man hands cane from the pile to another who sits by the mill; the second feeds the cane stalks, one or two at a time into the grinding part of the mill, while a mule walks round and round the mill turning it; the juice squeezed out runs into a barrel; it is dipped in buckets from the barrel and strained into a barrel just over the cooking pans; it is drained out of this feed barrel through a spigot into the pans."

"*Women skim the impurities from the cooking syrup with long handled 'shovels'; the cooked syrup is drained off at the opposite end of the pans, measured in gallon cans, and strained into a barrel. The mill is a portable one and the mill owner gets every sixth gallon for making the syrup. Children, a baby, and some of the women were at the cane grinding mill more for sociability than for work and all of them seemed to be enjoying it.*"

SALT RISING, OR YEAST

🦎 *This kind of yeast will be found convenient when you get out of other kinds; it does not rise quite so soon as the hop yeast, yet it makes excellent bread. Make a quart of water lukewarm, stir into it a tablespoonful of salt, and make it a tolerably thin batter with flour; mix it well, sprinkle on the top a handful of dry flour, and set it in a warm place to rise, but be sure you do not let it get hot, or it would spoil it. Turn it round occasionally, and in a few hours it will be light, and the top covered with bubbles. . . .*
— Lettice Bryan, <u>The Kentucky Housewife</u>, 1839

Salt-Rising Bread

☞Three 8 × 5 × 3-inch loaf pans, greased

The Starter

12 oz. (about 6 small) red boiling potatoes, thinly sliced, not peeled

2½ tsp. salt

2½ tsp. sugar

2 Tb. white cornmeal (water-ground only)

2 Tb. all-purpose flour

4 c. boiling water

The Sponge

4 c. flour

1 tsp. baking powder

1 tsp. salt

The Dough

¾ c. milk

2 Tb. butter

5–6 c. all-purpose flour

Combine the raw sliced potatoes and the dry ingredients for the starter in a large bowl. Toss well and pour over the boiling water. Stir around to dissolve the dry ingredients. Cover and store in a warm place 15–18 hours, until frothy and sour smelling. If you have doubts, it is not ready.

Strain the fermented starter well. Gently press the potatoes but do not break them up or force through the strainer. Discard the potatoes.

Sift together the flour, baking powder, and salt for the sponge. Add to the yeasty starter and beat very well. Cover and let rise until doubled.

Reserve 1 cup of the sponge and refrigerate for the next batch if you intend to bake again soon. It will not hold more than 2 or 3 days.

For the dough, heat together the milk and butter until the butter melts. Reserve 2 tablespoons of this liquid for glazing the loaves. Add the rest of the liquid to the sponge along with the flour. Beat well until a stiff dough forms. Turn out onto a floured surface and knead very well, at least 10 minutes. Divide into 3 loaves (24 ounces each). Place in the greased loaf pans, cover, and let rise about 2 hours or until doubled. Slash the top of the loaves with a very sharp knife, brush with the reserved milk, and bake in a preheated oven at 400° F. for 15 minutes. Reduce the heat to 350° F. and bake for about 40 more minutes. ✖ *3 loaves*

Potato Yeast

2 baking potatoes, peeled and
    sliced
4 c. water
¼ c. all-purpose flour

2 Tb. light brown sugar
2 tsp. salt
1 pkg. dry yeast

Put the potatoes and the water in a saucepan, bring to a boil, then simmer until tender. Drain the potatoes, reserving the water, and put them through a fine strainer. Add the cooking water, whisk thoroughly, and let cool to about 90° F. Mix the flour, sugar, salt, and yeast and stir into the potato liquid until smooth. Store, covered, in a warm place about 6 hours until thoroughly frothy. It is now ready to use. To store, shake down, bottle, and refrigerate until needed.

Refrigerated, Potato Yeast will keep about 2½ weeks. Test it by adding a little sugar and flour to a bit of the yeast at room temperature. It should bubble if active. If the starter is still good, use the last cup to begin the next batch, substituting it for or using it in conjunction with the dry yeast. ✖ *6 cups*

A Good White Loaf

1 c. Potato Yeast starter
  (opposite), at room
  temperature*
1 c. milk
4 Tb. butter

2 Tb. sugar
2–2½ tsp. salt
5–5½ c. all-purpose flour
Milk and butter for glazing

Heat the milk, butter, sugar, and salt together, stirring just until the butter melts. Add to yeast and beat in 2 cups of the flour. Cover and let sit in a warm place about an hour, until very light and spongy.

Beat the starter well and incorporate 3–3½ cups flour. Turn out on a floured surface and knead very well, 8–10 minutes.

Form as desired. This amount of dough will make 2 loaves in 6-cup pans, or about 30 rolls, or a combination of the two. Pans for baking should be lightly greased.

Cover and let rise until doubled, about 1 hour. Do not stint on rising time. Also, it is very important that the dough not dry out on the surface during rising. Sprinkle the baking sheet lightly with water before covering rolls with wax paper or plastic wrap. Just before baking, glaze lightly with a little melted butter mixed with milk. Slash loaves and/or rolls with a very sharp knife just before baking.

Bake in a preheated oven at 375° F. The loaves will take about 45 minutes, rolls 20 minutes. Glaze again, once breads begin to brown. Bake until golden brown. ✴ *2 loaves or about 30 rolls*

* *To substitute dry yeast, see p. 74.*

Big Mama's Everlasting Rolls

Big Mama's Everlasting Rolls are a delicate, slightly sweet and sour company or Sunday bread. They are known in every region of the South and are prized in every household. The rolls are always served warm and have a characteristic light dusting of flour on the top surface. Manchet, the fine, white bread of the English aristocracy, is the likely ancestor of these little breads; typically, Southern cooks have enriched the parent dough with sugar, eggs, and fat for better keeping in the hot, humid climate. Use this same dough as the base for many other breads. It keeps a week refrigerated; once baked, it's gone! Four variations follow.

3 Tb. lard	2 eggs, beaten
3 Tb. butter	6½ c. flour
1 c. milk	1¾ tsp. salt
½ c. sugar	½ tsp. baking soda
1 pkg. dry yeast and 1 c. Potato Yeast starter (p. 78) at room temperature *or* 1½ c. Potato Yeast starter	1 tsp. baking powder
	Melted butter for glazing

Combine the lard, butter, milk, and sugar in a saucepan and heat, stirring, until the fats melt. Let cool to lukewarm.

Dissolve the dry yeast in the lukewarm milk mixture and stir in the Potato Yeast. Let sit 15 minutes. Beat in the eggs and enough flour to make a light dough. Add the salt, soda, and baking powder. Beat vigorously, then turn out on a floured surface. Incorporate as little flour as possible while kneading hard for 8–10 minutes. The dough should remain soft. Put in a large bowl and cover with a damp towel. Let rise in a warm place until double, about 2 hours.

At this point the dough can be refrigerated either in whole or in part. Tightly covered, the refrigerated dough will last about 7 days.

To make rolls, roll the dough out on a floured surface to a thickness about ⅜ inch. Cut into 2-inch rounds. Use the back of a chef's knife to crease the circle on the diameter. Fold the roll over to make a half-moon shape so the crease is on the outside and transfer to an ungreased baking sheet, giving the ends of the roll a pull to elongate slightly. Sprinkle very lightly with warm water. Cover again with a damp towel and let rise until double, about 40–50 minutes. Do not stint on rising time; the rolls must be very light or they will lose their charm. Preheat oven to 400° F.

Brush each roll lightly with melted butter. Bake for 10 minutes, until lightly browned. Serve warm with butter.

✕ *64 ounces dough, about 60 rolls*

Scuppernong Wine
Christmas Loaf

☞ Loaf pan, approximately 3½ × 6½ inches, greased

◆ ◆ ◆ ◆ ◆ ◆ ◆ ◆

Loaf

⅓ c. chopped glacéed fruit (cherries, citron, orange, pineapple)
¼ c. chopped pecans
1 Tb. dry scuppernong wine or sherry
10 oz. (about 2 c.) Big Mama's Everlasting Rolls dough (opposite)
1½ tsp. melted butter

Glaze

6 Tb. powdered sugar
4 tsp. dry scuppernong wine or sherry

Toss together the glacéed fruit, pecans, and wine. Let stand 10 minutes.

Turn the dough out and knead the macerated fruits and nuts into it. Shape into a small loaf and place in the greased pan. Brush with the melted butter, cover lightly, and let rise until light and doubled in volume, about 90 minutes. Slash the top of the loaf with a sharp knife to prevent splitting while baking.

Bake in an oven preheated to 375° F. for about 30 minutes or until golden brown. Turn the heat off, but leave the loaf in the oven. Mix together the powdered sugar and wine for the glaze; spoon over the bread evenly until it is all absorbed. Leave the loaf in the oven with the door ajar for about 5 more minutes, then remove to a rack and cool. Refrigerated or frozen, this pretty loaf keeps well. *1 loaf*

Cinnamon Rolls

• • • • • • •

24 oz. (about 4½ c.) Big Mama's
    Everlasting Rolls dough
    (p. 80)

3 Tb. butter
1 c. minus 2 Tb. light brown
    sugar
½–¾ tsp. cinnamon

Roll the dough into approximately an 18 × 9-inch rectangle.
Leaving a ¾-inch margin on both long sides, dot the butter over the
dough. Sprinkle the brown sugar over the butter and top with the
cinnamon. Brush the far long side with a little water. Roll up jelly-
roll fashion, starting at the near long side. Press lightly to seal. Slice
about 2 inches thick and place cut side down in a lightly buttered
pan. The rolls should be close to, but not touching, each other.
Cover and let rise until light and doubled in volume, about an hour.

Bake the rolls in an oven preheated to 350° F. for about 25–30
minutes or until golden. ✖ *10 rolls*

Pineapple Rolls

24 oz. (about 4½ c.) Big Mama's
    Everlasting Rolls dough
    (p. 80)

1 recipe Pineapple Filling
    (p. 288)

Roll the dough, not too thinly, to an 18 × 9-inch rectangle.
Prepare and bake as for cinnamon rolls using the Pineapple Filling,
instead of the brown sugar/cinnamon filling. ✖ *10 rolls*

Persimmon Rolls

Use about 10 small, sweet native persimmons rubbed through a colander to eliminate skins and seeds for this filling. Persimmon puree can be frozen to last through the winter.

10 oz. (about 2 c.) Big Mama's
   Everlasting Rolls dough
   (p. 80)
1 Tb. butter
6 Tb. raw persimmon puree

2 Tb. peach or apricot preserves
¼ tsp. powdered ginger
1 egg, beaten
¼ c. chopped pecans
⅓ c. light brown sugar

Thinly roll the dough out to about a 14 × 7-inch rectangle. Leaving a ½-inch margin all around, dot with butter. Beat the persimmon puree, preserves, ginger, egg, and nuts until well mixed. Spread over the dough respecting the free borders. Sprinkle the brown sugar over.

Moisten the far long side and roll up loosely, jelly-roll fashion, starting at the near long side. Tuck the ends in and press to seal the edges. Transfer to a lightly buttered baking sheet. Cover with a damp towel and let rise until light and doubled in volume, about 50 minutes.

Bake in a preheated oven at 375° F. for about 30 minutes or until golden brown. Let rest 10–15 minutes before slicing on the diagonal to serve. ✖ *4–6 servings*

MORAVIAN SUGAR BREAD

The Moravian settlement at Winston-Salem, North Carolina, was only one of many German settlements in the South, but it was (and is today) by far the most famous and still the most traditional. When the Rev. Charles Woodmason proselytized among the pioneers of upland Carolina for the Anglican Church, he detested almost all the slothful ways he saw, but in the Moravian towns he was amazed: "They have Mills, Furnaces, Forges, Potteries, Founderies All Trades, and all things in and among themselves . . . they are all *Bees,* not a Drone suffer'd in the Hive."

The restored village of Old Salem presents authentic crafts and folkways for tourists, but the religious, musical, and cooking heritages are all still very much part of the modern life of the community. The Moravian Sugar Bread, usually associated with the Christmas holidays, has been enjoyed in the South for generations, but it always carries its cultural identification as specifically Moravian.

Moravian Cake

Sift a quart of fine flour, sprinkle into it a small spoonful of salt, two powdered nutmegs, a spoonful of cinnamon, one of mace, and four ounces of powdered sugar. Rub in with your hands four ounces of butter and two beaten eggs; when they are completely saturated, add four table-spoonfuls of good yeast, and enough sweet milk to make it into a thick batter. Put it in a buttered pan, cover it, and set it by the fire to rise, but be sure you do not let it get hot, or the cake will be spoiled. When it looks quite light, superadd four ounces of sugar, and a handful of flour; sprinkle a handful of brown sugar over the top, and bake it in a moderate oven.
—*Lettice Bryan, <u>The Kentucky Housewife</u>, 1839*

Moravian Sugar Bread

☞ Two 12 × 9-inch baking dishes, greased

◆ ◆ ◆ ◆ ◆ ◆ ◆ ◆ ◆

The Bread

1½ c. Potato Yeast starter (p. 78) or 1½ pkg. dry yeast*
3 Tb. plus ½ c. sugar
¾ c. milk
1 tsp. salt
½ c. butter
3 eggs, beaten
7½–8½ c. all-purpose flour

Sugar Topping

¾ c. butter
Pinch of salt
1 lb. light brown sugar
1 tsp. cinnamon
½–¾ tsp. freshly grated nutmeg
Extra butter (about 2 Tb.)

Combine the yeast and 3 tablespoons sugar. Set aside until frothy. Heat the milk with ½ cup sugar, salt, and butter. Stir until the butter melts. Let cool to lukewarm. Add the yeast and beat in the eggs.

Make a starter by adding 2½ cups flour to the liquid. Beat very well, cover, and set in a warm place until very light and bubbly, about 40 minutes.

Beat down and beat in the flour. Add just enough flour to make a manageable, not stiff, dough. Turn out on a floured surface and knead thoroughly. Divide into 2 equal portions (32 ounces each) and place in greased baking dishes approximately 12 × 9 inches. Cover and let rise 1 hour or until doubled in volume.

Combine the ingredients for the sugar topping, except the extra butter, in a heavy-bottomed saucepan and heat, stirring, until melted.

Poke the dough all over with a finger, especially around the edges. Pour the sugar topping equally over the 2 pans of dough, being sure to fill the indentations. Dot the bare surfaces with the extra butter. Bake in a preheated oven at 375° F. about 30 minutes, until brown and bubbling. Serve warm. *2 loaves or 24 servings*

* *To substitute dry yeast, see p. 74.*

Sweet Potato Yeast Bread

This Mississippi bread has just about everything going for it — a fine, rich crumb, delicious flavor, excellent keeping qualities, and high nutritive value. It is often braided — glazed with a little egg and milk it comes out spectacularly golden brown. I usually make one braided loaf and one regular loaf pan form. It is a treat just toasted with butter.

This very delicious and nutritious recipe came to me from a friend in Mississippi. Similar recipes are published in local cookbooks throughout the Southern coastal regions, wherever blacks live in large numbers. The bread is most likely of African and West Indian heritage, which has loaves prepared from starchy tubers such as cassava, tanyah (elephant's ear), yams, and arrowroot.

This loaf is delicious for sandwiches or spread with cream cheese and watercress or cucumbers. It goes surprisingly well with spicy seafood salads of crab and shrimp. The contrasts of piquant and savoury fillings with the slight sweetness and spiciness of the bread is a welcome change.

The Bread
2 pkg. dry yeast
¼ c. warm water
1 c. milk
¼ c. sugar
1½ tsp. salt
½ c. butter
1½ c. mashed, cooked, cold
    sweet potatoes

1 tsp. cinnamon
⅓ tsp. freshly grated nutmeg
4½ c. all-purpose flour
1 c. rolled, uncooked oats

The Glaze
1 egg beaten with 2 Tb. milk

Dissolve the dry yeast in the warm water.

Heat the milk with the sugar and salt, stirring until dissolved. Remove from heat and let cool to room temperature.

Cream the butter and the sweet potatoes well. Add the dissolved yeast, the milk mixture, and then all dry ingredients. Beat very well, then turn out onto a floured surface. Knead vigorously until satiny, about 10 minutes.

Place the dough in a bowl, cover, and let rise in a warm place until doubled, about 1 hour. Punch down and divide into 2 equal portions. To braid the bread, divide 1 portion into 3 parts. Roll each part out to form a rope. Place side by side on an ungreased sheet. Braid by alternately bringing the left hand rope over the middle one, then the right. Repeat until the braid is formed. Tuck the ends under. Cover loosely and let rise about 1 hour or until double.

Bake in a preheated oven at 400° F. for about 20 minutes, then brush with the glaze and continue baking 15 minutes more for a total of 35 minutes. If the bread is baked in a conventional loaf pan (9 × 5 × 3 inches), cook about 45 minutes. The loaves should be a lovely, deep honeyed color. ✂ *2 braids or 2 loaves*

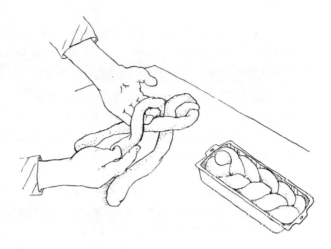

Patent Yeast

🐝 *Apart from ale barms, beer yeasts and the new distillery or compressed yeasts, nineteenth-century bakers and housekeepers used specially brewed ferments from which they extracted their yeast for bread. Such yeasts were often known as patent yeasts. There are scores of different recipes and methods to be found in published cookery books, and many variations appear in MS. receipt books. They really were used and were successful.*
— Elizabeth David, <u>English Bread and Yeast Cookery</u>, 1977

Patent yeasts were the homemade forerunner of today's compressed and dried yeasts. In the South, they were prepared with cornmeal, and sometimes with curious substitutions for the hops that kept the yeast from souring.

🐝 *Put half a pound of fresh hops into a gallon of water and boil it away to two quarts, then strain it and make it a thin batter with flour; add half a pint of good yeast, and when well fermented, pour it in a bowl and work in as much corn meal as will make it the consistency of biscuit dough; set it to rise, and when quite light, make it into little cakes, which must be dried in the shade, turning them very frequently; keep them securely from damp and dust. Persons who live in towns, and can procure brewer's yeast, will save trouble by using it; take one quart of it, add a quart of water, and proceed as before directed.*
— Mary Randolph, <u>The Virginia House-wife</u>, 1824

Fig Leaf Yeast

This patent yeast from South Carolina replaces hops with the leaves of the fig.

🐝 *Take a double handful of leaves and put on them one quart of cold water; boil them until it makes a strong tea; when cold, strain; add as much flour as will make a thick batter; set it aside to rise; when bubbling add as much corn meal as will make it into cakes.*
— <u>The Rural Carolinian</u>, October 1872

Pain de Babeurre

Pain de Babeurre is buttermilk bread, a New Orleans twist on the classic fine-grained Pain de Mie from France. It makes an excellent light loaf and absolutely superb and beautiful rolls. The sweet-sour combination is much to Southern tastes, and the bread with its high fat content keeps well in the hot, humid climate. You can make your own endless variations on the theme. I'll show you one with cornmeal and also its similarity to perhaps the most beloved yeast bread of the South, Sally Lunn of the English tradition.

1½ c. buttermilk	2 Tb. warm water
½ c. butter	4½ c. flour
⅓ c. sugar	1 tsp. salt
1 pkg. dry yeast	Cornmeal (about 1 Tb.)

Heat the buttermilk, butter, and sugar, stirring to dissolve. Remove from the heat and cool to lukewarm. Add yeast softened in the water. Set aside until frothy.

Turn into a bowl, add the flour and salt. Beat very well until smooth, then turn out and knead thoroughly, about 10 minutes.

Let rise, covered, for an hour or so until doubled. Punch down.

For rolls, pinch off the dough in 1¼-ounce portions, about the size of a large egg. Shape like an egg and place on a baking sheet sprinkled with cornmeal. Let rise again covered until doubled. Just before baking, slash the rolls about ½-inch deep across the top to allow expansion. Bake at 375° F. in a preheated oven for about 15 minutes or until well browned.

This recipe makes two small loaves — slash the tops deeply and stuff a little butter in the gashes. Bake at 375° F. for about 40 minutes or until well browned. ✖ *24 rolls or 2 small loaves*

Pain de Babeurre au Mais

This very pretty golden loaf is a creole classic.

1 recipe Pain de Babeurre
   (above) with the following
   changes:

Stir ½ cup yellow cornmeal and 2 tablespoons yellow corn flour into the warm milk mixture. Proceed, adding yeast, then enough flour, about 4 cups, to make a firm but soft dough. ✖ *1 loaf*

SALLY LUNN

BISCUITS, SPOONBREAD, AND SWEET POTATO PIE

Sally Lunn is among the aristocrats of Southern breads, a rich egg bread resembling brioche in its delicacy. This loaf found its original fame in England, most say at the spa of Bath, taking on the name of a tea-shop proprietress. There's little or no evidence for this nice story, but it's prettier than seeing the name as a corruption of *solimeme*, a similar Alsatian bread.

Corruption does occur with time, though, and what has happened to the elegant Sally Lunn in the past century is shameful. A fast little cupcake all puffed up with baking powder and sweetened beyond good taste masquerades under the grande dame's name. The recipe here should restore the original's deserved respectability.

The proportion of ingredients for Sally Lunn is close to that of Pain de Babeurre, with the addition of 4 eggs. The extra liquid makes a softer dough that will almost pour.

☞ 9-inch diameter tube pan,
   greased

• • • • • • • •

1 c. milk
½ c. butter
⅓ c. sugar

1 pkg. dry yeast
2 Tb. warm water
4 eggs, well beaten
4½ c. flour
1 Tb. salt

Heat the milk and butter in a saucepan with the sugar, stirring to dissolve. Remove from the heat and cool to lukewarm. Add the yeast softened in the water. Set aside until frothy.

Turn into a bowl, add the beaten eggs, flour, and salt. Beat well, if by hand count 400–500 strokes. If you use an appliance, the dough should be smooth, shiny, and, though very soft, not too sticky. Cover and let rise until doubled, about an hour. Beat down again and turn into a greased tube pan. Let rise again for about an hour or until doubled.

Bake in a 375° F. preheated oven for about 40 minutes or until golden. Let rest a few minutes out of the oven, then invert and remove from the pan to complete cooling. ✘ *1 large loaf, about 15 thick slices*

Mrs. Mason's Sally Lunn

I like this recipe for its sensitivity to the seasons. Well-risen yeast means Potato Yeast.

🦑 *One & a half pounds of flour — 1 pint of milk warmed, & Two ounces of butter melted in the milk. Three eggs. 1 cup of well risen yeast. 1 spoonful of sugar or two teaspoonful. Beat all well together. Grease a baking pan, pour in the batter & set it to rise. In summer make it at 12 o'clock & in winter at 9 for tea. Observe that it is twice as high in the pan as before it began to rise. Then bake it, & when baked serve immediately. It is improved by slicing off the top, buttering & replacing it.*

First beat the egg yolks & whites together, then mix in alternately the flour batter & milk & lastly put in the yeast with the sugar in it.

The two ounces is just a teacup of butter — . Have your pan a little warm & in winter set it over a little warm water in the tea kettle, on the end of your range or close by the side of it. In summer it does not matter.
— Manuscript Recipe, Cameron Collection

Martin's Cheese Bread

☞ 9-inch diameter tube pan, greased

♦ ♦ ♦ ♦ ♦ ♦ ♦

1 recipe Sally Lunn (opposite)
4 oz. grated sharp cheddar, about 1 heaping c.

1 oz. grated Parmesan, about ¼ cup
1 tsp. coarsely cracked fresh pepper

Prepare the Sally Lunn according to the recipe. Add the cheeses and pepper just after the flour. Proceed to work the dough as for Sally Lunn. ✖ *1 loaf*

Christmas Sally

Amounts of exotic ingredients such as saffron are never specified in old Southern recipes. They mostly depend upon availability and occasion. In the old days, even the smallest pinch of saffron was a signal for celebration and special occasions. This bread finds its ancestry in southernmost England where saffron was once an important crop. In the American South it is served with tea.

Add a good pinch of pulverized saffron and zest of a tangerine or an orange to infuse in 1 cup warm milk. Plump 2 tablespoons raisins in 2 tablespoons orange liqueur. Chop ½ cup citron and ½ cup candied cherries. Toss with ¼ cup flour.

Make Sally Lunn (p. 90) as directed with the above flavored milk. Beat the dough well, then add the fruits prepared above. Beat well again but do not mangle the fruit. Proceed to let rise and bake as for Sally Lunn.

FROM·OUR· BRITISH· HERITAGE

Manchet or Rolls

Cracknels

Southern Baps

Bannocks

Southern Crumpets

Muffins

Velvet Cakes

Wigs

Breakfast Rusks

Tea Rusks

Scones

Irish Soda Bread

Irish Fruit Bread

FARM LIFE

Farm life is about producing food, from planting sweet potatoes to plowing even while the previous season's crop is still in the field. There are annual tasks such as hog killings and daily tasks such as churning butter.

And there is the joy of a well-stocked pantry and a romp in a stream while the corn is being ground at the grist mill.

MANCHET

Manchet is an old English roll, rather large, made of the finest white flour for aristocratic tables. Elizabeth David in *English Bread and Yeast Cookery* (1977) writes, "the manchet seems to have been the common ancestor, no less, of most of our breakfast breads, baps, tea cakes, muffins, soft rolls, even of lardy cakes and dough cakes, as well as of the eighteenth-century fine breads known as French rolls and French bread." Mrs. David's proportions for manchets are: 1¼ pounds flour, ½ ounce yeast, 1 tablespoon salt, 1 ounce softened butter, a little over ½ pint of milk and water. These same proportions of ingredients are found frequently in Southern recipes for light white breads. When such a dough is to be baked as a loaf, all water can be used, but when making rolls the directions usually run to Eliza Leslie's order from *Miss Leslie's New Cooking Book* (1847): "Rolls — Are made as above, except they are mixed with warm milk instead of water, and a little fresh butter rubbed into the dough."

Other than in early manuscripts, the word manchet rarely appears in Southern recipe collections, though the bread itself is ubiquitous. *Martha Washington's Booke of Cookery* (1981) calls for "toasts of manchet," "a little manchet cut like dice," and an oven that "is as hot as for manchet," but never specifies the making of the bread.

Manchet or Rolls

1 c. milk
1 tsp. salt
½ pkg. yeast
2 Tb. warm water

2¾–3 c. all-purpose flour
2 Tb. butter, at room
　　temperature
Cornmeal

Heat the milk gently with the salt to dissolve and let cool to lukewarm. Dissolve the yeast in the water. Add the liquids to the smaller amount of flour, beat well, and incorporate the butter. Knead well, 8–10 minutes, adding more flour if the dough is too soft. Place the dough in a bowl, cover, and let rise, then turn out onto a lightly floured surface. Shape into 8 oval or round rolls and place on a baking sheet lightly dusted with cornmeal. Let rise, loosely covered, for about 1 hour or until doubled.

Slash the tops deeply with a sharp knife just before baking in a preheated oven at 350° F. for about 25 minutes or until lightly browned. For a loaf, bake about 1 hour, until a good, hard crust forms.
✄ *8 rolls or 1 loaf*

Cracknels

Cracknels are thin, yeast crackers made from the manchet-type dough. *The New Dixie Cook-Book* of 1889 and *The Picayune Creole Cook Book* of 1901 contain similar recipes.

    Cracknels. — To one pint of rich milk put two ounces of butter and spoon of yeast. Make it warm, and mix enough fine flour to make a light dough; roll thin and cut in long pieces, two inches broad. Prick well, and bake in slow oven.
— *The New Dixie Cook-Book*, 1889

Earlier, cracknel could signify something else indeed. Martha Washington had a recipe "To make cracknells" calling for caraway, sugar, and rosewater. Other, older recipes from England called for throwing the dough into boiling water before baking it. The *Oxford English Dictionary* cites its shape as significant: "A light, crisp kind of biscuit, of a curved or hollowed shape," and quotes a 1706 authority, "Cracknels, a sort of Cakes made in the shape of a Dish, and bak-d hard, so as to crackle under the Teeth." If not in other ways, these Southern cracknels are related to their namesake in the auditory sense.

Use the Manchet (p. 97) dough, roll thin, cut into long thin rectangles about 2 × ½ inch, and bake on an ungreased sheet at 325° F. for about 15 minutes or until crisp and lightly colored.

BAPS, BANNOCKS, AND CRUMPETS

Baps, bannocks, and crumpets are three traditional breads of the British Isles once popular in the South, rarely prepared today. None of the three has escaped transformation, sometimes radical, in Southern kitchens.

Elizabeth David in *English Bread and Yeast Cookery* (1977) surveys the myriad recipes for the baps, the national morning roll of Scotland, and quotes Lady Clark of Tillypronie, "to the effect that baps are made from flour, salt, yeast, and water only. *No milk, butter, or eggs,* Lady Clark says firmly. And adds 'the dough to be made very slack.' Professional bakers evidently agree with Lady Clark, except that they seem to favour a half and half milk and water mix rather than plain water."

Harriott Pinckney Horry, mistress of an eighteenth century South Carolina plantation, recorded in her eighteenth-century day book a recipe for baps that is a confusing but fair facsimile of the Scots:

> *Take about a pound of flour and rub into it a pap spoonfull of Butter then add as much Milk as will make it into a very thick Batter then put it into a marble Mortar and beat it till 'tis quite light drop it upon tin Sheets (about a large spoonfull in a drop) and bake them. They are to be split and butter'd.*

The last note puts this bap clearly in the English small bread tradition of crumpets, muffins, biscuits — split and buttered. Victor MacClure in *Good Appetite My Companion* (1955) writes, "But don't attempt to tackle it as some people, for 'politeness,' treat a crisp roll — that is, broken and buttered in pieces. To this method the bap, somehow, doesn't seem to answer."

Sarah Rutledge was the cousin of Harriott Pinckney Horry and she published her version of baps in *The Carolina Housewife* (1847). The recipe grows richer and farther from its source:

> *One pint of milk, three eggs, one spoonful of butter, four spoonfuls of flour. Mix them well together, and bake in plates, and in a quick oven. They ought to be buttered while hot, and put one above another before sent in.*

Another recipe further corrupted the name and style. It appeared in 1879 as Box Bread in *Housekeeping in Old Virginia:*

> *One quart of flour, one teacup of yeast, one teacup of melted lard or butter, four eggs, one teaspoonful of salt. Let it rise as light bread, and when risen, make it into square rolls, without working it a second time. Let it rise again and then bake it. — Mrs. R.E.W.*

Though no liquid is given, I believe it is understood, 4 eggs will not make 4 cups of flour into anything resembling "light bread." At any rate, the emphasis on the light touch in handling the dough, and the shaping ties the recipe to its original. Again from *English Bread and Yeast Cookery:* "Miss Elizabeth Craig, in *Scottish Cookery* (André Deutsch, 1956) . . . directs that the baps be 'squarish in shape.' "

My recipe is basically the Scots one, with the Southern enrichments held in check. The dough is very soft but is easy enough to handle with copious flour on the board.

Southern Baps

Breakfast is a good time for these rolls even today. Make up the dough in the evening and leave in the coolest part of the kitchen without refrigerating it. Quickly shape in the morning and let rise in a warm place. Baps may be large as a plate or smaller than a cupcake. I use about 2½ ounces of dough for each bap. Since there is no kneading there's less mess about and the second rising need not double. The crust has substantial but tender crunch and the insides are well perforated with air pockets ready for butter. A tradition well worth reviving.

1 pkg. dry yeast	2 c. milk, tepid
¼ c. warm water	4 Tb. butter
1 Tb. sugar	5–5½ c. flour
1¾ tsp. salt	2 eggs, beaten

Proof the yeast in the water with the sugar. Dissolve the salt in the milk. Rub the butter through 5 cups of the flour with the fingertips as for pie dough. Stir in the liquids and the eggs and beat well. The dough is too soft to knead. Set aside, covered, to rise for 1–1½ hours until double in volume. Beat down and drop a plum-size piece of dough onto a well floured surface. By working quickly and lightly, tossing it around, you should be able to give it some shape. If not, beat in a little more flour, but add more cautiously. Drop the shaped dough — ovals or squares — onto a lightly greased and floured sheet. Sprinkle lightly with flour and set aside about 25 minutes to rise some just short of doubling. Before baking, punch each bap right in the middle with the index finger. Bake at 400° F. for about 25 minutes. The baps should brown only lightly. ✕ *20 baps*

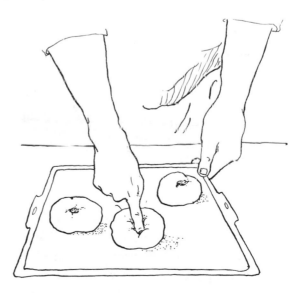

Bannocks

🦐 *The word Bannock is from the Gaelic* bannach, *a cake; that is, a large, round girdle scone or oatcake in the whole piece. A bannock is a thing of substance and may be made of oatmeal, wheatflour, barley, or pease meal.*
— *Mrs. E.M.L. Douglas, of Innerleithen,* <u>A Concise Encyclopedia of Gastronomy</u>, *1952*

🦐 *So-called oaten breads are nearly always flat, griddle-baked bannocks or oatcakes, although recipes for yeast-leavened oatmeal muffins appear in eighteenth- and nineteenth-century English cookery books, and Yorkshire oatcakes were often made with a natural or sour leavening.*
— *Elizabeth David,* <u>English Bread and Yeast Cookery</u>, *1977*

A Southern bannock shows little resemblance to its oaten forebears. Cornmeal is always present as in its New England cousin of the same name, but in the South it is, typically, enriched with eggs, butter, and sugar.

🦐 *Cream one pound butter with one and one-fourth pounds brown sugar, add six eggs whipped to a cream, one teaspoon ginger, one and one-fourth pounds white Indian meal and same of flour. Bake in small cakes in cups or gem pans and leave in them until cold.*
— *Estelle Wilcox,* <u>The New Dixie Cook-Book</u>, *1889*

This bannock is a very moist cake, but when cooked slowly on a griddle and turned once when well browned, it will split nicely for buttering. It is quite delicious and goes well with roasts and gravies as a starchy dish in place of rice, noodles, or potatoes.

2 c. boiling water	¾ tsp. salt
1 c. cornmeal	½ c. rye flour
4 Tb. butter	Very small pinch of powdered
1 Tb. brown sugar	ginger, optional
2 eggs	

Pour the boiling water over the cornmeal, beating well. Cream the butter and add the brown sugar. Add one egg, beat well, then add the other. Beat the butter-sugar-egg mixture into the cornmeal along with the salt, rye flour, and ginger. Beat well and drop the batter by the ¼ cup on a lightly greased griddle over low heat. When well browned, after about 6 minutes, turn and cook about 5 more minutes. ✖ *10 bannocks*

To bake: Separate the eggs. Add the yolks as directed for the whole eggs and beat the whites until stiff. Fold the whites into the batter. Turn into a greased and cornmeal-dusted 9-inch cake pan. Bake in a preheated 400° F. oven for about 35 minutes, until lightly browned and the bannock pulls away from the edges. ✖ *4–6 servings*

Southern Crumpets

Southern Crumpets match up very well to their originals, with the addition of a cooked cereal base. Grits or rice put through a sieve extend the notoriously short life span of a crumpet. Elizabeth David says, "Personally, I find crumpets edible only when freshly cooked, warm and soaked in plenty of butter. Toasting makes them tough and alters the whole structure." These richer Southern Crumpets are undeniably at their best just off the bakestone, but rewarming is kind to them, as is toasting. The rings for baking come from tinned fish on the grocery shelf. English muffin tins from cookery stores are too shallow for crumpets; I like them about 1½-inches high. If all the tuna tins are of the pressed bottom, two-part sort, check out the pet food section for traditional three-part tins.

My two youngest, Elliott and Madeline, being the final arbiters of taste in the household, want their crumpets like this: slightly toasted, and still warm, spread with fresh cream cheese, topped with crushed strawberries, and sweetened with a tad of honey. We celebrate spring with crumpets in the garden.

☞ Rings, greased; griddle, bakestone, or cast-iron skillet

 • • • • • • • •

2 c. milk
1 Tb. sugar
2 Tb. butter
2 Tb. cornmeal

1 c. Plain Cooked Grits (p. 29) or well-cooked rice, sieved
1 pkg. dry yeast
4 c. all-purpose flour
2 tsp. salt
½ tsp. baking soda
¾–1 c. warm water

Heat the milk, sugar, and butter until lukewarm. Stir in cornmeal, cooked grits or rice, and yeast, and set aside for 20 minutes. Beat in the flour and salt and continue beating for 3–4 minutes. Cover and let ferment 1½–2 hours or leave in a cool place to work overnight.

Dissolve the soda in ¾ cup water and beat into the dough that should now resemble a batter. Cover and let rise again 30 minutes. Pour into well-greased rings and cook on a lightly greased griddle, bakestone, or in a cast-iron skillet over fairly low heat, about 15 minutes the first side, 5 the other. If you are new to crumpets, cook a test one. The top should be full of holes when ready to turn. If not, thin the batter with water. If the batter runs under the rings, add more flour. In case of any alteration, the batter should rest 20 minutes or so before proceeding. ✖ *12 crumpets*

Muffins

Muffins are essentially free-form crumpets, but the batter is heavier. Make the recipe for Southern Crumpets (p. 103), but add enough extra flour, about 1 cup, to make a fairly stiff, yet not kneadable dough. Do not add the soda or the final water. After rising, shape lightly by hand and let rest 15–20 minutes on a well-floured surface. Cook oven-top without rings, turning once. Muffins are about half the height of crumpets. ✹ *12 muffins*

Velvet Cakes

Crumpets rich from eggs were also popular. An 1848 recipe of Hester Ann Harwood, printed in *Maryland's Way,* is of the same proportions as the following, called Velvet Cakes in South Carolina at least as early as 1847.

Two eggs, one quart good milk, a piece of butter or lard size of a hen egg and flour enough to make a batter as stiff as a pound cake. About two or three tablespoonsful of good yeast. If wanted for tea, set about twelve o'clock, bake in muffin rings, cut open and butter before sending to the table. This combination makes a very delicate tea cake.
— *The Rural Carolinian*, December 1872

☞Rings, greased; griddle, bakestone, or cast-iron skillet

· · · · · · · ·

	½ pkg. dry yeast
	2 Tb. water
	2½ c. all-purpose flour
1½ c. milk	2½ Tb. butter
1¼ tsp. salt	1 egg, beaten
¼ tsp. sugar	

Bring the milk up to blood warmth, stirring, with the salt and sugar. Dissolve the yeast in the water. Rub the butter through the flour as for pie dough and add all the liquids. Beat very well until the gluten is exercised, and the batter changes into an elastic, thin dough. Let rise until very light, more than doubled, beat down, and let rise again. Heat a heavy iron skillet, griddle, or bakestone, lightly greased, and bake in greased 3-inch rings over a burner at medium-low heat about 10 minutes each side. Use about ⅓ cup dough per cake being careful not to deflate the dough as you pour it into the rings. Split, butter, and eat while warm. ✹ *8–10 crumpets*

WIGS

His round halfe-penny loaves are transformed into square wiggs, (which wigges like drunkards are drowned in their Ale).
—J. Taylor, *Jack-a-Lent*, 1620

The *Oxford English Dictionary* tells us a wig is a "wedge, wedge shaped cake. A kind of bun or small cake made of fine flour." Originally they were lenten cakes, but came to be enriched with all sorts of spices, seeds, dried fruits, and wine by dunking. Elizabeth David, in *English Bread and Yeast Cookery*, finds an assumed knowledge of wigs in antique English recipes. "Not one of the eighteenth-century ladies gives us a clue as to the shape of these wiggs — it was taken for granted that readers knew what they should look like — but since wigg is said to derive from *Weig*, an old Teutonic word meaning wedge, it seems fairly obvious that the cakes should be triangular. . . ."

While English wigs are baked, in South Carolina they were cooked on the griddle in rings much like crumpets, and split, not wedged. The proportions otherwise are nearly the same as for Elizabeth Raffold's recipe in *Experienced English Housekeeper* (1769):

To three quarters of a pound of fine flour put half a pint of milk made warm, mix in it two or three spoonfuls of light barm, cover it up, set it half an hour by the fire to rise, work in the paste four ounces of sugar, and four ounces of butter, make it into wigs with as little flour as possible, and a few seeds, set them in a quick oven to bake.

Miss Rutledge's more aromatic, Southern version:

Two pounds of wheat flour, half a pound of butter, half a pound of sugar, one pint of milk; mix these ingredients well together, and add three table-spoonfuls of good yeast, a little cinnamon and rosewater; cover the mixture, and set it in a warm place to rise; when light, bake in rings, and split and butter them while hot.
—Sarah Rutledge, *The Carolina Housewife*, 1847

Here's a modern approximation of Miss Rutledge's recipe, formed in the English manner.

3¼ c. all-purpose flour	2 Tb. warm water
½ c. butter	1 tsp. salt
½ c. sugar	½ tsp. cinnamon
1 c. milk	½ tsp. powdered ginger
1 pkg. dry yeast	4 Tb. rosewater

Sift the flour into a bowl. Melt the butter and sugar gently in the milk over low heat and let cool to lukewarm. Activate the yeast in the water. Combine all the ingredients and beat very well. Set aside to rise until double, about an hour.

Beat the risen dough down and, on a floured surface, divide into 2 portions. Shape each as a round about 9 inches in diameter and transfer to a lightly greased baking sheet. Make 4 slashes across the top of each cake so later there will be 8 portions or wedges. Cover and let rise again, but short of doubling in volume, in a warm place about 30 minutes. Bake in a preheated 375° F. oven for about 25 minutes or until light brown and aromatic. Cool on a rack.

Wigs are best warm; to reheat, break (not cut) into ragged wedges along the slash lines. Warm gently, but enough to toast up the edges. Lemon Snow is delectable alongside as a dessert. ✖ *16 wedges*

RUSKS

A rusk is a sweet roll that is usually baked, then split and baked again to be served up warm and toasted at tea time as Mary Randolph in *The Virginia House-wife* (1824) directs: "bake it in small rolls; when cold, slice it, lay it on tin sheets, and dry it in the oven." From *Maryland's Way* (1966): "When fresh they are delicious cut in slices ½ inch thick, buttered and toasted a light golden brown. Stale rusks may be sliced and dried in a slow oven until a fine golden color."

These tea rolls were much practiced in the eighteenth and nineteenth centuries. Eliza Pinckney, the noted woman planter who discovered the secret of indigo cultivation in the mid-eighteenth century gave the recipe to her daughter Harriott Pinckney Horry. *The Picayune Creole Cook Book* has a traditional recipe in its 1901 edition, but that is about the last time it appears in Southern cookbooks. By 1930, in *Two Hundred Years of Charleston Cooking,* the rusk has become a common though delicious sweet muffin.

From the *Recipe Book* of Eliza Pinckney dated 1756:

Take half a pint of good Leaven or Yeast, half a pint of warm Milk, six oz. Butter half a pound of Sugar and six Eggs — beat up your Eggs and Butter together and mix it in with half your flour ading your Leaven and Milk etc., leave it till 'tis well risen, then mix in the rest of your Flour knead it well and let it rise again.

Breakfast Rusks

Although the name might lead you to expect something very unusual, Charleston breakfast rusks are really only very delicious muffins.
1½ tablespoons butter
¼ cup sugar
1 egg, well-beaten
1 cup milk
1¾ cups flour
¼ teaspoon salt
3 teaspoons baking powder
Cream the butter and sugar, add the well-beaten egg and beat well. Mix and sift the dry ingredients and add to the first mixture alternately with the milk. Turn into well-greased muffin tins and bake in a hot oven (400 degrees F.) for about twenty-five minutes. Makes about nine muffins.
— Mary Leize Simons, Two Hundred Years of Charleston Cooking, 1930

Tea Rusks

The following is a true rusk and is delicious warm from the oven. The old way, though, is to split the baked roll, spread lightly with butter, and bake at about 300° F. until toasted and crisp, about 20 minutes.

1 c. milk
¼ c. heavy cream
½ c. sugar
1½ tsp. salt
1 pkg. dry yeast
2 Tb. warm water

3 eggs, beaten
5 c. all-purpose flour
½ c. butter, at room temperature

Optional Glaze
Cream and sugar

Heat the milk and cream with sugar and salt to dissolve, then cool to lukewarm. Dissolve the yeast in the water. Add these liquids along with the eggs to the flour and beat well. Beat in the butter, bit by bit. Continue beating about 15 minutes or until dough is very smooth and elastic — a long, vigorous exercise. Cover and let rise about an hour or until double in volume.

Beat down and form into small rounds about the size of an egg or about 1½–2 ounces in weight. Do not handle the dough too much. Place on a lightly floured sheet and sprinkle with flour. Cover loosely (wax paper works well) and set aside to rise about 1 hour or until doubled. Bake in a preheated oven at 350° F. for about 25 minutes, until golden. The cakes can be lightly glazed with cream, then sprinkled with sugar just before baking. ✖ *18 rusks*

Scones

Scones originally were Scotch griddle cakes; today they are almost universally oven baked. They can vary greatly in their flour make-up — from all wheat, white or brown, to barley and oats. Scones also have been enriched over the years in the British Isles as well as in the South. Butter, sugar, dried fruits have all been incorporated, but the original nature of this scone is that of a biscuit minus the fat. It has much in common with the Irish Soda Bread. The singular crust and crumb of a scone is often obscured by shortening. Not surprisingly, and like so many British tea breads, the scone does not keep.

The traditional shape of a scone is more or less triangular. A round loaf is cut into wedges before baking. Each wedge can be called a farl, an Old English word meaning fourth part, or quarter.

2¾ c. all-purpose flour	2 tsp. baking powder
½ tsp. salt	1¼ c. buttermilk
½ tsp. baking soda	

Sift the dry ingredients together and stir in the buttermilk until just smooth. The dough should be soft. Turn onto a floured surface. Divide the dough into 2 pieces. Shape each into a round approximately 6 inches in diameter. With a very sharp knife, cut each round into 6 wedges. Separate the wedges and bake on an ungreased sheet at 375° F. for about 15 minutes. Brown off the tops, if necessary, with top (or broiler) heat. Serve with lots of butter, jam, fresh cheeses. ✷ *12 scones*

Irish Soda Bread

Most Irish Soda Breads in this country have lost their hearthside character, weakened by the exclusive use of white flour. Most are more like cakey biscuits. Oatmeal and rye add character to these loaves. Big, rough, and peasanty, these loaves have two distinctively different and complementary crusts: rough and crackled on the top, smooth and crunchy on the bottom. They are best served slightly warm with butter, good cheeses, soups, and stews, and like most quick breads, should be torn, split, or broken, but never cut. No bread can compare to this, given the time, energy, and expense involved.

☞Two 9-inch cake rounds, greased, or baking sheet, greased	2⅔ c. all-purpose flour
	1½ tsp. baking soda
◆ ◆ ◆ ◆ ◆ ◆ ◆ ◆	2 tsp. salt
1 c. oatmeal	1½ c. plus 2 Tb. buttermilk
⅓ c. rye flour	

Grind the oatmeal in a food processor or blender until it is as fine as cornmeal. Sift with the rye, wheat, soda, and salt into a large bowl. Check the rough meal left in the sifter. Either add it as is for a rougher texture, or grind it again. Stir in 1½ cups buttermilk and mix quickly but well. Shape the dough into 2 rounds about 6 inches in diameter. Put on a greased baking sheet or into greased cake rounds. Slash a deep X across the tops, pour 1 tablespoon of buttermilk into the center of each cake, and bake for 5 minutes in an oven preheated to 450° F. Reduce heat to 375° F. and continue baking for about another 30 minutes, until the tops are lightly browned, the bottoms well browned. Remove to rack for cooling. ✷ *2 breads*

Irish Fruit Bread

The rather austere Irish Soda Bread can be enriched and turned out as a loaf with similarities to the Southern fruit cakes. Irish Fruit Bread is a delightful warm breakfast or teatime cake.

Follow the Irish Soda Bread recipe (p. 109) for the dry ingredients. Heat the buttermilk gently and add 6 tablespoons butter and 4–5 tablespoons molasses to it. When butter is melted, remove from heat and stir in 1 cup currants or raisins. Let cool, then stir into the dry ingredients along with ½ cup diced glacéed orange and ½ cup diced glacéed pear or citron.

Turn the dough into 2 small, well-greased loaf pans (8½ × 4½ × 3 inches). Smooth out, then cut a deep slash down the middle. Pour a little buttermilk in the slash, then bake as for Irish Soda Bread. Remove to a rack for cooling.

RICE · RYE · WHOLE-WHEAT · AND · OATMEAL · BREADS

Philpy

Carolina Cooked Rice

Rice Griddles

Carolina Rice and
Wheat Bread

Ashley Rice Bread

Yeast-Leavened
Rice Bread

Rye and Indian Bread

Brown Bread

Alamance Brown Bread

Oatmeal Poppy
Seed Bread

THE LOW COUNTRY

The magnificent cities of the South were built on the labor in the fields.
The bucolic photograph of rice planting in South Carolina does little to
convey the heat and humidity of the Southern summer. Yet while planters and
their families escaped to their sea breeze—oriented townhouses, there was haunting
beauty even in the mill ponds built for threshing rice.

RICE BREAD

&✺ *Captain Alston is a gentleman of large fortune and esteemed one of the neatest planters in the State of South Carolina, and a proprietor of the most valuable ground for culture of rice. His house which is large, new and elegantly furnished, stands on a sand hill, high for the country, with its rice fields below, the contrast of which, with the lands back of it, and the sand and piney barrens through which we passed, is scarcely to be conceived.*
—*George Washington, April 29, 1791*

By the time the President toured the Southern states, rice had made a fortune for many a planter in the Carolinas and Georgia and would continue to be the economic basis of the Low Country for another century. Rice was first planted sometime prior to 1686, according to Mr. A. S. Salley, Secretary of the Historical Commission of South Carolina in 1936. The seed came from Madagascar and was a gift from John Thurber, a New England ship captain, to Dr. Henry Woodward. "Dr. Woodward planted this seed, had a very good yield and distributed the seed among his friends for further planting, and by 1690 the production of rice in South Carolina had so advanced that the planters asked that it be specified as one of the commodities of the province with which they might pay their quit rents, and by 1700 its production was declared by the collector of customs to have been so great that there had not been ships enough at Charles Town that year in which to export it all."

The rice crop was so successful because the deep, murky, black alluvial soil had been collecting for centuries in the coastal swamps, which were fed by tidal rivers. In order to cultivate rice, planters constructed an elaborate system of gates, dams, and sluices. The fields were flooded with fresh river water three times during the growing season. The first inundation sprouted the newly planted seed. The second drowned the weeds and grasses. The third matured the crop. Twice every day, salt water at high tide had to be checked. The mechanics were fairly simple but relied upon hard slave labor. The periodic influx of upland water laden with leached minerals and sediments renewed the fields. Unlike the other major commercial crops of the South—indigo, cotton, and tobacco—that depleted the soil rapidly, the growing ground for rice was constantly renewed because of the flooding. Thus the continuing cultivation of rice seemed ensured—that is, until the end of the nineteenth century.

At this point, three factors contributed to the ultimate demise of rice on the Atlantic seaboard—the first, of course, being the emancipation of the slaves. Bankrupt in 1865, Southern planters could not pay real wages for land cultivation, and blacks sought employment in other areas. Second, when agricultural machines were developed to sow and harvest the crop, the new technology spread into the Mississippi valley. Texas, Louisiana, Arkansas, eventually even Missouri became the centers of production. With corporate financing, buying, processing, and marketing — the beginning of modern agribusiness — these states overwhelmed the Low Country economy, which was still tied to the ancient English system of middleman factors.

Finally, it was the weather that broke the old rice plantations. One Carolina grower wrote, "A rice planter gambles with nature, and Nature throws the dice." When the hurricane of 1893 struck, another Charleston planter remembered, "it was months before anyone could get around the fields in anything but a rowboat. I did not make a pint of rice, nor did scarcely anyone on the river." One storm alone could not destroy the return of the crop, but 1898 was again disastrous, as was 1910: "in three hours a scene of activity and prosperity was changed into one of stillness and desolation. Nothing left to the rice planter but another year's hopes." Another year brought another storm and the end of rice on the Atlantic seaboard. On August 27, 1911, planter D. C. Heyward was in Charleston. "I saw the ocean actually coming up Meeting Street, until all the lower part of Charleston was under water. As the water receded, I could see timbers from a wrecked vessel floating down Meeting Street, going out with the tide to the sea. When daylight came the waves still pounded against the high wall of the Battery, striking with such force that their spray was dashed as far away as Church Street, a block away. I knew that night that on Combahee we were having a repetition of the destruction of the year before, and I knew also that the death knell of rice planting in South Carolina was sounded."

More than two hundred years of cultivation put rice at the heart of much Southern cooking. It is the basis of many of our famous dishes such as hopping john and jambalaya. The Low Country cooks alone developed a number of rice breads. Sarah Rutledge published thirty of them in *The Carolina Housewife* (1847). They range from quick breads much like corn breads to fritters and yeast-raised loaves. Rice breads in general have a fine, crisp crust due to the grain's high-starch, low-protein makeup. Many people express amazement at how delicious a rice bread may be. Unfortunately, most of the traditional Southern rice breads are no longer made. A few recipes appear in local cookbooks, Philpy most frequently.

Philpy

½ cup milk
½ cup flour
½ teaspoon salt
¾ cup soft, cooked rice
2 teaspoons melted butter
1 egg, well beaten

🦋 *Add milk slowly to flour and salt, beating to avoid lumping. Mash rice until fairly smooth. Combine with flour mixture; add butter and egg; bake in a greased layer cake tin in a 450 degree oven for 30 minutes. When done, split open and butter generously. Serves 4–6*
— Mrs. Alston Ramsey, <u>Charleston Receipts</u>, 1950

Carolina Cooked Rice

Charlestonians have been cooking rice their own way — boiled in much water, then steamed — for centuries. Eliza Pinckney got a nicely detailed receipt from Mrs. Blakeway and entered it in her day book in 1756.

🦋 To Boil Rice. *Take a pint of rice well picked and Clean'd Set on a saucepan with one Gallon of water and a handful of salt, when the water boils put in the rice, about a quarter of an hour will boil it according to the quickness of the fire or by tasting it; but be sure to avoid stiring the rice after tis in the saucepann for one turn with a spoon will spoil all. When tis tender turn the rice into a sieve; when the water is quite drained off return it to the same pann and let it stand near the fire for an hour or more to be kept hott and if the process is well observed it will be white, dry, and every grain Separate.*

The sieve for steaming developed into a specialty of the Low Country. Such steamers are still available in Charleston hardware stores. Miss Leslie knew the method and approved of it, publishing it as the "Carolina way of Boiling Rice" one hundred years later.

🦋 *To cook rice for use in breads, waffles, etc., add 1 cup rice to 6 cups boiling water. Cook at a low boil for about 35 minutes, or until the grains are perfectly tender and starting to split. Drain and reserve for further preparation. Makes 4 cups cooked rice.*

Rice Griddles

In Charleston, the old ways persist, even in recipe writing. Anna Wells Rutledge, who was related by marriage to the family of Sarah Rutledge, wrote in her introduction to the University of South Carolina Press's facsimile edition (1979) of *The Carolina Housewife:* "I am a little surprised to find that some young people today aren't familiar with the *gill* as a unit of measurement: it's pronounced 'jill' and merely means a quarter of a pint (i.e., half a cup)." This is the incipient pun of the old English saying "Every Jack shall have his Jill."

Boil soft one gill of rice; while hot, stir into it a dessert-spoonful of butter. Beat two eggs very light, and mix them with the rice, after it becomes cold. — Add one gill of rice flour and half a pint of milk. Stir all together just before baking. Bake quickly in a hot griddle, and the cakes will rise much.
—Sarah Rutledge, The Carolina Housewife, 1847

One teacup of cold hominy, one egg, one teacup of sour milk, one teacup of rice flour, one quarter teaspoonful of soda, a little salt; bake on griddle and serve hot.
— The Rural Carolinian, May 1870

Carolina Rice and
Wheat Bread

Simmer one pound of rice in two quarts of water until it is quite soft; when it is cool enough, mix it well with four pounds of flour, yeast and salt as for other bread; of yeast, four large spoonfuls. Let it rise before the fire. Some of the flour should be reserved to make the loaves. If the rice swell greatly, and requires more water, add as much as you think proper.
—Sarah Rutledge, The Carolina Housewife, 1847

Ashley Rice Bread

The batter for quick rice bread adapted from Miss Rutledge's book will serve nicely for griddles, but it is even better for waffles or baked in a pan in the oven. Rice flour is available at oriental food stores.

☞Griddle, greased; or waffle iron; or 9-inch cake pan, buttered

• • • • • • • •

1¾ c. buttermilk
2 c. rice flour
2 Tb. melted butter
1 tsp. baking powder
¾ tsp. baking soda
¼ tsp. salt
2 tsp. sugar
2 eggs, separated
2 c. well-cooked rice (see Carolina Cooked Rice, p. 116)

Stir the buttermilk into the rice flour until smooth. Add the butter. Stir in baking powder, soda, salt, and sugar. Add well-beaten egg yolks and rice. Beat the egg whites stiff and fold in.

To cook, drop on a lightly greased griddle for pancakes or cook in a waffle iron. ✖ *24 of either*

To bake: Pour the batter into a well-buttered 9-inch cake pan. Bake in an oven preheated to 375° F. for about 30 minutes, until the bread is set and very lightly browned. Cut into wedges and serve immediately. ✖ *4–6 servings*

Yeast-Leavened Rice Bread

☞ One 5 × 9-inch or two 3 × 5-inch loaf pans, buttered

• • • • • • • •

1½ c. well-cooked rice (see Carolina Cooked Rice, p. 116)

1 egg

2 Tb. butter

1 Tb. sugar

1 c. very warm water or milk

1 pkg. dry yeast

4 c. or more all-purpose flour

2 tsp. salt

Beat the rice, egg, butter, sugar, water, and yeast together briefly. Set aside to proof well, 30 or 40 minutes until barmy. Pour into a sieve and rub the rice through. Unlike most sieving operations, this one goes quickly. Beat in the flour and salt until smooth. The dough should be quite soft, but not liquid. Add a little more flour if necessary and let rise in the bowl, covered, until doubled, about 1 hour. Beat down vigorously. Shape in 1 large loaf and place in a buttered 5 × 9-inch bread pan or make 2 loaves for 3 × 5-inch bread pans. You can shape the dough into egg-size rolls. Let the loaves or rolls rise, covered loosely, until double in volume, about 1 hour.

Slash the loaves or rolls deeply just before baking. Place the bread into a preheated 450° F. oven and immediately decrease the heat to 400° F. Bake until light brown, about 40 minutes for loaves, 20 minutes for rolls. ✄ *1 large loaf, 2 small loaves, or 24 rolls*

Rye and Indian Bread

Rye and Indian meal bread was commonly baked at home throughout the nineteenth century all along the eastern seaboard. As with all rye breads, the loaf is dense, moist, and long keeping. Neither rye nor corn has the gluten necessary to enable a dough to rise much, so don't despair at the volume of the bread. You will find it delicious with savoury items such as mustard, cheeses, cold cuts, or just on its own.

Originally this bread was baked in a Dutch oven in the fireplace. Nineteenth-century Southern cookbooks refer to the technique: "In the olden time it was placed in a kettle, allowed to rise, then placed on the hearth before the fire, with coals on top of the lid, and baked." My children are enthusiastic about all fireplace cooking and so this is the way we prepare Rye and Indian Bread. A few live coals are scraped to the side of the hearth, and the Dutch oven is placed over them. My pot has three legs to stand above the coals; for a legless pot, cover the coals well with ashes and set the pot directly on them. Scatter a good shovelful of coals and ashes on the lid. Give the pot a quarter turn every 10 minutes or so to keep the side nearest the open flames from scorching. You can also use a Dutch oven in a conventional kitchen range, setting it on the middle rack. The thick cast-iron walls give a crisp, honeycombed crust that cannot be duplicated by any other method of baking, but baked in an ordinary loaf pan, the bread is still delicious.

☞ 4½ × 8½-inch loaf pan

• • • • • • • •

1 c. boiling water
2 c. cornmeal
1½ tsp. dry yeast
¼ c. warm water

1 c. rye flour
2 Tb. molasses
½ tsp. salt
½ tsp. baking soda
About ½ c. water

Pour the boiling water over the cornmeal and beat hard. Dissolve the yeast in the warm water. Add to the cornmeal and work in the rye, molasses, salt, and soda. Add enough water, about ½ cup, to make a stiff, but workable dough. Turn out and knead very well. Set to rise in a bowl, covered, until double in volume, about an hour. Grease a 4½ × 8½-inch loaf pan and dust lightly with cornmeal. Beat the dough down and shape into a loaf. Place it in the pan to rise again, covered, until just shy of double, about 40 minutes. Set in a preheated oven and bake at 375° F. for about 50 minutes, until the loaf is lightly browned and pulls away from the sides of the pan. Turn out and cool on a rack.

✂ *1 loaf*

BROWN BREADS

Our current obsession with health foods, and particularly dietary fiber, actually has roots in a movement well over one hundred years old. Two Americans whose names are now almost immortal in merchandising — Sylvester Graham and John Kellogg — gave the original impetus to the movement. In 1830, the Reverend Graham began preaching temperance and a nutritious diet, and the bread he advocated was made of whole-wheat flour including the bran. As the movement spread, even popular journalism took up the cause, especially when Americans renewed their identification with the classical world as the centennial celebration of their declaration of independence drew near. Whole-grain breads were called "Roman meal" (as one commercial brand still is today), in connection to the early Roman republic. In 1876, a writer from the Baltimore *Sun* counseled his readers: " 'what is wanted' says an intelligent writer on this subject, 'is a wholesome, healthful, nourishing wheat food — a whole-wheat flour in the fullest and broadest sense of the term. It should be made from the choicest and ripest wheat, wholly (bran, or cortical portion, and all) reduced to a uniform fineness of quality, and well put up for family use, and whoever will give his earnest and honest efforts to furnish such a flour, and will keep its manufacture up to this high standard all the time will confer a lasting benefit upon his race and generation and find a remunerative market for all he can produce.' "

The monthly agricultural journal *The Rural Carolinian* was even more righteous: "why raise a pale, feeble, nervous and small sized race of people upon flour because flour bread looks white and light, and therefore is considered nice?"

The propaganda was effective. In antebellum Southern cookbooks there is scarcely a mention of whole-wheat flour, indeed no mention of it in the popular classics *The Carolina Housewife, The Virginia House-wife,* or *The Kentucky Housewife.* In 1889, however, *The New Dixie Cook-Book* published thirteen recipes for whole-wheat breads and admonished: "Most persons find it palatable, and it promotes health." Even a much less comprehensive recipe collection, *Woman's Club Cook-Book of Southern Recipes* from Charlotte, North Carolina, of 1908, had ten versions of Graham flour bread. These breads are often steamed rather than baked and are rarely yeast raised, the health food converts being suspicious of any form of fermentation.

Whole-wheat flours can vary as widely as cornmeal in terms of texture and moisture content. Both variables will obviously affect your loaves. Only experience in handling whole-grain doughs will help you to adjust to the differences; you must learn through your fingers. Whole-grain doughs will be stickier than those of refined flour, but it is not the kind of stickiness or softness resulting from too much liquid. Avoid the temptation to add too much flour; excess flour will make the dough stiffer, but its texture will still be sticky. If your dough is too stiff, you can add liquid in small increments. This is more neatly accomplished in a food processor or with a mixer and its dough hook than on a board, but hand kneading should always follow. The most common fault in home bread making is the use of too much flour; when baking with whole grains, the danger is greater if you are not familiar with these rougher, more irregular grains.

Another point to watch for is the irregularity of milled flour, especially stone-ground. Examine your flour closely before you begin baking. Rub it lightly through your fingertips feeling for the variation within the grind and sensing the moisture content. A coarser grind will be slower to absorb liquid, but as you work it and let it rest, the flour will absorb moisture eventually. A moister flour will require slightly less liquid or more flour than the recipe specifies. Doughs that seem initially slick and unhomogeneous may change dramatically as they are kneaded and will even continue to change, absorbing liquid, as they rise. The coarser the grain, the more likely this is to occur.

Brown Bread

☞ 8½ × 4½-inch loaf pan, greased

1½ c. milk
1½ c. cornmeal
1½ c. whole-wheat flour
¾ c. buttermilk
¾ tsp. salt
1 tsp. baking soda
¼ c. molasses

Bring the milk just to the boiling point and pour into the cornmeal. Beat well and let cool. Add the flour and, again, beat very well. Stir in the rest of the ingredients. Pour into the loaf pan that has been greased and dusted with cornmeal. Bake in an oven preheated to 375° F. for about 50 minutes. When top is well browned, turn out and cool on a rack. ✗ *1 loaf*

Alamance Brown Bread

This is a traditional North Carolina brown bread, that's been around almost one hundred years.

☞ 8½ × 4½-inch loaf pan, greased

• • • • • • • •

1 tsp. salt
¼ c. sugar
¾ tsp. baking soda
½ c. cornmeal

½ c. all-purpose flour
1 c. whole-wheat flour
1 egg
1 c. buttermilk
¼ c. molasses
¼ c. raisins tossed with 1 Tb. all-purpose flour

Sift all the dry ingredients together. Beat the egg well, then add the buttermilk and molasses to it. Add all the liquid to the dry ingredients and beat very hard. Stir the flour-tossed raisins into the dough. Pour into the greased loaf pan dusted with cornmeal. Bake in an oven preheated to 375° F. for about 50 minutes, until well browned.
✖ *1 loaf*

Oatmeal Poppy Seed Bread

I made this loaf by combining several old Southern recipes. It is as attractive as it is nutritious and delicious.

¼ c. molasses
¼ c. shortening
2 tsp. salt
1½ c. water
1 c. plus 3–4 Tb. rolled oats

1 Tb. poppy seeds
1 pkg. dry yeast
¼ c. warm water
3 c. whole-wheat flour
1¼ c. all-purpose flour

Put the molasses, shortening, salt, and water in a pot and bring to a boil. Pour over the oats and poppy seeds and let cool, stirring occasionally. Dissolve the yeast in the warm water and add to the oats when cool. Beat in the flours. Turn onto a well-floured board and knead vigorously 5–8 minutes. Place in greased bowl, cover, and let rise in a warm place until doubled in volume, about 1 hour. Turn out onto a lightly floured surface; knead well and divide into 2 equal pieces. Shape as long pointed ovals and place on a greased baking sheet lightly sprinkled with oats. Chop roughly 2 tablespoons of oats and sprinkle over the tops of the loaves. Cover loosely with wax paper and set aside for a second rising, just short of doubling. Slash each loaf at a diagonal about 4 or 5 times with a very sharp knife. Bake in a preheated 375° F. oven for about 45 minutes. The oatmeal on top will be crisp and brown.
✖ *2 loaves*

CONFECTIONS· AND·SAUCES

Pamelas

Chocolate Glaze
for Pamelas

Stuffed Dates

Rum Balls

Apricot Coconut Balls

Sherried Pecans

Peach Leather

Bynum Ridge Fudge

Pralines

Brittles

Benne or Pecan Brittle

Scotch Toffee

Divinity

Sea Foam

Candied Flowers

Custard Sauce

Fruit Sauces

Plum Sauce

Sour Cherry Sauce

Hard Sauce

Caramel Sauce

More Than Fudge Sauce

Soured Cream

CONFECTIONS

In the heat and humidity of the South, confectionary first developed as a domestic art. The natural tendency of cane sugar to crystallize and turn grainy in cooking is exacerbated by our climate. As a result, the famous candies of the region are rather simple and a product of the home cook. Most of them are produced during the winter holiday season when cool temperatures and high barometric pressure are the confectioners' angels. My mother used to give a candy pull every year after Christmas. She would boil a huge pot of molasses and butter and then force all of us into an unheated room to stretch the taffy out by hand until it was slick and hard enough to cut with scissors. Before candy-making could be done by large-scale commercial producers in the South more stable liquid corn sweeteners had to be developed — and that didn't happen until the twentieth century.

In the old days black women in particular made candies and they would sell them on the streets of the big towns and cities. The pralines and brittles, which are popularly identified with the city of New Orleans, are African in origin, as are the peanuts and benne (or sesame) seeds that studded them. The Africans brought with them to the New World a tradition of working with cane sugar in a similar climate. Both Africa and the Canary Islands had fed the ever increasing sweet tooth of the Europeans long before the settlement of the Americas. Unfortunately, raising and harvesting sugarcane depended on slave labor, and the system was transferred to the New World. Of the twenty million or more Africans enslaved for manual labor in the Americas, more than two thirds of them were absorbed by the sugar plantations. In the early days of settlement, sugar culture was attempted in South Carolina, Georgia, Florida, and Louisiana, but it usually failed due to the harshness of the mainland winters. Cane would grow the year round in the Indies, but the frost on the continent arrested its ripening. In 1797, a cold-resistant strain of sugarcane, the Otaheiti, that was introduced to Louisiana finally ensured the success of the crop.

The South has a wealth of sweeteners other than cane sugar, many much older. The Indians extracted the sap of cornstalks and bled maple trees for syrup. Honey from native trees such as the tupelo and the sourwood are much prized. Sorghum was probably brought from Africa; its stalks were pressed to make molasses throughout the region. It has always been considered a healthful food and something of a tonic. In *Plain Southern Eating* (1988), Tommie Bass, a famous herbalist from Alabama, remembers the process: "We began to make molasses about the end of August. You started pulling off the fodder, the leaves from the sorghum stems. Then you went along with a mowing blade and cut off the heads. In the old days a syrup mill — it was turned by a mule — came around to the field. Most every farmer had his own syrup patch. If you had a small patch, you took the stems to the one mill for grinding. When the juice came from the mill, it was cooked in what they called a pan. It was something similar to a pot, but more like a bread pan. They called it a syrup pan, made out of solid copper."

The sorghum mills that Tommie Bass describes still made the rounds when I was young, but, like mules, they are no longer part of the Southern scene. Store-bought molasses is often bitter, nothing like the thick, dark syrup we sopped our biscuits in.

Pamelas

Pamelas are a part of the Christmas-kitchen bustle of my memories, a time set apart from the daily necessities of getting a meal on the table for a large family. Each child had something to contribute. The first task for the youngest cook was to roll the candies and fruits in pans of white, grainy sugar — a simple job made rich by a joint effort in a heady atmosphere of toasting nuts, preparing the orange peel and cranberries, getting out the bourbon and brandy along with much, much chatter.

The Southern penchant for bitter flavors is typified by the holiday preference for crystallized grapefruit peel. Orange and lemon work well, too, if the rind is thick enough, and all three can be prepared together. When dry, Pamelas can be lightly glazed by dipping them lengthwise into chocolate to coat just one half.

I think the name Pamela must be a corruption of the French word for grapefruit, *pamplemousse*. Whatever they are called, they are an indispensable part of the Southern pantry. Orange and lemon Pamelas, especially, find their ways into all sorts of cookies, pies, and cakes throughout the winter.

4 oz. (about 1 c.) grapefruit peel, white pith trimmed away to a thickness of ¼ inch

1 c. sugar
1 c. water
Extra sugar for coating

Cut the trimmed peel to a width of ½ inch, lengths being about 2½–3 inches. Cover well with cold water in a saucepan. Bring to the boil and cook for 1 minute. Drain and rinse well with cold water. Repeat this process 5 times.

Combine the sugar and water and bring to the boil. Cook 5 minutes. Add the drained peel, reduce heat, and cook slowly until the water is almost completely evaporated and the sugar absorbed, about 45 minutes. Watch very closely at the end of cooking; do not let the sugar caramelize.

Turn the candied peel onto a sheet heavily sprinkled with granulated sugar. Toss well and remove the Pamelas to a rack for drying. The time required for drying will depend on heat and humidity. One good dry day should suffice. I prefer the Pamelas when they are short of crisp, still possessing a slightly chewy center. Store airtight. ✖ *2 cups*

Chocolate Glaze for Pamelas

☞ Double boiler

◆ ◆ ◆ ◆ ◆ ◆ ◆ ◆ ◆

2 oz. semisweet chocolate
1½ Tb. butter

1 Tb. strong coffee
2 tsp. sieved powdered sugar
Pinch of salt
1 recipe Pamelas (p. 129)

Combine all ingredients in the top of a double boiler. Heat gently until chocolate is melted and the mixture is smooth upon stirring. Dip each Pamela into the chocolate just enough to coat it by half. Cool on a piece of lightly oiled wax paper. ✗ *½ cup glaze*

Stuffed Dates

Southern children begin the winter holidays rolling these stuffed dates in plates of sugar. My sister and I could hardly reach the countertop when we first helped make these Christmas candies.

☞ Double boiler

◆ ◆ ◆ ◆ ◆ ◆ ◆ ◆ ◆

Pitted dates
Sherry, rum, brandy, or bourbon

Lemon juice
Pecan halves
Granulated sugar
Lemon zest

Put the dates in the top of a double boiler. Sprinkle very lightly with sherry or liquor and add a quick squeeze of lemon juice. Cover and steam over boiling water for about 10 minutes, until plump and soft. Cool, stuff with a pecan half, and roll in granulated sugar mixed with a little lemon zest. Let dry on a rack for several hours, then store airtight; age for a week before serving.

Rum Balls

Every Christmas, at least one child should feign inebriation after eating a couple of these. And at least one child should learn how to make these simple confections for gift-giving. Adults can use the food processor for grinding the wafers and nuts, but give children the rolling pin for pounding — and give them lots of encouragement.

3 c. ground vanilla wafers, about one 12-oz. box
¾ c. powdered sugar
1 c. ground pecans
⅓ c. cocoa
⅓ c. light corn syrup
⅓ c. dark rum
Powdered sugar for rolling

Mix together all the ingredients except the powdered sugar. Work by hand until it forms one big ball. Break off pieces ½ ounce, or the size of a large grape. Shape into a ball and roll in powdered sugar. Store airtight; let age a week or more before serving. ✖ *About 45 candies*

Apricot Coconut Balls

☞ Double boiler
◆ ◆ ◆ ◆ ◆ ◆ ◆ ◆
1 c. dried apricots
¼ c. orange liqueur
1 Tb. water
1 c. grated coconut
1 c. finely chopped pecans
Grated zest of 1 lemon
2 Tb. powdered sugar, optional
Granulated sugar

Toss the apricots with the orange liqueur and water. Steam, covered, in the top of a double boiler for about 10 minutes. Let cool, then chop fine or grind; do not puree. Knead with the coconut, pecans, lemon zest, and powdered sugar if desired. Form into small balls, about ½ ounce or less, the size of a small grape. Roll in granulated sugar, let dry on a rack for several hours, and store airtight in a cool, dry place. Hide them so they can age a bit, for 3 or 4 days at least. ✖ *25–30 confections*

Sherried Pecans

Winter's low humidity is a blessing for Southern cooks. Many sugar preparations doomed to failure in warmer months are then successful. These sherried pecans are a good example. A sticky disaster in the summer, in winter the nuts can be wrapped in a crack caramel. If the sugar does grain up, more water and a rapid boildown seems the correction. You can further dry the nuts in a very low (150° F.) oven with the door ajar. Once cool, store airtight. Almonds prepared in this fashion were once street fare in New Orleans. *The Picayune Creole Cook Book* in 1901 provides a delicate portrait:

> *There used to be an old colored woman who supplied the judges and attorneys of the Civil District Court, near the St. Louis Cathedral alley, with lunches. She made these ancient Creole "Amandes Pralines" a specialty, and served each almond separately, in a little cornet of paper, just as the ancient Creole dames do when serving them at their elegant festivities.*

☞ Cast-iron skillet

◆ ◆ ◆ ◆ ◆ ◆ ◆

2 c. pecan halves	Grated zest of 1 tangerine or orange
1 c. lightly packed light brown sugar	1 Tb. dry sherry
1 Tb. white vinegar	½ tsp. salt
	¾ c. water

Toast the pecans over low heat in a heavy skillet, turning frequently, until they begin to smell delicious. Add the rest of the ingredients, increase heat, and stir constantly until the sugar is at the caramel or hard-crack stage. Remove and let dry separately on a lightly oiled baking sheet. There should be just enough caramel to coat each nut. Store airtight. ✗ *2 cups*

Peach Leather

Peach or Apricot Leather has been treasured in the Low Country of South Carolina for centuries. The technique may have been learned from the Native Americans, who certainly practiced it. Harriott Pinckney Horry's recipe is still valid.

🐾 *To Dry Peaches. Take cling Stone peaches, pare them and cut them into as large thick slices as you can cut, put them into a stew pan (say about 4 lb) pour ½ pint of Water to them and sprinkle on them two heaped spoonsful of powdered Sugar, put them on the fire and let them scald (but not boil) then pour them into a sieve and let them drain well, then spread them thin on dishes and put them in the sun to dry, remove them on clean dishes every day and put them in the Sun 'till they are dry.*
—*Harriott Pinckney Horry*, A Colonial Plantation Cookbook, *1770*

Sarah Rutledge's recipe from *The Carolina Housewife* (1847) is more precise: "to four quarts of pulp add one quart of good brown sugar" or 4 cups fruit to 1 cup sugar. All recipes say cook 1 or 2 minutes only. Use metal cookie sheets and spread the conserve thin. For sun drying, in the past, some had iron tables with screens to keep out the insects. Mosquito netting or cheesecloth can be used, wrapped tightly around. Plastic screening is inexpensive at the hardware store and can be cut to order. Marion Brown's recipe in her comprehensive volume from the University of North Carolina Press says: "Someone should sit and watch leather, to see that no insects crawl under netting." If that caveat doesn't place this recipe in another age, I don't know what does!

When dry, after three days most likely, sprinkle with sugar (granulated or powdered) cut into strips, and roll up. Store in a tin for long keeping. Should the weather turn, a very low oven can be used, but don't try to hurry up the process. This is *dried*, not cooked fruit.

Bynum Ridge Fudge

I first tasted this fudge when I lived in Bynum, North Carolina, a village on the rocky Haw River. In those days, Bynum hosted a kayak competition on the mill sluice in February. Contestants, drawn from Maine to Florida, were fed by the women of the local churches at the Ruritan Club building. Everyone in town came, set up folding chairs on the banks of the Haw beneath the leafless trees, and, when their feet were cold, headed indoors for steaming bowls of pinto beans, ham hocks, and onions; country ham and sausage; plus a countless variety of pies. One cook offered this fudge, studded with the astringent black walnuts of the Southern woods and carefully wrapped in wax paper.

☞ Candy thermometer; 8 × 8-inch
pan, buttered

• • • • • • • •

3 oz. unsweetened chocolate
1 c. lightly packed light brown
    sugar
1 c. white sugar

2 Tb. light corn syrup
⅔ c. heavy cream
Pinch of salt
2 Tb. butter
½ c. black walnuts
1 tsp. vanilla
1 Tb. brandy, rum, or bourbon

Bring the chocolate, sugars, syrup, cream, and salt to a boil in a heavy saucepan and cook, without stirring, to 234° F. or to the soft ball stage. Remove from the heat and cool to lukewarm without stirring or agitating the pan. When cooled, beat in butter, walnuts, and flavorings. Beat hard until the candy thickens, about 3 minutes. Spread it in the pan and cut into 1-inch squares before it hardens.

✗ *About 64 small pieces of candy*

Pralines

Praline, according to the *Larousse Gastronomique,* is sugar cooked to the caramel stage with toasted nuts added. We call that a brittle in the South and know it doesn't hold up for long. In New Orleans, where the weather never dries out, cooks adapted the candy, made it richer, softer, and capable of lasting longer in the city's year-round heat and humidity. Praline in Southern cooking no longer calls for sugar cooked to the caramel stage. Most recipes use brown sugar instead; those using white sugar cooked to the caramel stage are often designated "burnt sugar." This is true of the caramel cake icings and ice cream as well. Below is the old-fashioned praline with its "burnt" base. Modern commercial pralines are a travesty of the originals using coconut oil instead of butter, corn syrups for cane sugars, and artificial flavorings.

☞ Candy thermometer;
   baking sheet, buttered

• • • • • • • •

1½ c. sugar
½ c. milk

⅛ tsp. salt
1½ c. lightly toasted pecans
3 Tb. butter
1 tsp. vanilla
1 Tb. rum, bourbon, or brandy

Bring 1 cup of the sugar, the milk, and salt to a boil in one saucepan while caramelizing the remaining ½ cup sugar in a second, heavy saucepan. Cook to a slightly-darker-than-peanut-butter brown. Remove from the heat and quickly, but carefully, pour in the hot milk while averting your face from the pan. Return to heat, stirring, and add nuts. Cook to 242° F. or the upper range of the soft ball stage. Remove from the heat and continue to stir vigorously. Beat in the butter, then the flavorings. Continue to beat hard until the candy starts to lose its sheen and thickens slightly. Drop by the tablespoon onto a buttered baking sheet. Cool, then individually wrap the pieces and store airtight or in the refrigerator. ✖ *24 pralines*

Brittles

Brittles are one of the South's easiest candies to make. They're cooked so long that the danger of crystallization, as in fudge and pralines, is eliminated. My sister and I used to make peanut brittle from an old Alabama recipe which said, "cook until the peanuts pop." That was a reliable measure of temperature then, but I find that the larger, drier Virginia-type peanuts sold in small burlap bags don't pop as audibly as the short, round ones we raised on our farm. So use a candy thermometer and cook to 293° F.

Southern cooks make three types of brittle — peanut, benne, and pecan — the most common being peanut, often called groundnut. The peanut came to the South from Africa, though it originally grew in Brazil, and so did the Atlantic coastal specialty, the benne (or sesame) plant. The benne seeds are used in a number of Afro-American specialties, both sweet and savoury, and often in brittle. In the deep South, especially Louisiana, there are pecans for brittle. Occasionally an almond brittle surfaces.

An Excellent Receipt for Groundnut Candy. *To one quart of molasses add half a pint of brown sugar and a quarter of a pound of butter; boil it for half an hour over a slow fire; then put in a quart of groundnuts, parched and shelled; boil for a quarter of an hour, and then pour it into a shallow tin pan to harden.*
—Sarah Rutledge, The Carolina Housewife, 1847

Candy thermometer; 12 × 15-inch baking sheet, buttered

1¼ c. sugar
¾ c. light corn syrup
2 Tb. water
½ tsp. salt
2½ c. peanuts, skins on
4 Tb. butter
¾ tsp. baking soda

Combine sugar, syrup, water, and salt in a heavy saucepan. Bring to the boil. Add peanuts and stir constantly over medium heat until peanuts pop, brown lightly, or the temperature reaches 293° F. Remove from heat and stir in butter and soda. The candy will foam up. Pour onto the well-buttered sheet and spread out. When cool, break into pieces; store airtight. *About 1½ pounds brittle*

Benne or Pecan Brittle

Benne, or sesame, was brought from Africa and cultivated throughout the Carolina Low Country by blacks who prepared cakes and candies from it for home and for sale in Charleston. Make as for peanut brittle, substituting lightly toasted benne seeds for the peanuts. Omit the baking soda. Pecan brittle is made with chopped pecans; the baking soda, again, is omitted. ✂ *About 1½ pounds brittle*

Scotch Toffee

My son Elliott says this is the world's largest Heath Bar,* but it predates any commercial candy bar in the South. Adjust the sweetness of the chocolate glaze to your taste.

☞ 9 × 13-inch pan, buttered

• • • • • • • •

1 recipe Brittles (opposite), using chopped, blanched almonds in place of peanuts and omitting the baking soda

2 oz. semisweet chocolate
1 oz. unsweetened chocolate
1 c. finely chopped toasted, blanched almonds

Prepare the brittle and pour into the well-buttered pan. Spread thin and let cool. Melt the chocolate. Spread half of it over the candy and sprinkle with ½ cup nuts. Turn out of the pan and repeat, glazing the other side with chocolate and nuts. Present whole and let children break it into pieces. ✂ *About 1¾ pounds*

Divinity

Divinity is a tricky confection to make under the best circumstances — almost impossible under less than good. The recipe in one community cookbook advises a short consultation with the local meteorologist: "Please remember candy doesn't set unless the barometer reads 30 in. or over; doesn't make any difference whether it's raining or not, just watch your t.v. for the barometric pressure." Divinity like most other Southern candies shows up around the winter holidays. It is a sort of companion piece to fudge in Christmas gift boxes. A candy thermometer is a necessity; the only other trick is beating it long enough; mixer beating is fine for adding the syrup, but I find it takes good hard hand beating to finish it off properly.

☞ Candy thermometer

½ c. raisins	½ c. light corn syrup
¼ c. sherry	⅛ tsp. salt
2¼ c. sugar	2 egg whites
½ c. water	1 c. chopped pecans or black walnuts
	1 tsp. vanilla

Plump the raisins in the sherry over low heat for 2–3 minutes. Pour off excess sherry into a heavy saucepan and to the excess add the sugar, water, syrup, and salt. Bring to the boil and cook to 255° F. Meanwhile, begin beating the egg whites until they are lightly whipped. Hold if necessary until syrup is ready. When the syrup is at 255° F., pour it very slowly into the egg whites, beating constantly and at high speed. Continue beating after the syrup has been added until the candy is thick, cooled, and very fluffy. Add raisins, nuts, and vanilla. If the candy seems gooey or sticky instead of rather fudgelike, beat more. Drop by the spoonful on buttered wax paper or spread in a buttered dish to cut into squares. ✗ *About 60 candies*

Sea Foam

If you use brown sugar in place of white and/or dark corn syrup in the Divinity recipe, you make Sea Foam. Both candies can be topped with a little semisweet chocolate, or flavored with glacéed fruits or crystallized ginger.

CANDIED FLOWERS

Edible flowers are rather faddish right now, but Southerners have been consuming roses, violets, dandelions, nasturtiums, and many other blossoms for centuries. The caveat now is pesticides. Just be sure you know exactly who grew the flower and how it was grown. Beware of anything picked on the roadside or even in a field. A field sprayed during cultivation last year is not necessarily safe this year although it's lying fallow. I garden at home and I have no tolerance whatsoever for injecting our mother planet with poisons. I take what I can get and share the rest begrudgingly with the other denizens of my garden.

A sick rose does not please me, but I know I haven't killed the bees or contaminated the ground water. And it's all safe for children to romp in. Children will also be more than happy to bring in your flowers to candy them, and, since they typically pick the shortest stems, it doesn't matter for all you need is the blossom. Deep rose and violet hues persevere, white usually looks quite dirty. Violets, Johnny-jump-ups, pansy petals, rose petals are all reasonably available. In the dead of winter, it is luxurious to toss a big handful of sugared rose petals over a whipped cream covered cake. A whole rose may be carefully composed of individual petals to place in the center of a cake.

To Candy Flowers. Take any kind of flower you think pretty; clarify and boil a pound of fine sugar until it is nearly candied; when the sugar begins to grow stiff, and rather cool, dip the flowers into it; take them out immediately, and lay them one by one on a sieve to dry.
— *Sarah Rutledge, The Carolina Housewife, 1847*

This method is easier than Miss Rutledge's and can defy the weather.

1 egg white	Granulated sugar
2 tsp. water	
½ c. flower petals or blossoms	

Beat the egg white with the water until frothy. Dip a small blossom or a large petal into the liquid coating well but removing excess. Dip in granulated sugar. Dry on a rack in a slow oven (150° F.). Store airtight. Use for decorating and garnishing. ✗ *1 cup*

DESSERT SAUCES

Dessert sauces are largely neglected these days. If someone rubs a package of frozen strawberries through a sieve, he will receive adulation, and this unfortunately is true even in our country's best French restaurants. In the South, however, sauces for the final course were and still are of great variety and frequency. Mrs. Randolph in *The Virginia House-wife* (1824) calls for a wine sauce but doesn't give directions other than "sugar, butter, and nutmeg." Miss Rutledge in *The Carolina Housewife* (1847) gives an explicit recipe for wine sauce, but that only. Mrs. Bryan in *The Kentucky Housewife* (1839) gives five sauces for puddings. But in the last half of the nineteenth century, cookbooks devoted whole chapters to dessert sauces. *The New Dixie Cook-Book* of 1889 has fifty-two sauces just for puddings!

The epitome of the genre is the classic custard sauce or *crème anglaise*. Many Southern cooks keep it on hand at all times. It can be served warm or cold. Then, there are many fruit sauces to be prepared in season. Refrigerated, these keep very well — weeks to months — and freeze perfectly. Fruit sauces are best used as a contrast, blackberry sauce on lemon ice; they also replace syrups for pancakes and other breakfast breads. Small portions are used to flavor ice creams, bavarians, hard sauces, and whipped cream. They are indispensable and can turn a plain dessert into something quite fancy.

There are also candy sauces, such as fudge and caramel, fine for indulging, but they lack the finesse of the other dessert sauces.

Custard Sauce

☞ Double boiler

◆　◆　◆　◆　◆　◆　◆　◆

2 c. milk
1 c. heavy cream
6 egg yolks

2 eggs
10 Tb. sugar
⅛ tsp. salt
Flavoring: vanilla, rum, or
　　brandy to taste, about 1 Tb.

Heat the milk and cream in a saucepan but do not let boil.

Combine the egg yolks, eggs, sugar, and salt in the top of a double boiler. Beat well. Pour in the hot milk and cream, whisking steadily. Place over, not in, simmering water and stir continuously until the egg yolks are cooked, that is, until mixture thickens somewhat, coats a spoon, and feels hot to the touch. Remove from the double boiler and continue to whisk off the heat. Stir in the desired flavoring: vanilla, rum, brandy, whatever. If the custard is to be served cool, continue to whisk occasionally as it cools to allow steam to evaporate; otherwise, it can become watery. ✖ *4 cups*

Fruit Sauces

These fruit sauces before they are pureed are simple compotes. One way to use them is for breakfast: Split, butter, and lightly toast some day-old biscuits in a baking dish. Pour some stewed fruit over the biscuits, return them to the oven, and bake until hot. In the old days, my grandmother served such biscuits with clabber; today we use yogurt or soured cream.

	Raspberry	Blueberry	Strawberry
Fruit	2 c.	2 c.	3 c. sliced
Sugar	½ c.	½ c.	½ c.
Water	½ c.	½ c.	½ c.
Optional Flavorings	Lemon juice to taste	Lemon juice to taste *or* Port *or* Campari	Lemon juice to taste *or* white rum

	Mango-Cantaloupe	Blackberry
Fruit	1 c. chopped, each fruit	2 c.
Sugar	½ c.	½ c. + 1 Tb.
Water	½ c.	½ c.
Optional Flavorings	1 Tb. lemon juice *or* 1 Tb. or more sherry *or* white rum	1 Tb. or more Port *or* Campari

Combine the fruit, sugar, and water in a saucepan, bring to a boil, and cook 3–5 minutes. Pass through the very fine screen of a food mill or a sieve to remove any peel, pulp, or seeds. Season to taste after straining. These sauces can be used to flavor and color whipped cream and can be frozen to make a sherbet. If a thicker sauce is desired, boil down rapidly, but do not add flour or cornstarch. ✕ *2 cups*

Plum Sauce

Plums make sauces as beautiful as they are delicious, but they require longer cooking than most other fruits. Use any of the plums in the market — from the icy green to the black Japanese ones. Wash them, pit them, slice them, but do not remove the skins. For every 2 cups sliced fruit, add ½ cup each sugar and water. Bring to a boil, then simmer gently about 1 hour, until the fruit is completely tender. Puree in a blender or processor, then rub through a strainer or food mill. Season with cinnamon, lemon, orange, brandy, rum, or whatever you desire. ✕ *2 cups*

Sour Cherry Sauce

1 c. pitted sour cherries, reserving
    the stones
1 c. sugar

1 Tb. cornstarch
3 drops almond extract

Put the pitted cherries with their cracked stones in a saucepan. Mix the sugar and cornstarch well; stir into the fruit. Add the almond extract. Bring to boil over medium heat and cook until the fruit is tender, about 10 minutes. Strain. Serve hot or cold. ✖ *1 cup*

Hard Sauce

Hard sauce is the traditional accompaniment to hot puddings and pies and is especially popular during the winter holidays. The name seems contradictory but reflects its true nature — a sweet composed butter served cold to melt on the dish, not a sauce at all.

Hard sauce can be adapted in numerous ways to suit a dish. A little of any of the fruit sauces may be beaten in. Crushed shredded mint with lemon zest or toasted, finely chopped almonds are both candidates as is almost any proposal of the imagination.

1 c. butter, at room temperature
¾ c. sugar

2 Tb. heavy cream
4 Tb. brandy, bourbon, or rum

Beat the butter until very light. Slowly add the sugar. Then beat in the cream first, then the liquor. ✖ *1¼ cups*

Caramel Sauce

1 c. sugar
Pinch of salt
½ c. water
¾ c. heavy cream
2 Tb. butter

½ c. chopped lightly toasted
   pecans
Flavoring: bourbon, rum, or
   brandy, about 1 tsp.

Caramelize the sugar in a heavy saucepan to a rich amber color. Remove from heat. With great care, add salt, water, and cream. Bring back to a gentle boil and cook 15 minutes, stirring until the caramel is completely dissolved. Stir in the butter and pecans off the heat. Flavor with bourbon, rum, or brandy. ✖ *1½ cups*

More Than Fudge Sauce

More than fudge because the sugar is cooked right up to the caramel stage giving more depth to the flavor and more tack to the texture.

⅓ c. milk
2 Tb. heavy cream
½ c. sugar
2 oz. semisweet chocolate,
   roughly chopped

1 Tb. butter
2 Tb. strong coffee
Pinch of salt
1 Tb. brandy

Cook the milk, cream, and sugar in a heavy-bottomed saucepan, stirring up the bottom of the pot well, until it is a light caramel. Off the heat, add the chocolate, butter, coffee, and salt and stir gently until smooth. Flavor with brandy; thin if desired with a little water, cream, or coffee. Pour, hot, over ice cream. To reheat, use a double boiler. ✖ *¾ cup*

Soured Cream

Dairy products are in as sorry a state in the South today as in the rest of the country. Historically, we have never been strong in dairy production. The long, hot summers are not conducive to it, and pasturage in antebellum times was neglected in favor of export crops such as tobacco and cotton. Both dairy and beef cattle were often turned out to forage in the forest. The scientific management of the dairy industry, which began late in the nineteenth century, has led only to the thin, characterless, over-pasteurized products of the supermarket.

The best cream and butter of the South were home products. Well into the twentieth century, many people, even in town, kept a cow for their own needs. My grandparents' cow and I hated each other; as soon as my grandmother would look away, I'd get kicked. But it did give us the fresh milk for making clabber, a wonderfully nutty cultured cream curd, much like the famous French *crème fraîche*. Both are raw milk products; they cannot be made from pasteurized milk, and are lost to us today. It is possible to put some life back into our cream by inoculating it with a little cultured buttermilk or sour cream. I call it Soured Cream — it is thicker and it lasts longer in the refrigerator than unimproved cream. If I don't have any Soured Cream on hand, I sometimes use the following short cut, although it's not as good. Whip 1 cup of heavy cream to soft, firm peaks, then beat ¼ cup sour cream well and fold it into the whipped cream.

Here's an easy way to put some life back into modern ultra-pasteurized dairy products. In the summer, it's no problem to maintain the temperature. In the winter, set the mixture near a pilot light or by the hearth.

1 c. heavy cream	2 Tb. sour cream

Beat the 2 creams together. Cover and let ripen at a constant temperature of 85° F. until thickened, about 18 hours. Refrigerate.

FRUIT · DESSERTS

Tomatoes with Claret

Ambrosia

Almond Stuffed Prunes

A Christmas Compote

Late Summer Compote

Brushy Mountain
Apple Bake

Rum Baked Bananas
or Plantains

Other Fruits Baked
in Rum

Applesauce

Strawberry Gratin

Apricots in Rum

Brandied Fruit

FRUIT

The Carrboro Farmers' Market is particularly frenzied in the early spring mornings when the first fruits appear. Everyone is anxious to get the little sweet strawberries or the sour baking cherries before the stock runs out — and it always does unmercifully early. Right now, Madeline and Elliott are in the kitchen trying to sort out what we brought home today. Late as usual and perfect prey to shoppers' panic, we went our separate ways around the market and ended up buying most things three times. It's a blessing actually; I usually feel too greedy to take all the sour cherries when the supply is so limited and the demand for them so great, but with this windfall I'll have enough to put some up in brandy to eat later in December and remember this day.

Spring came early this year and has stayed around longer than usual. Strawberries are still with us in cherry season, and the first apricots are coming in. Mulberries and raspberries are just a few days away. From now to July there is a torrent of fruit rushing towards blackberry season, to be chased by peaches and summer's swan song, the luscious, little brown figs. In the fall, the farmers bring in the apples forgotten by the grocery stores — Arkansas blacks and pippins and golden russets. Out at Whippoorwill Farm, Charley Thompson collects the rare apple varieties of the South and grows them organically. He never has enough of the spicy, red-fleshed Yates apple that was first grown in Georgia in 1813. They are gone almost by the time Charley has his stand set up. The hard green pears, which are perfect for pies and chutneys, and the exotic pomegranates appear just before the frost makes the persimmon sweet. There is fresh, local fruit in the market until it closes in early December, when the traditional gift and stocking citrus fruits arrive from Florida. For the rest of the winter dried fruits served the South in the old days. My grandfather, though, packed the last of the fall harvest away in straw, and he had apples and pears along with green tomatoes well into January. His major feat was pulling out a perfectly ripe watermelon on Christmas Day. That will always seem like magic to me.

As for preparing fruits in Southern kitchens, the simplest ways are usually preferred. Compotes have always been popular; some are only fresh raw fruit lightly sugared; sometimes the fruit is poached or baked. Pureed fruits mixed with sweet cream are traditional English summer fruit desserts that appeared frequently on Southern tables in the eighteenth and nineteenth centuries. Southern cooks avoid baking in the hot months whenever possible; they may offer stove-top dumplings instead or the more elegant fritter—a deep fried, batter-coated fruit that New Orleans, Charleston, and Mobile (cities with large French and Spanish populations) particularly fancied. A few oven-baked pastries such as cobblers were the exception, but the general rule for all Southern fruit desserts in any season is: Keep it simple.

OUR RICHES

When I was young, I was sent out to gather wild plums, strawberries, and blackberries. Fruits are a gift in the South for which no Southerner is ever thankless—I think because our ties to the land are so deep. No matter how much we depend on the staple crops of grains and the work of men, it is women and the bounty of nature that compose the song that sustains us.

Tomatoes with Claret

Tomatoes with Claret is the simplest form of a summer compote and reflects the shifting boundaries often encountered at the Southern table where a pumpkin may appear as a soup, vegetable, or dessert. The same goes for sweet potatoes, peaches, and peanuts among a number of other equally versatile fruits and vegetables. Southerners probably give the most license to the tomato, which begins to move around the menu even in its green state as pickles, relishes, fried vegetable, jelly, and pies. Once it's ripe, its uses are legion.

Choose firm, solid, but fully ripe tomatoes, scald them and remove the skins; slice, spread in a dish, sprinkle generously with white sugar, and pour claret wine over the whole.
— *The Rural Carolinian*, October 1869

Ambrosia

Ambrosia is a gift of the West Indies to the South and it must have seemed like the food of the gods when the oranges, pineapples, and coconuts arrived by ship at the Southern ports from New Orleans to Baltimore in the winter months. The proportions of fruit vary; bananas can rightly be included by geography and tradition, but the miniature marshmallows that occasionally show up these days should be banished. Ambrosia can be layered or lightly mixed and it should come to the table in a clear glass bowl or crystal dishes. All Southerners consider it one of the most special desserts of our kitchens.

8 large seedless oranges	Sugar
1 medium pineapple	Rum or Grand Marnier
1 small coconut	

Remove all the peel and white from the oranges. Cut across in thin slices. Peel the pineapple and remove the eyes. Discard the core and cut in thin wedges. Crack the coconut, remove the brown skin, and grate the white flesh. Layer the fruits in a clear bowl with a very light sprinkling of sugar, taste to determine how much — it depends on the fruit — but probably about ¼ cup total. Sprinkle lightly with white rum, or, for very special parties, Grand Marnier. Use just enough sugar and liquor to bring out the flavor of the fruits, but don't mask them. Let sit about 4 to 6 hours before serving. Serve with whipped cream, pound cake, or a simple cookie. ✖ *10–12 servings*

PRUNE COMPOTES

In winter, the richness and complexity of prunes are a better reminder of summer's warmth than all the acrid green fruits on the grocer's rack. The following recipes and variations are based on my grandmother's simple compote, which she kept in the pantry at almost all times. Serve such prunes warm with French toast, or cold with custard as a tiny treat with a cup of tea, or as a condiment with pork, game, or fowl. They are always better eaten on a cold day in front of a roaring fire.

Almond Stuffed Prunes

18 large pitted prunes	4 Tb. sugar
18 whole blanched almonds	2 slices lemon
½ c. dry scuppernong wine or dry	1 piece vanilla bean
sherry	3 Tb. water

Stuff each prune with a whole blanched almond.

Combine the wine, sugar, lemon, vanilla, and water in a small saucepan and bring to the boil. Add the prunes, reduce the heat, and simmer very gently until the prunes are soft and the liquid reduced to just a glaze. Cook slowly, an hour or more. Serve warm with Soured Cream or Custard Sauce or refrigerate. A plain cookie, such as a basic brown sugar wafer, is delicious with the prunes.

For a more exotic version, stuff the pitted prunes, either before or after stewing, with a piece of crystallized ginger the size of an almond. ✖ *18 prunes*

A Christmas Compote

1 recipe Almond Stuffed Prunes	9–10 pieces chocolate glazed
(above)	orange Pamelas (pp. 129–30)
Brandy or orange flavored liqueur	
to taste, about 6 Tb.	

Prepare the recipe for Almond Stuffed Prunes with this exception: Do not stuff the prunes but stew the almonds loosely along with the fruit. Let cool. Add the liqueur and refrigerate overnight. Before serving, cut up the Pamelas (no smaller than necessary), and stuff the prunes with them. Spoon the sauce and almonds over the fruit. Very rich. At tea, one prune would suffice. ✖ *6–18 servings*

Late Summer Compote

The *Picayune Creole Cook Book* of 1901 gives thirty-one different compotes made of fruits from plantains to cranberries. The general directions are as follows:

> *Compotes are fruits preserved in very little sugar, and made as needed in the household. The fruits are always blanched, and a little sugar is added for them to absorb, and then they are put into dishes, and the syrup is poured over them. The Creoles often cut the fruits into many pretty shapes, especially apples and peaches. . . . All compotes may be served as desserts or entremets.*

Apples are the most frequently encountered fruit in nineteenth-century compote recipes. Mary Randolph in *The Virginia House-wife* (1824) and Sarah Rutledge in *The Carolina Housewife* (1847) both have excellent apple compote recipes. Estelle Wilcox in *The New Dixie Cook-Book* (1889) recommends compotes for digestive problems:

> *Compotes are very easily prepared, and are said to be the most wholesome manner of serving fruits for those who cannot eat raw fruits or the richer preparations requiring a larger proportion of sugar. Fresh fruits are much more delicious served raw, but the compote is far better than ordinary stewed fruit, makes a nice dessert dish that can be hastily prepared, and apples are very acceptable served thus.*

A judicious blend of late summer and autumn fruits is a perfect end to a heavy meal. These fruits are also good for breakfast.

6 c. water	1 large green apple
1 c. sugar	2 firm but ripe pears
1 piece cinnamon stick *or* 6 whole allspice	3 ripe peaches, blanched and peeled
3 strips lemon zest	Seeds from 1 large pomegranate*

Combine the water, sugar, cinnamon or allspice, and lemon zest in a medium saucepan, bring to a boil, and cook for 5 minutes.

Peel and core the apple. Slice ½-inch thick and drop into the poaching liquid. Simmer for 10 minutes. Meanwhile, peel, core, and quarter the pears, then add to the pot and cook. After 5 minutes add the peaches cut into ⅓-inch slices. Poach 2 minutes and let cool in the liquid. Refrigerate.

Serve cold, adding the pomegranate seeds at the last minute.

---

* To seed a pomegranate — *Lightly score the outer peel with a very sharp paring knife as if cutting into quarters. Slightly pierce, crosswise, both the blossom and stem ends. The pomegranate with a little effort should open without the seeds being pierced. Gently extricate the seeds from the pith with the fingers.*

Brushy Mountain Apple Bake

Almost all the southeastern states share the Appalachian backbone whose height provides welcome cool weather to low-landers in the summers and whose slopes produce fine fall apples. I lived a few miles from the Blue Ridge Parkway after graduating from college. Among my favorite mountain memories are autumn drives through the gorgeously colored forests, picnics on rocky outcroppings, and the ice-cold freshly squeezed cider and crisp apples picked up along the way. This recipe always makes me think of those halcyon days before the winter storms put an end to our weekend junkets.

1½ c. all-natural apple cider
2–4 Tb. honey
4 tsp. currants
4 good-size baking apples
4 whole glacéed cherries, diced

1½ tsp. diced homemade orange Pamelas (p. 129) or glacéed oranges
1 Tb. diced citron
1 Tb. finely chopped pecans

Preheat oven to 375° F.

Combine the cider and honey in a saucepan, bring to a hard boil, and reduce to 1 cup. Add the currants and remove from the heat. Peel the apples and core. Place closely together in an 8 × 8-inch baking dish. Drain and add the currants to the other fruits and nuts, mix well, and use to fill the cavities of the apples. Spoon the reduced cider over the apples and into the cavities.

Bake, uncovered, for about 30 minutes, until the apples are very tender and well cooked but still, tenuously, holding their shapes. Serve warm with very lightly sweetened whipped cream, Soured Cream, or Custard Sauce, if desired. ✕ *4 servings*

Rum Baked Bananas
or Plantains

This baked compote is from the West Indies, though now identified with New Orleans, and especially Brennan's restaurant where it is flamed tableside. That's an easy enough step to add to this recipe. Just before serving, gently heat ¼ cup rum in a saucepan. Ignite the rum with a match — in a darkened room — and pour the flames over the fruit. All this is a sort of instant version of the original from the West Indies: barely ripe plantains, slowly baked for a good while in a sauce of brown sugar, lemon, and rum with the plantains becoming almost candied as they become tender enough to eat. If you find plantains at the market, use them for this recipe but cover and cook them a little longer than called for.

1 banana not quite ripe, or ripe
   plantain, split lengthwise
3 very thin slices lemon
2 Tb. light brown sugar

1 Tb. butter
1 Tb. dark rum
1 tsp. water

Place the banana in a buttered dish, top with the lemon slices, and sprinkle with sugar. Add butter, rum, and water. Bake in a preheated 350° F. oven for 25 minutes or until tender. Baste every 5 minutes.
✂ *1 serving*

Other Fruits Baked in Rum

Though baked bananas are the classic, other semitropical fruits are prepared the same way. One of the following can be paired with bananas, or the three may be baked together, but bananas *and* all three together lose focus.

Ripe figs, peeled and split
Ripe peaches, blanched, peeled
   and split

Ripe mangoes, peeled and sliced

Applesauce

Applesauce is often served at breakfast with grits, ham, eggs, and biscuits. At other meals, it may be served as a vegetable or a dessert.

3 lbs. cooking apples, peeled, cored, and quartered
1¼ c. water

Sugar to taste, about ¼ c.
1–2 Tb. dark rum
1–2 Tb. butter

Cook the apples and water together in a heavy-bottomed saucepan over medium heat. Roughly stir about from time to time. When tender, beat with a whisk until reasonably smooth. Add sugar to taste, rum, and butter. Serve warm in small cups or ramekins with cream barely whipped. ✗ *3 cups*

Strawberry Gratin

The best fresh fruit as it comes into season hardly needs embellishment to reveal its charms. The following simple treatment can be used throughout the summer as cherries, strawberries, raspberries, blackberries, then peaches, figs, and pears appear in the market. Arrange the fruits carefully in a single layer, close but not layered or overlapping. Peaches, apricots, and the like should be blanched first, then peeled and cut into quarters. Mixed fruits are delicious if carefully chosen for complementing flavors. Raspberries, for instance, in a mixed dish should be used with restraint, as accents for peaches, mangoes, and blueberries. Too many soft berries will end up mushy. Serve with a simple cookie or shortbread.

1 c. small, perfect strawberries
1 Tb. Triple Sec

1½ Tb. heavy cream
1½ tsp. sugar

Cap but do not cut into the strawberries and sprinkle with the Triple Sec. Let sit at room temperature for 20 minutes. Arrange the strawberries carefully in an ovenproof dish stem end down, points up. Pour any liqueur over the berries. Carefully spoon a little cream over each berry, then sprinkle each very lightly with sugar. Treat each separate piece of fruit rather reverently.

Run under a very hot broiler for 3 or 4 minutes. The sugar should just melt and slightly caramelize. Do not overcook. Serve immediately while hot with cream or Custard Sauce if desired. ✗ *2 servings*

Apricots in Rum

Here's a simple country dessert or breakfast dish. Use two whole apricots for each person. Split them, remove the pits, and place in a gratin dish. Top with brown sugar — a good teaspoon per half — sprinkle with dark rum, add a little cinnamon, and a piece of butter. Broil until tender, 10–20 minutes depending on the apricots. Serve warm with cold cream. A few fresh cherries, treated as above, combine well with the apricots, or can be prepared alone. Similarly, in Old Salem, North Carolina, the cavities of split peaches are filled with honey and butter and broiled and are usually served alongside ham or chicken.

Brandied Fruit

Brandied Fruit is a treasured cake, pudding, or ice cream topping for special events. By Christmas, the fruit has all of the previous summer's flavor intensified by brandy. Betty Lewis, my piano teacher, would serve it at winter musicales during my high school years. She kept a seemingly eternal stock in a heavy glass crock in the kitchen pantry.

This is a simple preparation if you measure and keep the mixture cool. The first year I made it with visions of Christmas gifts solved, I found it in full runaway and throwaway fermentation in August's heat.

Start with the first spring fruits. Peel if necessary and remove the pits. Pour 1 quart brandy (or white rum, if you like) into a crock, stir the fruit in, and for every cup of fruit, add 1 cup of sugar. For each quart of brandy you may add up to 20 cups of fruit. Stir it about daily until all is added.

In the fall, Southerners often finish off the mix with 1 cup of pecans and/or raisins (no sugar for these). Good fruit choices are pineapple, strawberries, cherries, raspberries, apricots, peaches, figs. Apples, bananas, and pears are either too hard or too mushy.

FOOLS

🐝 *"Your cheesecakes, curdes, and clouted creame, Your fooles, your flaunes."*
— *Ben Jonson, 1637*

Mr. Jonson's catalogue sounds more like curses than sweets, but these dishes represent some of the best English desserts. The culinary fool was first described in 1598 as "a kinde of clouted creame called a foole or a trifle in English." The *Oxford English Dictionary* says now it is a "dish composed of fruit stewed, crushed, and mixed with milk, cream, or custard." The charm of all fools is their simplicity — perfectly ripe fruit, rich cream, sugar — nothing else need complicate the picture. The name fool does not often appear in early Southern recipes. Such dishes are often called creams as in Lettice Bryan's *The Kentucky Housewife* (1839):

🐝 Strawberry Cream. *Pick the leaves and stems from a quart of English white strawberries, mash them to a perfect marmalade, add three quarters of a pound of powdered white sugar, press it through a sieve, stir it into a quart of rich sweet cream, beat it till light, and serve it in cups or glasses. Raspberry cream may be made in the same manner.*

Many Southern ice cream recipes are simply frozen fools. As opposed to custard-based ice creams, these are often called old-fashioned, as in the following recipe from *Marion Brown's Southern Cook Book:*

🐝 Old Virginia Fresh Peach Ice Cream.
One gallon
    Pare and stone 1 quart of very soft peaches. Add to them 2 cups of sugar, and mash them thoroughly. When ready to freeze, add 2 quarts of rich cream. (Freeze in hand-turned freezer.) When frozen, this will fill a dish holding 4 quarts.
— *Mrs. J. E. Timberlake, Stevenson's Depot, Va., 1951*

Apricot Fool

My great-grandmother froze this sort of fool in an ice tray in the freezer part of the refrigerator. It works well for an ice cream if you do not stir it while it is setting up. I freeze it in individual ramekins and serve it with a small dollop of whipped cream and a matching or contrasting fruit sauce. A mulberry or blackberry sauce is especially good with apricots.

1¼ lbs. ripe apricots
½ c. water
1 c. sugar

¾ c. heavy cream
Sugar to taste, about 3 Tb.

Blanch, peel, and remove pits from the apricots. You should have about 2 cups fruit. Stew the fruit with the water and sugar until tender, about 20 minutes. Rub through a fine sieve and refrigerate until quite cold.

Whip the cream with the sugar until stiff; the amount of sugar to be added depends upon the sweetness of the fruit. Fold into the fruit puree and chill again. Serve from a dish set over ice if possible.
✖ *4 servings*

A Fool for Spring

This is a wonderful dessert served out-of-doors early in the spring. In the best of years, there is a crop of strawberries by late April.

1 c. chopped rhubarb stalk, *no*
  leaves
½ c. sugar
½ c. water

1½ c. whole, capped strawberries
1 c. heavy cream
1 Tb. sugar

Cook the rhubarb, sugar, and water together until the stalks are very tender, about 30 minutes. Raise the heat and boil away the water until the mixture is syrupy and thick. Immediately toss in the berries, remove from heat, and cover. Let sit 15 minutes. Rub through a sieve, discarding pulp and seeds. Chill.

Whip the cream with the 1 tablespoon sugar to soft but firm peaks. Fold about half of it into the chilled fruit puree. Reserve the rest for garnishing the dessert. ✖ *4 servings*

DUMPLINGS

High summer is the season for fruit dumplings. Almost all the berries are available. Sometimes strawberries, surely raspberries, and blueberries are still to be found, and the first blackberries are just coming in. An early season peach or two may show up in the farmers' market. It's an exciting time to shop, but a wearying one to cook in due to the inevitable heat.

Fortunately dumplings are stove-top cooking, and quick at that. No Southern cook wants that oven on by late June. The fruit needs a fast simmer—about 5 minutes, and the dumplings a few more—15 minutes should see you done.

A sweet potato dumpling poached in blackberries is a delicious and exotically Southern dessert, but various combinations of fruits and berries are all delectable. Strawberries, raspberries, and peaches together are irresistibly beautiful and delicate. Blackberries and blueberries together are intensely violet colored and complexly flavored. Later, apples, pears, and plums extend the season of the dumpling, but mostly by fall, these fruits fill pies and other oven-baked dishes.

Be light-handed seasoning the fruits. The ripeness and the variety of the particular fruits will determine how much seasoning to use — more than a recipe can tell you. Use a little lemon juice to heighten flavors at the end of cooking. Port pairs well with blackberries and blueberries. Use spices sparingly, if at all. A hint of nutmeg or cinnamon may pass muster but remember not to overwhelm the flavor of the fruit.

For breakfast or dessert in the summer, split stale biscuits. Spread with butter and toast lightly. Pour some stewed fresh fruit over, return to oven, and bake for 8–10 minutes, until just hot.

Egg Dumplings

1 c. plus 2 Tb. all-purpose flour	¾ c. milk
1½ tsp. baking powder	1½ tsp. melted butter
1 tsp. sugar	1 recipe Basic Stewed Fruit
½ tsp. salt	(opposite)
1 egg	

Sift the dry ingredients together into a large bowl. Beat the egg, milk, and melted butter together. Combine quickly with the flour mixture. Do not overbeat.

Drop the dumpling batter by the tablespoonful into simmering, sweetened fruit. Cover and cook gently 5–8 minutes depending on the size of the dumplings. ✄ *6 servings*

Basic Stewed Fruit
for Dumplings

This is also used as a breakfast compote, formerly with clabber, now with yogurt.

4 c. fruit (peeled, seeded, cored, whatever is necessary)
2 c. water

1 c. sugar
Lemon juice, Port, or orange liqueur

Combine fruit, water, and sugar in a heavy-bottomed saucepan. Bring to a rapid boil, reduce heat, and simmer until just tender. Do not overcook.

Season lightly and appropriately with lemon juice, Port, or orange liqueur. Add dumplings and continue to cook at a simmer, covered.

Serve hot with whipped cream, or, better, a small scoop of vanilla ice cream. ✖ *6 servings*

Sweet Potato Dumplings

1¼ c. all-purpose flour
2 tsp. baking powder
1 tsp. sugar
½ tsp. salt
Scant c. milk

6 Tb. mashed, cooked sweet potato
1½ tsp. butter, melted
1 recipe Basic Stewed Fruit (above)

Sift the dry ingredients together into a large bowl. Beat the milk and mashed sweet potato together until smooth. Beat in the melted butter, and combine quickly with the dry ingredients. Do not overbeat.

Drop the dumpling batter by the tablespoonful into simmering, sweetened fruit. Cover and cook gently 5–8 minutes depending on the size of the dumplings. ✖ *6–8 servings*

ROLY POLY

Roly Poly is an old-fashioned fruit dumpling poached in simmering water. A cloth is wrapped around the pastry to keep it intact while cooking. It was a very popular early Southern dessert.

Cooks used to have special pudding cloths shaped like a stocking cap for steaming and poaching. In 1889, *The New Dixie Cook-Book*'s instructions:

> *Pudding Bags are either knitted or made of firm white drilling, tapering from top to bottom, and rounded on corners; stitch and fill seams, which should be outside when in use, and sew a tape to seam, about three inches from top . . . Pudding-cloths, however coarse, should never be washed with soap, but in clear, clean water, dried as quickly as possible, and kept dry and out of dust in a drawer or cupboard free from smell.*

The Roly Poly needs only an 18-inch square cloth for rolling, cheesecloth or unbleached muslin will do. If you have or want to make a pudding bag, double the amount of fruit, mash it well, stir it into the dough, and cook the batter in the bag.

Few cooks make any sort of boiled or steamed puddings anymore. A Roly Poly isn't much trouble; in fact, it's rather fun to assemble and cook in its archaic fashion. Despite the number of steps, the dish is easy to compose and the first slice that reveals the tucked-away fruit in its sauce inside always seems a little magical. Nineteenth-century cooks were quite serious about the little Roly Poly as the next few recipes reveal.

Raisin Rolls

Make a paste of flour and fresh suet, minced fine, or butter, allowing one pound of flour to half a pound of the suet or butter; mix in as much cold water as will make it into good paste, knead it well, and roll it out into oblong sheets about one fourth of an inch thick. Having seeded and cut in half some raisins, stew them tender in a very little water; then mix in some brown sugar, and spread a smooth layer of them over each sheet of paste, roll them up evenly and closely into a scroll, close the side by pressing it together with your fingers, trim the ends smoothly, and close them also securely, by pressing them smoothly together; then sprinkle them thickly with flour, tie them up in separate cloths, taking care that you do not bend or spoil the shape of them, and boil them in a vessel sufficiently large to contain them at full length; there should be plenty of water to keep them well covered till done, which should be boiling when they are put in. Serve them up in a flat dish of suitable size, grate a little sugar over them, and eat them warm with cream sauce, or cold butter, powdered sugar, and nutmeg. Peaches, pears, quinces, apples, gooseberries, grapes, cherries and plums will all make nice rolls by first stewing them tender in a little water, and sweetening them with sugar.
— Lettice Bryan, The Kentucky Housewife, 1839

A few suggestions from 1889:

For Apple, Orange and Peach Rolly-Poly the fruit should be sliced, and for Cherry, stoned; sprinkle the fruit well with sugar, and some add bits of butter before rolling up, with a little grated peel over the oranges, and cinnamon or nutmeg over the apple. Some use Plain or Suet Paste or raised biscuit dough, rolling a quarter inch thick. This dessert may be varied by making into several small rolls, or shaping into balls with a spoonful fruit in center of each. Some sprinkle in a few currants with the apples and use raisins with jelly, jam, apple butter or marmalade. For Fig Rolly-Poly spread with figs cut in small pieces and for Lemon cook the pulp of three lemons with cup and a half sugar twenty minutes, then spread the dough and roll as above. Or some simply mix the juice with teaspoon each flour and sugar for each lemon and spread over the paste, or use the Lemon Butter. Chopped pie-plant, thickly sprinkled with sugar is nice used as above. A Dixie Rolly-Poly is made in two or three rolls, using any of above mixture for spreading, and placed in pan four or five inches deep with cup sugar, half cup butter and hot water enough to cover. Bake half an hour.
— Estelle Wilcox, The New Dixie Cook-Book, 1889

Roly Poly

This Roly Poly is also often baked in the South, but the dough must be stiffer. Increase flour to 2¼ cups and bake at 375° F. for 40 minutes or until brown. Serve with a like fruit sauce, whipped cream, or ice cream.

The Dough
1½ c. flour
1 tsp. baking powder
½ tsp. baking soda
½ tsp. salt
1 Tb. sugar
2 Tb. lard
1 egg
¼ c. buttermilk
1 tsp. vanilla

Fruit Filling
2 c. fruit such as 1½ c. blueberries and ½ c. mulberries, 1 c.
each blueberries and blackberries, ¾ c. raspberries, and
1¼ c. chopped peaches
¼–⅓ c. sugar
Cinnamon, optional
2 Tb. plus 3 Tb. flour

Sift the dry ingredients together for the dough. Rub in the lard. Beat the egg with the buttermilk and vanilla. Stir the liquid into the flour and chill the mixture 10 minutes.

In the meantime, prepare the filling. Sweeten the fruit to taste with sugar and cinnamon and toss with 2 tablespoons of the flour. Mash slightly.

To assemble, dip an 18-inch square cloth into boiling water, spread out on a smooth surface and sprinkle with an even layer of flour, about 3 tablespoons. Put the chilled dough in the center and very lightly roll out the dough to a 10-inch square. Leaving a 1-inch margin of pastry, pat the fruit into the center of the square. Roll the dough over on itself; the cloth should pull away. If the dough sticks, gently scrape it loose with a long, flexible knife blade. Then wrap the cloth fairly tightly around the roll. Tie each end securely.

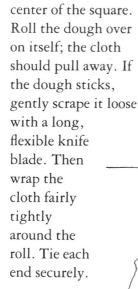

Poach in simmering water for 1 hour and 20 minutes or until it is firm. A fish poacher with a tray is ideal for this, but the dumpling is substantial enough for easy removal from any pot large enough to accommodate it. Drain well, remove the cloth, and serve warm with custard, whipped cream, or Hard sauce. ✖ *6–8 servings*

A Sweet Potato Roly Poly

Prepare the Roly Poly (opposite) recipe but work 1 cup sieved, baked sweet potato into the dough with the milk and egg. This is very pretty with dark berries; some spice — cinnamon, nutmeg, or allspice — can be put into the dough.

Pear and Plum Cobbler

☞ Baking dish about 11 × 13 inches, buttered

♦ ♦ ♦ ♦ ♦ ♦ ♦ ♦

Fruit

1¼ lbs. plums, stoned and sliced to yield 3 c.

1¾ lbs. pears, peeled, cored and sliced to yield 4 c.

Grated zest of 1 orange, lemon, or tangerine

Pinch of salt

½ tsp. cinnamon

1½ c. sugar

¼ c. flour

Topping

½ c. butter

⅓ c. lightly packed light brown sugar

⅓ c. white sugar

⅛ tsp. salt

1⅞ c. all-purpose flour

½ tsp. baking powder

1 Tb. chopped, crystallized ginger

¼ c. water

½ c. chopped walnuts or pecans

Toss the fruits with the seasonings, sugar, and flour. Pour into a buttered dish for baking.

For the topping, cream the butter well and beat in the sugars. Sift the salt, flour, baking powder together, and add the chopped ginger. Work into the butter and add enough cold water to make a crumbly dough. Stir in the nuts. Drop the dough roughly all over the fruit. Bake in an oven preheated to 350° F. for about 45 minutes or until fruit is bubbly and top is lightly browned. Serve warm with whipped cream. ✗ *6–8 servings*

Peach Cobbler with
Clabber Biscuits

My grandmother kept a milk cow and made her biscuits with clabber —a sort of cross between yogurt and a fresh cheese that cures overnight; the result of enzymes working on fresh, not pasteurized, milk. The combination of yogurt and cream in this recipe approximates clabber's rich and sour taste. These biscuits can be baked alone, rather than only as a topping for the fruit.

☞ 9 × 13-inch baking dish, buttered

Fruit
6 c. peeled, pitted, and sliced peaches
½ c. pitted sour cherries *or* raspberries
4 Tb. flour
1½ c. sugar
Dash of cinnamon *or* nutmeg
Juice of ½ lemon

Biscuits
2 c. flour
2 Tb. sugar
3 tsp. baking powder
1 tsp. salt
1 tsp. baking soda
4 Tb. butter
¾ c. plain yogurt
¼ c. heavy cream

Toss the fruit with the flour, sugar, spice, and lemon juice. Pour into the well-buttered baking dish.

Sift the flour, sugar, baking powder, salt, and baking soda. Cut in the butter until the flour resembles coarse meal. Stir in the yogurt and cream. Turn the dough out on a lightly floured surface and knead gently 10 or 12 strokes. Pat out about ½-inch thick and cut into 10 rounds. Place the rounds on top of the fruit. Cut the scraps into small diamonds and fill in the spaces between the biscuits with the smaller pieces. Bake in an oven preheated to 425° F. for about 25 minutes, until the fruit is bubbling and the biscuits are golden brown. Serve with whipped cream or ice cream. ✄ *10 servings*

Fruit Crackle

Fruit Crackle is a real midsummer celebration of fresh fruits and should be adapted to what's at hand. It's a simple country dessert; don't fuss over it too much or it will lose its charm.

☞ 8 × 8-inch baking pan, buttered

* * * * * * * *

6 medium ripe peaches
3 medium ripe plums
1 c. blueberries, raspberries, blackberries, mulberries, or a combination of the four

½ c. plus ⅔ c. sugar
1 c. all-purpose flour
¼ tsp. salt
½ tsp. cinnamon
½ c. butter

Blanch, peel, and slice the peaches thickly. Slice the plums *without* peeling. Put the peaches in the bottom of the buttered baking pan, top with plum slices, then the berries. Sprinkle with ½ cup sugar.

Sift the flour, ⅔ cup sugar, salt, and cinnamon together. Work in the butter until crumbly. Sprinkle over the fruit and bake about 35 minutes in an oven preheated to 375° F. or until the fruit is bubbly and the top is lightly browned. Serve warm with cream, custard, or ice cream. ✕ *6 servings*

Fruit Fritters

Fritters in the South take two forms, one savoury, one sweet. Usually, but not always, the savoury fritter — whether seafood, corn, or ham — is more of a thin pancake fried in some, but not deep, fat. The sweet fritter is usually a slice of fresh fruit, such as apple, peach, banana, dipped in a batter and deep fried. The fruit is often marinated a bit before frying in brandy or liquor. Smaller fruits — apricots, large strawberries, figs — can be fried halved or whole. Very small fruits such as cherries should be pitted, stirred into the batter, and dropped by the spoonful into the fat.

Lard was the frying medium of choice; today, tasteless oils such as peanut or vegetable shortening are used. Whipped cream flavored with rum and a bit of fruit sauce make a fancier dish.

Fritter Batter
1 egg, separated
1 tsp. peanut oil
1 Tb. sugar
Slight pinch of salt
½ c. beer

⅔ c. flour, sifted
1–2 Tb. water

• • • • • • • •

Fruit, about 2 cups
Powdered sugar

Beat the egg yolk, oil, sugar, and salt briefly. Stir in the beer and add the flour. Beat just until smooth. The batter should be as thick as boiled custard. Thin with cold water if necessary.

Set aside at room temperature for at least 30 minutes. Just before using, beat the egg white until stiff and fold gently into the batter. Dip the fruit in the batter or mix smaller fruits with batter. Fry at about 360° F. for 3–4 minutes until brown. Drain on brown paper. Sprinkle with powdered sugar and serve immediately. ✖ *4 servings*

DRIED FRUITS

Mountain cooks still dry their bumper crops of fall apples, much as my grandmother did when I was young. The peeled, sliced apples would be set out on large, clean white cotton sheets, each piece carefully placed to shrivel up without touching its neighbor and then covered with cheesecloth to keep off the insects. Every evening before the damp came out, the sheets were rolled up and brought inside. As soon as the morning dew dried, the apples went back to the sun.

We had a much beloved neighbor who lived the traditional rural life in a ramshackle log cabin in the midst of a garden of irises and lilies. When we were young, we visited regularly, for she would talk to us unceasingly about flowers, cows, weather, and neighbors as if we mattered. She dried her apples threaded and hung like garlands around the stone fireplace and looped over the woodstove. They had their own peculiar smoky flavor.

One long summer, constant construction went on behind the old homestead. By fall, the original house was pulled down to expose a modern, brick ranch with an all electric kitchen—built-in ovens and an avocado green refrigerator. All the earthy odors were gone, all the shadows chased out by fluorescent lights. Yet the food was as good as ever, which did not make sense even to us youngsters, until one day we were invited downstairs. The new house had been built over the old root cellar. Here were all the odors of the previous years—the apples in great bows, sweet potatoes, red peppers drying. In the middle of the cellar the old woodstove was fired up; biscuits were baking. For years this was our secret, held in trust with our mighty cook. For others, she cooked downstairs, but brought the dishes up and kept them warm on the electrical units of the new kitchen—her guests never knew the source of such good cooking.

Dried fruits from the store won't have the smoky nuances or summer memories attached, but they do have an intensity that fresh fruits lack. Unfortunately they vary widely in water content, texture, and sweetness. Many commercially packaged fruits are put up to remain moist and rather puffy. Health food store products are usually offered in bulk and are less expensive, much drier, and more intense in flavor. Cooking time, liquid, sweetening will have to be adjusted for the inconsistencies.

Stewed Dried Fruit

	Peaches, Apricots	Apples, Pears
Dried fruit	4 oz. (equals about 1 lb. fresh)	4 oz. (equals about 3 lbs. fresh)
Water	2½ c.	3 c.

Cook the fruit and water about 40 minutes over low heat, covered, until the fruit is completely tender. Add more water if necessary. Drain, mash coarsely, and season to taste. Start with ¼ cup sugar for each batch. Cinnamon, nutmeg, cloves, ginger, a little lemon juice are often used — about ¼ teaspoon powdered spices total to start off. If desired, beat in a teaspoon or 2 of butter.

⚔ *About 1 cup stewed peaches or apricots or 2 cups apples or pears*

Fried Pies

Fried pies are a constant feature of the Carrboro Farmers' Market every Saturday morning from April through November. Constant, that is, if you get there early on. The social shoppers arriving around 10 a.m. or so, miss the pies as well as the baby okras, the organic watercress, the little brown figs, and Sarah Llewellyn's blowsy lotus blossoms on 4-foot stems. For those who do get there by 7:30 a.m., hot coffee, stacks of fried pies, biscuits, ham and sausage, and the baby rose buds of "Cecile Brunner" are the early bird's worm.

When we first offered fried pies at the restaurant Crook's Corner, the response was overwhelming. Southerners see these pastries as symbols of the traditional life of the region. Hardly anyone prepares them at home anymore, but most Southerners, like me, remember fried pies from when they were about eye-level with an iron skillet. The fillings are usually stewed dried fruits. Sometimes jam or jelly is used. The dough is either biscuit or pie dough, depending on what your grandmother used. Mine (both) used biscuit dough and fried it in just a film of fat in the skillet. Other cooks deep fat fry. In either case, a little lard mixed in with cooking shortening or oil will improve the flavor and texture.

1 recipe Biscuit Dough (refer to pp. 44–5)
1 c. Stewed Dried Fruit (above)

Powdered sugar
Fat for deep frying: oil, shortening, lard, or a combination

Prepare the biscuit dough as directed and pat out to a ¾ inch thickness. Cut into 2-inch rounds. Roll each round out thinly to a 5-inch diameter. Put a good tablespoon filling in the center. Moisten the

BISCUITS, SPOONBREAD, AND SWEET POTATO PIE

edges and fold over to form a half circle. Press the edges together with a fork. Remove to a sheet of parchment or wax paper lightly sprinkled with flour while preparing the rest. Fry in a heavy skillet in a small amount of fat (¼ inch of oil, shortening, lard — any or a combination) over medium heat. The pies should brown up nicely in about 3 minutes. Turn and brown the remaining side.

Drain on brown paper, sprinkle with powdered sugar, and serve immediately. The hand is usually the serving dish, but fried pies may be served on a plate with whipped cream or ice cream.

✖ *About 12 pies*

COOLING · OFF
FROZEN DESSERTS

Frozen Strawberries

Ruby Red Grapefruit Ice

Planter's Ice

Lemon-Lime Ice

Orange Ice

Pomegranate Ice

Honeydew Ice

Mulberry Ice

Pear Ice

Banana Sherbet

Green Tea Sherbet

Dragoon's Punch Sherbet

Roman Punch

Snow Cream

Strawberry Ice Cream

Other Ice Creams
Vanilla Custard Ice Cream
Coffee Ice Cream
Jamaican Ice Cream
Chocolate Ice Cream
Milk Punch Ice Cream
Cherry Bounce Ice Cream
Fig Ice Cream
Bananas Foster Ice Cream
Lemon Ice Cream
Burnt Fruit Ice Cream
Butter Pecan Ice Cream
Eggnog Ice Cream
French Vanilla Ice Cream
Blackberry Bombe

FROZEN DESSERTS

In the history books, 1799 may be noted for Napoléon's rise to power, the composition of Beethoven's *Sonate Pathétique,* and the births of Balzac, Pushkin, and Heine, but in Charleston the momentous event was the day that ice first arrived for sale, cut from frozen lakes, packed in sawdust, and transported by boat from the northern states. A commercial ice depot was established and from that time on summers became more tolerable with iced drinks and frozen desserts.

Before ice, there were ingenious solutions to cooling off. To keep a drink cool, it would be set in a small wooden bucket of water and placed where there was a breeze. The eccentric Cooper River planter Francis Cordes "so disapproved of higher education that a nephew was left his property on condition that he abstained from colleges. . . . Every night his grog was mixed of French Brandy, sugar, and water in a large silver mug. This was stood in a cedar piggin filled with cool spring water, out on the piazza where any shift of breeze would cool it. From it he poured and drank until sleep was assured."

In the winter, nature provided snow and ice for making frozen desserts. The frozen precipitation was packed in a pan with rock salt and a shallow metal tray containing cream or custard was set over it. As the cream froze on the bottom of the tray, it was periodically scraped up and incorporated into the rest of the mixture. The practice is ancient, the technique simple, and arguments over who first served ice cream in America are rather silly when you come to think of it. Those who could afford them used pewter cylinders for freezing ice cream. These were the forerunners of the churn, but they still required manual mixing. Mrs. Bryan describes the method: "Having prepared your cream, put it in the freezer, set it in the tub of ice, pressing up the ice closely to it; cover it with a folded carpet, turn it round constantly, taking care not to let a drop of the salt water get in, which would injure very much the taste of the cream. Raise the cover frequently, and with a long-handled spoon scrape down the ice from the sides of the freezer." Churns were common by the end of the nineteenth century; the continuous motion resulted in a finer texture and a reduced freezing time. Mrs. Bryan had found her whole process to take about 4 hours the old way.

Another alternative was snow cream, a mixture of fresh snow and cream. Even in Charleston, it could be made occasionally and was always a treat. Emma Holmes of Charleston kept a diary during the Civil War. She wrote on March 19, 1861:

🏃 *To our astonishment when we woke this morning, we found it snowing hard, but it stopped between seven and eight. It was about two inches thick on the shed and everything looked beautifully, but the sun shone forth very brightly and dissipated the picture. We enjoyed it while it lasted and though we did not make snowballs, we made milk sherbert or punch.*

Fantastic ice cream gardens, usually operated by French or Italian immigrants, were built in all the large Southern cities once the supply of ice was assured. In Charleston, the fashionable Mount Vernon Garden "with its fountains, statues, arbors, and music" was Miss Holmes' favorite. In Richmond, the best families were seen at Pizzini's. As the horrors of the Civil War drew closer, the ice cream garden's lure of escape grew dearer. Mrs. D. Girard Wright's memoirs of her adolescence during the war years, *A Southern Girl in '61*, tell: "I find recorded in letters at this time, in spite of the gnawing anxieties which were weighing down the hearts of all serious people, that sundry delightful parties were organized to partake of strawberries and ice cream at Pizzini's." A few years later, Charleston evacuated, Emma Holmes found herself a refugee in the Carolina interior. Ice cream was a nostalgic comfort, a reminder of peaceful days.

🏃 *The weather was bitter cold — thermometer being at 12 deg. — one of the coldest spells for years. Lander's creek was frozen and even the foam from the mill floated congealed like huge water lilies. The carriage broke ice an inch thick on the road, and in many places, it was deeper.*

The girls determined to take advantage of it and enjoy some ice cream. We had much amusement in collecting the materials, finally borrowing eggs and churn. . . . After many quakings and considerable excitement, at half past ten we were regaled with an excellent Confederate article, sorghum & lemon combined, having produced chocolate cream equal to the palmy days of Mount Vernon Garden.

All sorts of frozen desserts exist in the Southern repertoire. There are crushed fruits heavily sugared and frozen without churning, ices of the Italian type made with juice and a syrup, sorbets with pureed fruit, strongly alcoholic punches, creams of the English tradition like frozen fools, nogs and custards, and rich, silky bombes from the French. Fruits are important in all Southern frozen confections; fortunately they come into season when we need cooling off the most.

Frozen Strawberries

Frozen fruit in general is a type of confection unto itself, not to be confused with ice creams, sorbets, or ices. Quite sweet, dense, even chewy, these dishes have all but disappeared from the modern southeastern states. A few years ago, I was elated to find frozen fruits are perfectly made in the city of Oaxaca, Mexico. The origin must be Spanish, for frozen fruits were a nineteenth-century favorite of New Orleans, the most Spanish city of our region. They are not well suited for a dessert; they are refreshments, in the strict sense, in small portions for tropical revivals.

1 lb. ripe strawberries	Juice of 1 lemon
¾–1 c. sugar, to taste	Good dry red wine such as
½–¾ c. water, to taste	Cabernet Sauvignon

Cap and slice the berries. There should be about 3 cups. Toss with the sugar and mash well with a pestle or potato masher. You want to break the cellulose structure down for easy sugar absorption while avoiding a puree. The sense of whole fruit should remain. Add a little water and lemon juice. Taste; it should be quite sweet. Set aside for 1 hour to macerate, then pour into a shallow pan and freeze. Stir it up every hour for 6 hours until firmly set, but do not try to incorporate air or try to make it fluffy. Serve with a tablespoon (you can add more) of the dry red wine over each serving. ✗ *8 servings*

Ruby Red Grapefruit Ice

Grapefruits are relatively new to the world of food. They first were farmed commercially in Florida in 1885, and Florida now produces the overwhelming majority of the world crop. But before the grapefruit, a near relative called the shaddock — after the English Captain who brought it from Indonesia to Barbados in 1696 — was used to make sweets in the South. Like most citrus fruits before the acquisition of Florida, the shaddock was grown as far north as Charleston, and Sarah Rutledge had a method of preserving them whole. Today shaddocks are found in home gardens from the Carolina Low Country southward, but they are little used in cooking.

The grapefruit remains a symbol of welcome cool weather in the late fall and early winter. The following ice is sophisticated in its bitter and sweet play and is an excellent wrap up for a formal winter dinner. The Ruby Red grapefruits from Texas make the prettiest ice, but you can use any pink, or even the yellow flesh, grapefruits. It goes well with chocolate glazed shortbread, a surprising combination.

☞ Electric ice cream maker or small manual churn

2 large red grapefruit
½ c. honey
⅓–½ c. sugar, to taste
½ c. water
Pomegranate seeds, optional
Port or Campari, optional

Section the grapefruit in the following manner. Slice off both the blossom and stem ends to reveal the flesh. Turn on one end and with a very sharp knife pare away the outer peel and the inner white pith right down to the flesh of each section. Then cut in a V-fashion on each side of the membrane to free a segment of the grapefruit with absolutely no white pith, skin, or membrane attached. Repeat for all the segments of the fruit and squeeze out the membrane when through to extract all juice. Two grapefruits should give you 16 ounces or a heaping 2 cups of fruit and juice.

Combine all the ingredients in a food processor or

blender and give it a quick whirl to break up, but not liquify, the fruit. Let stand 10 minutes. Stir well, then freeze in a churn or ice cream maker. Garnish each serving with pomegranate seeds when serving, and/or a spoonful of Port or Campari. ✖ *3–4 cups*

Planter's Ice

The pineapple is a symbol of hospitality. A native of the West Indies, the pineapple was placed as a sign of safe approach at the entrance of Indian villages. Gates leading to colonial mansions in Georgia and South Carolina were often topped by wooden replicas of the fruit (it actually isn't a fruit, but the union of individual flowers forming a juicy, fleshy mass). Mary Randolph in Virginia made ice cream from it. In Charleston, which has much closer ties to the exotic foods of the Indies, Sarah Rutledge made several pineapple sherbets, a pudding, preserves, and beer. Pineapples are still used in the South for producing homemade vinegars.

1 lb. ripe pineapple, peeled	½ tsp. Pernod or Herbsaint
1 c. sugar	liqueur
2 Tb. white rum	Mint leaves for garnish
2 Tb. fresh lime juice	

Finely chop the pineapple and put into a bowl with the sugar. With a potato masher or a large, strong whisk, bruise the fruit well with the sugar. Leave to macerate 15 minutes. Add the rum, lime juice, and Pernod. Stir well and pour into a shallow pan. Cover and freeze in the frozen food compartment of the refrigerator. Garnish with mint leaves when serving. ✖ *1 quart*

Lemon-Lime Ice

My children Madeline and Elliott occasionally persuade me to provide the goods for a Saturday afternoon bake sale on the front porch. Our neighborhood is pretty well traveled by joggers, cyclists, and baby strollers, and it isn't difficult to lure customers to their glorified lemonade stand for lemon and chocolate chess pies, popcorn, strawberry cream puffs, Lemon-Lime Ice, and herb teas. Madeline and Elliott usually manage to put away most of the ice — it's their favorite — but they still bring in enough cash to buy comics at the Nice Price Book Store down the street. Both the lemon and orange ices can end a meal beautifully with a contrasting sauce such as blackberry, blueberry, raspberry.

☞ Electric ice cream maker or small manual churn

3 c. water
1½ c. sugar

Zest of 1 lime and 1 lemon, cut in strips
Juice from 3 lemons and 2 limes to measure ½ c.

Boil the water, sugar, and zests together for 5 minutes. Chill the syrup, then strain.

Add the juice to the syrup and freeze it in a churn or an ice cream maker until very hard. ✳ *1 quart*

Orange Ice

3 c. water
1½ c. sugar
Zest of 2 oranges, cut in strips

1 c. orange juice
Juice of 1 lemon

Proceed as for Lemon-Lime Ice (above). ✳ *1 quart*

Pomegranate Ice

☞ Electric ice cream maker or small   2 oranges
       manual churn   3 Tb. honey

♦   ♦   ♦   ♦   ♦   ♦   ♦   ♦   ½ c. sugar
4 good-size pomegranates   1 Tb. lemon juice

Release the seeds from the pomegranate by lightly scoring the fruit's skin twice around stem to blossom end. Pull into halves, then quarters and loosen the seeds into a bowl. If you are careful, the job is not at all messy and goes quickly. There should be 3½–4 cups of the seeds. Spin them quickly — *using the plastic blade* — in a food processor and then press lightly in a sieve to extract the juice. Now, there should be 1½ cups liquid.

Section the oranges, discarding all peel, seed, and membrane. Add any juice to the flesh, and, again, give a quick spin in the food processor to break up but not to liquify the orange. About 1¼ cups should measure out.

Combine the strained pomegranate juice with the pulpy orange juice. Sweeten with the honey and sugar; add the lemon juice. Taste and adjust. Freezing will diminish the sweeteners, but, still, don't be heavy handed. You'll want to relish, not mask, the slightly bitter quality of the pomegranate. Freeze in a churn or ice cream maker. Producing a flavor as intense as the color, the ice should be served in small cold dishes. ✄ *3 cups*

Honeydew Ice

When summer afternoons stretch interminably into what should be night, this Honeydew Ice makes the passing of time more palatable. Cocktail hours are often inappropriate in the debilitating heat. Offering an ice such as this as an alternative to stronger drink during the summer is a thoughtful gesture to one's guest. Add a small splash of rum and a sprig of mint, and you create a daiquiri.

Use melons as they come into market. Cantaloupes and watermelons will make beautiful ices by this recipe. Adjust the sugar by the melon's sweetness.

☞ Electric ice cream maker or small manual churn

1 large ripe honeydew, about 2½ lbs.

1½ c. sugar
1½ limes, juice and zest
½ c. dry white rum

Scoop out the flesh of the melon, cover it with sugar, lime juice, and the lime zest. Set aside for about 1 hour.

Puree the sugared fruit and rub through a sieve so it will be very fine. Stir in the rum and freeze in a churn or an ice cream maker.

✖ *6 cups*

Mulberry Ice

The Mulberry Tree every-where amidst the Woods grows wild: The Planters, near their Plantations, in Rows and Walks, plant them for Use, Ornament and Pleasure: What I observed of this Fruit was admirable; the Fruit there, was full and ripe in the latter end of April and beginning of May, whereas in England and Europe, they are not ripe before the latter end of August. A Manufactory of Silk well encouraged might soon be accomplisht, considering the numerousness of the Leaf for Provision, the clemency and moderateness of the Climate to indulge and nourish the Silkworm: To make tryal of its Success, was the Intention of those French Protestant Passengers transported thither in His Majesties Frigat the Richmond *being Forty Five, the half of a greater number design'd for that Place; but their Design was too early anticipated: the Eggs which they brought with them being hatch'd at Sea, before we could reach the Land, the Worms for want of Provision were untimely lost and destroyed.*
—*Thomas Ashe,* Carolina, *1682*

Mulberries come along in May with the first strawberries and before the general deluge of summer fruits and berries. Blueberries and cherries may be showing up spottily at the Farmers' Market, but the price is dear. Mulberries, on the other hand, are never found in the market, but they're free and easy to get if you have neighborhood children. My two, Elliott and Madeline, and their friends, Taylor, Amanda, and Frankie, brought in a bumper harvest this spring. Our teeth, hands, bare feet, and clothes all bore the mark of the purple berries, for it is a fruit determined to set a stain.

Mulberries were widely planted in the South as food for the silkworm. Over and over, speculators from colonial days through the late nineteenth century tried to establish a Southern silk industry. Town names such as Silk Hope, North Carolina, bear witness to the attempts, but today mulberries are neglected by most adults. In fact, the entire crop of a tree is usually turned over to the children and the bluejays. The flavor is sweet and a little musky; the fruit needs a little lemon or other sharp flavor to bring it alive.

☞ Electric ice cream maker or small manual churn

• • • • • • • •

3 c. water

1½ c. sugar

Zest in strips of 1 lemon

4 oz. (about ½ c.) fresh ginger, thinly sliced

4 c. fresh mulberries

¼ c. or more Port

¼ c. or more lemon juice

Combine water, sugar, lemon zest, and ginger in a heavy saucepan and boil 5 minutes. Add the mulberries, bring back to the boil, then remove from heat and let cool. Puree briefly in a food processor or blender, strain, and rub the berries to release all juice. Add ¼ cup each Port and lemon juice and taste. It may need a little more sugar or lemon juice depending on the berries. Freeze in a churn or an ice cream maker. Garnish with a splash of Port or a squeeze of lemon juice when serving.

✘ *5½ cups*

Pear Ice

Pears, perfectly ripe, give the finest texture to frozen desserts. This is a real hybrid recipe. Highlighting the cool weather fruit in this delectable ice are the decidedly Caribbean flavors of rum and citrus.

☞ Electric ice cream maker or small manual churn

• • • • • • • •

4 c. peeled, chopped, cored ripe pears, about 2 lbs. before preparation

¼ c. white rum
1 Tb. Triple Sec
Juice of 1 orange
Juice of 1 lemon
½ tsp. Angostura bitters
1 c. sugar

Combine all the ingredients and let stand about 30 minutes, stirring up occasionally. Give it all a good spin in the food processor or blender and rub through a sieve. Freeze in a churn or an ice cream maker. ✘ *5½ cups*

Banana Sherbet

☞ Electric ice cream maker or small manual churn

• • • • • • • •

1 c. water
1½ c. sugar
Zest of ½ orange

Zest of ½ lemon
6 medium-size ripe bananas
2 c. orange juice
Juice of 2 lemons
¼ c. white rum

Make a syrup of the water, sugar, and zests. Boil for 5 minutes, cool, and strain. Puree the bananas with the juices and rum. Combine with the syrup and freeze in a churn or an ice cream maker. ✘ *About 6 cups*

Green Tea Sherbet

Tea was always the favorite base in Southern colonial society for punches and other drinks, and almost without exception it was the green kind that the old recipes call hyson, with the lovely Chinese meaning of "flourishing spring." The cultivation of tea was a short-lived English hope for the Southern colonies. In 1890, the experiment was revived briefly in Summerville, South Carolina. In 1987, Mack Fleming and Bill Hall began growing tea again at The Charleston Tea Plantation on Wadmalaw Island, South Carolina. Their plant stock came from Low Country bushes planted well before the Civil War. America's only home-grown tea can be ordered by writing to P.O. Box 12810, Charleston, South Carolina 29412.

☞ Electric ice cream maker or small
    manual churn

◆ ◆ ◆ ◆ ◆ ◆ ◆ ◆

1 c. water
1½ c. sugar

3 Tb. green tea
1 c. orange juice
Juice of 1 lime
Juice of 2 lemons
Angostura bitters, optional

Make a syrup of the water and sugar. Boil 5 minutes. Remove from heat, add the green tea. Cover and let steep 5 minutes. Strain and cool. Add the citrus juices and freeze in a churn or an ice cream maker. Serve in small portions with a dash of bitters over the top if desired.
✗ *About 4 cups*

Dragoon's Punch Sherbet

🐾 *I shall not easily forget such a frolic and [such] flirtation I have not enjoyed for a long time. . . . Edwin rode with Rosa and the Dr. with me, while Mr. B. followed on horseback and Dr. D. in his sulky. At the [Ashley Dragoons'] camp we found Dick Macbeth, Sam Wilson and Willie Vincent, all of whom I knew, & Mr. Maclaine a young Irishman . . . We waited for lunch, as I wanted to taste their famous camp pudding, of bread soaked in molasses & fried bacon. When it was ready, we went to the mess tent a few steps off, & I took lunch in true soldier style; a pine table with tin plates and a* calabash *from which to take a "slight refreshment." The bill of fare was beefsteak & bread & pudding. The latter with a little whiskey or "kitchen wasser" poured over it, the gentlemen declared, tasted like mince pie, but a few mouthfuls soon satisfied me.*
—*The Diary of Miss Emma Holmes, March 12, 1862*

Green Tea Sherbet becomes Dragoon's Punch Sherbet by adding rum and brandy. A dragoon originally was an eighteenth-century cavalryman; there is a famous Charleston punch (and many variants of it) created for the Ashley Dragoons of the Third South Carolina Cavalry. Servings of it run to something like 350 to 500 cups. You can manage this sherbet in a regular size churn.

> 1 recipe for Green Tea Sherbet   ¼ c. white rum
>   (p. 185)   2 Tb. brandy

Proceed as for Green Tea Sherbet, adding the liquors with the fruit just before freezing. ✗ *About 4½ cups*

Roman Punch

Make a rich lemonade (of limes, if they can be had), and to two quarts of the lemonade allow half a pint of old rum and half a pint of peach brandy; stir all well together, and freeze.
—*Sarah Rutledge,* The Carolina Housewife, *1847*

Roman Punch was one of a variety of frozen beverages served at fancy dinners to stimulate the inundated palate. These cleansing sorbets came back into American fashion in the 1970s as home cooks exercised their fascination with French cuisine, but the lower South had held onto them, especially for winter holidays. *The Picayune Creole Cook Book* (1901) described their currency at the turn of the century before listing its eleven punches:

Middle Course Drinks, Coup de Millieu. From earliest Creole days no elegant dinner or luncheon or supper was considered complete without a "Coup de Millieu," or a middle course, consisting of a form of iced sherbet or punch, into which fruit juices or fancy liqueurs were added. As the name "Coup de Millieu" indicates, these fancy punches were brought to the table in the middle of the feast, just before the roasts were served. The custom was a survival of an ancient French and Spanish usage, that in our day has been adopted by all leading northern caterers. . . . The "Coup de Millieu" is always frozen, but it must be remembered that it is never possible to freeze it entirely, on account of the alcohol in the liquors that enter into its composition.

1 recipe Lemon-Lime Ice (p. 180)	1 c. golden or dark rum
	1 c. champagne

Prepare the Lemon-Lime Ice as directed and freeze in a churn or an ice cream maker. When quite hard add the rum and champagne and freeze again. Serve in a tall chilled glass, such as a champagne flute.
About 5 cups

Snow Cream

A beautiful fall of pure snow is a rare treat for most of the South. Winter storms usually bring us a savage mix of freezing rain and sleet and the damage to vegetation is often heartbreaking. Along the Carolina coast the subtropical oleanders and palmettos freeze and split during the rare but inevitable onslaughts. Inland, the soft-wooded evergreens bend and crack. Otherwise silent, the winter nights of my childhood were often pierced with the creaking and splitting of pine trees broken under the weight of their icy burdens. But as I write this in January 1988, eight inches of snow has collected. It is undeniably beautiful, its twilight glow mysterious, reflecting the dying light, dispersing all shadows. And it is, blessedly, dry, light, pure snow, insulating, I hope, the year-old fig that has gone from drought to this. An occasional gust relieves the cedars of their accumulation. Only a snow such as this can be lovely. And only a snow such as this can provide the delight of Snow Cream.

Snow for Snow Cream must be gathered from a high place, never from the ground, unless a cloth is put out for it. Put the snow lightly into cold dishes; don't pack it down. Then pour thick cream sweetened with sugar, just lightly beaten, and flavored with vanilla over it, not too much. A good dose of bourbon in the cream will warm all. Make in small amounts so it can be eaten before it melts, and so little ones can constantly trek in and out with fresh bowls of snow.

In 1847, Sarah Rutledge published a different recipe called Snow Cream in *The Carolina Housewife*. From her Charleston home, she could only know infrequently the direct pleasures of frozen precipitation.

Put some thin slices of sponge-cake in the bottom of a dish; pour in wine enough to soak it. Beat up the whites of three eggs very hard; add to it two tablespoonsfuls of finely powdered sugar, a glass of sweet wine, and a pint of rich cream. Beat these well in, and pour over the cake.

Miss Rutledge sought other recipes to satisfy her image of the ephemeral ice. This confection is found in one form or another in most nineteenth-century cookbooks, but never so nicely written as by Miss Rutledge:

To make a Dish of Snow, take eight or nine apples, put them in cold water, and set them over a slow fire; when they are soft, put them upon a hair sieve to drain; take off the skin, and put the pulp into a bowl; then beat the whites of three eggs to a very strong froth; sweet it to your taste with sugar sifted very fine, and strewed into the eggs. Beat the pulp of your apples also into a stiff froth; then beat them together till they resemble snow. Lay this upon a china dish, and heap it up as high as possible, placing at the top a piece of myrtle, and ornamenting it round the bottom of the pyramid.

Strawberry Ice Cream

The basic eighteenth- and nineteenth-century ice cream recipes were simply frozen fools. The standard formula was 1 quart of fruit, pureed, to 2 cups sugar to 1 quart cream. Mary Randolph in *The Virginia House-wife* (1824) gives a custard-based "Strawberry Cream" but notes, "If rich cream can be procured, it will be infinitely better — the custard is intended as a substitute when cream cannot be had."

Ice creams in the past were often, once frozen, turned into myriad fancy molds. Different flavors were sandwiched in much more creative fashion than our "Neapolitan" descendant ("Neapolitan" then meant a custard-based ice cream). Estelle Wilcox in *The New Dixie Cook-Book* of 1889 says, "The variety of molds is very large, from the plain pyramid to the most elaborate combinations of figures, animals, flowers and fruits, corresponding to the flavor, as oranges for orange ice-cream, etc., and new designs and devices are brought out every year . . . All these molds have tightly fitting covers and tapering sides, to allow their contents to be easily turned out. In the final packing of salt and ice, and when molds are packed, if rock salt is used, have it in small lumps size of a pea." Mary Randolph directs that "when ice creams are not put into shapes, they should be served in glasses with handles."

☞ Electric ice cream maker or manual churn

• • • • • • • •

1 qt. ripe strawberries

1½ c. sugar
2 c. very cold heavy cream
1 c. heavy cream
¼ c. sugar

Hull the berries and crush them with 1¼ cups sugar. Let stand until the sugar is dissolved, then rub through a sieve to remove the seeds. Chill the juice well. Combine with 2 cups very cold cream and turn into a churn or an ice cream maker to freeze. Both juice and cream must be very cold so the freezing process can begin before the cream is churned to butter.

When this mixture is frozen to a soft mush, whip the third cup of cream with ¼ cup sugar to soft peaks. Fold into the strawberry cream and continue churning until well frozen. Make in 2 batches if using a small electric ice cream maker. ✖ *2 quarts*

Other Ice Creams

Raspberries, peaches, apricots, almost all other soft fruits can be used as described on page 189. Complex flavorings such as liqueurs and spices should be reserved for custard ice creams.

Vanilla Custard Ice Cream

Custard for ice cream is simply Custard Sauce sweetened and extended. It is true that cream alone was preferred by eighteenth- and nineteenth-century cooks, but today custard-based ice cream is held the finest, due most likely to the decline in the quality of commercial dairy products rather than to a change in taste.

☞ Double boiler; electric ice cream
   maker or manual churn

◆ ◆ ◆ ◆ ◆ ◆ ◆ ◆

2 c. plus 1½ c. milk
1 c. plus ½ c. heavy cream

6 egg yolks
2 eggs
1 c. plus 3 Tb. sugar
⅛ tsp. salt
2 tsp. vanilla

Heat 2 cups milk and 1 cup cream in a saucepan, but do not let boil. Combine the egg yolks, eggs, sugar, and salt in the top of a double boiler. Beat well. Pour in the hot milk, whisking steadily. Place over, not in, simmering water and stir continuously until the egg yolks are cooked. The mixture will thicken somewhat, coat a spoon, and feel hot to the touch. Remove the top from the bottom of the double boiler and continue to whisk off the heat. Add vanilla, 1½ cups milk, and ½ cup cream.

To make the ice cream, chill the custard well, then freeze in a churn. Freeze in 2 batches if using a small electric ice cream maker.
✗ *2 quarts*

Coffee Ice Cream

Mary Randolph's subtle, sophisticated recipe for coffee cream in *The Virginia House-wife* (1824) is one of my favorite frozen desserts. The coffee beans must be as fresh as possible, preferably purchased just before preparation. If a coffee roasting house is nearby, green beans may be purchased for home roasting, and this is, of course, the route to maximum flavor. Roasting can be done in the oven or on top of a burner. Use a heavy pan and a medium heat. The only trick is keeping the beans moving to avoid scorching. When roasting, they usually throw a lot of chaff that can be sifted away. Mrs. Randolph's method yields a delicate ivory color and the most refined coffee flavor.

Toast two gills of raw coffee till it is a light brown, and not a grain burnt; put it hot from the toaster, without grinding it, into a quart of rich, and perfectly sweet, milk; boil it, and add the yolks of eight eggs: when done, strain it through a sieve, and sweeten it — if properly done, it will not be discoloured. The coffee may be dried, and will answer for making in the usual way to drink, allowing more for the quantity of water, than if it had not gone through this process.

1 recipe Vanilla Custard Ice Cream (opposite)	2 Tb. brandy
1 c. whole, medium-roast coffee beans, slightly cracked	

When the initial milk and cream are heated for the Vanilla Custard Ice Cream, add the coffee beans. Steep gently over very low heat for about 30 minutes, until the liquid is quite aromatic. Strain out the beans and proceed with the custard recipe, adding the brandy along with the vanilla. ✕ *2 quarts*

Jamaican Ice Cream

Not as delicate as Mrs. Randolph's cream, but quick and delicious.

1 recipe Vanilla Custard Ice
    Cream (p. 190)
4 Tb. instant coffee

4 Tb. hot water
4 Tb. dark rum

Prepare the vanilla custard and chill. Dissolve the instant coffee in the hot water. Stir into the custard along with the rum. Freeze in a churn or in an ice cream maker. ✖ *2 quarts*

Chocolate Ice Cream

Prepare Vanilla Custard Ice Cream (p. 190) with the following changes.

4 oz. unsweetened chocolate
1¼ c. sugar

2 Tb. brandy

Melt the chocolate in the top of a double boiler. Prepare the custard base with a total of 1¼ cups sugar. Flavor with brandy and stir in the melted chocolate. ✖ *2 quarts*

Milk Punch Ice Cream

This is my favorite ice cream. It goes well with steamed puddings — Winter's Pudding or Persimmon Pudding — and fruit cakes during the winter holidays. Milk Punch Ice Cream can be served with first a little cream poured over, next a light dusting of nutmeg. Most sauces will either compete with or mask its subtlety.

1 recipe Vanilla Custard Ice
    Cream (p. 190)

¾ c. brandy
½ tsp. freshly grated nutmeg

Prepare the custard and set aside to cool. When ready to freeze, stir in brandy and nutmeg to taste. Freeze in a churn or in an ice cream maker. ✖ *2 quarts*

Cherry Bounce Ice Cream

Cherry Bounce is an old Southern homemade cordial. The recipe for it in *Charleston Receipts* (1950) begins, "Go to Old Market in June and get a quart of wild cherries." A quick bounce with sour cherries makes a delicate, delicious ice cream.

¾ c. sour cherries (such as
    Montmorency)
2 Tb. sugar
½ cup brandy or bourbon

1 recipe Vanilla Custard Ice
    Cream (p. 190), partially
    frozen

Crush the cherries (stems and pits are okay) with the sugar and let stand 3 hours. Add the brandy or bourbon, cover, and let stand 24 hours. Strain, pressing fruit lightly. Add to the Vanilla Custard Ice Cream when it is almost frozen. Continue churning/freezing until set. �֎ *2 quarts*

To make a Bounce for drinking: Combine cherries, sugar, and liquor in the same proportions as above. Let stand in a *cool* place for 2 weeks or more. Strain, bottle, and store in cool, dark place for a month before using.

Fig Ice Cream

The fig tree of my childhood made a jungle against the smokehouse that kept it from freezing in the winter. Under the tree's broad leaves was the coolest place to play in the summer.

1 recipe Vanilla Custard Ice
    Cream (p. 190)
3 c. fresh figs

¼ c. sugar
2 tsp. lemon juice
Port

Prepare custard and chill. Peel and mash figs with sugar and lemon juice. Churn or freeze custard until almost set, then add the figs. Continue churning/freezing until frozen. Serve with a splash of Port over the top. ✖ *3 quarts*

Bananas Foster Ice Cream

Breakfast at Brennan's restaurant is a New Orleans ritual that typically ends with bananas flamed in rum, served with ice cream. The dish was named for Richard Foster, a regular patron of the famous eatery. This ice cream incorporates the cooked fruit with the rum.

1 recipe Vanilla Custard Ice
   Cream (p. 190)
2 Tb. butter
2 Tb. water

4 Tb. light brown sugar
4 ripe bananas
Dash of cinnamon
⅔ c. dark rum

Prepare the custard and set aside to cool. Combine butter, water, and brown sugar in a small pan over medium heat. Thinly slice the bananas and add to the sauce when it is bubbling, along with a dash of cinnamon. Cook 3–4 minutes, until the bananas look slightly glazed. Remove from heat and cool to room temperature. Add the rum. Turn all into the custard base and freeze in a churn or ice cream maker. Serve with hot chocolate sauce. ✖ *3 quarts*

Lemon Ice Cream

1 recipe for Vanilla Custard Ice
   Cream (p. 190) omitting
   vanilla

2 lemons
2 Tb. sugar
A few drops orange flower water

Prepare the custard with the following changes: Remove zest in strips from the 2 lemons and add to the milk while heating. Let stand 10 minutes then strain into the egg yolks and proceed. Do not add vanilla.

Juice the lemons and dissolve the sugar in the liquid. Stir into the custard just before freezing with 4 or 5 drops orange flower water. ✖ *2 quarts*

Burnt Fruit Ice Cream

This is an early summer delight. This year I found apricots and sour cherries at the Farmers' Market on May 28, an undocumented record I'm sure, but it's been an early spring all around. Try this with peaches and raspberries later in the season.

1 recipe Vanilla Custard Ice
    Cream (p. 190)
1 c. pitted sour cherries
6–8 apricots

5 Tb. light brown sugar
1 Tb. white rum
1 Tb. Kirsch

Prepare the custard as directed and begin to freeze it in the churn or ice cream maker. Spread the pitted cherries about in a very lightly buttered baking dish. Blanch, peel, and slice the apricots and add to the cherries. Sprinkle with brown sugar and run under a hot broiler about 4 minutes, until bubbly and slightly caramelized. Let cool. When the ice cream is almost set, add the fruit, rum, and Kirsch. Continue churning/freezing until well frozen. ✄ *2 quarts*

Butter Pecan Ice Cream

This is a classic combination of favorite Southern flavors: a hint of bitter from the pecans, the burnt sweetness of caramel and bourbon, and a bit of salt that intensifies all the flavors.

1 recipe Vanilla Custard Ice
    Cream (p. 190)
1½ c. pecan halves
⅛ tsp. salt

2 Tb. butter
¼ c. sugar
¼ c. water
2 Tb. bourbon

Prepare the custard as directed. Bake the pecan halves with the salt and butter in an oven preheated to 325° F., stirring frequently, for about 10 minutes or until lightly toasted. Caramelize the sugar in a heavy saucepan. With great care, when it turns a rich amber, remove from heat and pour in the water. Stir until dissolved and cooled slightly. Add to the custard along with the pecans and bourbon. Freeze in a churn or ice cream maker until hard. ✄ *2 quarts*

Eggnog Ice Cream

☞ Double boiler; small manual
    churn

• • • • • • • •

6 eggs, separated
10 Tb. sugar
Pinch of salt

¼ c. brandy
¼ c. rum
2 Tb. dry sherry
1 c. milk
2 c. heavy cream
Freshly grated nutmeg

Cook the egg yolks, sugar, salt, brandy, rum, and sherry in a double boiler until very light and thickened. Off heat, add milk and cream; cool. Beat whites until stiff, fold them in, then freeze the mixture in a churn. Sprinkle with fresh nutmeg to serve.

For alternate method if you don't have a churn: Whip the cream to soft peaks, fold in before the egg whites, and freeze in the frozen food part of the refrigerator. ✗ *1 quart*

French Vanilla Ice Cream

"French" in America usually connotes richness and decadence, and that's the idea of this ice cream. A scoop of it would be about as much at home in a cone as Marie Antoinette in Lizard Lick, North Carolina. Its texture is not affected by freezer storage, but remains imperiously suave under all circumstances. Serve it in small portions with fresh fruit or chocolate sauces as a dessert.

☞ Double boiler; electric ice cream
    maker or small manual churn

• • • • • • • •

1 c. milk
1 c. heavy cream

½ vanilla bean, split lengthwise
4 egg yolks
Pinch of salt
⅝ c. sugar

Combine the milk, cream, and vanilla bean in a saucepan. Heat to scalding, remove from heat, and let cool. Remove the vanilla bean.

Combine the egg yolks, salt, and sugar and beat well. Add the warm milk, stirring, and cook in the top of a double boiler until slightly thickened and the taste of rawness is dissipated. Refrigerate until cool. Freeze in a churn or in an ice cream maker. ✗ *3 cups*

Blackberry Bombe

Any of the fruit sauces can be used in place of the blackberry. Try the cherry sauce and pour Cherry Bounce over.

1 recipe French Vanilla Ice Cream
  (opposite)
1 c. blackberry sauce (p. 141)

½ c. blackberry brandy or extra
  blackberry sauce

Follow the recipe for French Vanilla Ice Cream. When the custard is cool, stir in 1 cup homemade blackberry sauce. Freeze in a churn or in an ice cream maker. Turn into a bombe mold or other container suitable for unmolding. Place in freezer compartment of the refrigerator overnight. To turn out, dip mold quickly into warm water and invert. Pour the brandy or sauce over all and serve immediately.

The same procedure may be followed for any of the fruit sauces. Again, these are very rich, elegant frozen confections. ✕ *2 quarts*

DELECTABLES
CUSTARDS, BAVARIANS, CURDS, MOUSSES, JELLIES, AND PUDDINGS

A Trifle

A Light Pastry Cream

Grand Marnier Banana Pudding

Bavarian Cream

Orange Bavarian Cream

Sherried Bavarian Cream

Lemon Curd

Lemon Snow

Lemon Mousse

Lemon-Orange Curd

Peach Curd

Peach Sponge

Syllabub

Eggnog

Rum Bumble

Two Whiskey Chocolate
Mousse

Wine Jelly

Indian Meal Pudding

Winter's Pudding

Persimmon Pudding

Batter Puddings

Peach Pudding

Crumb Pudding

The Queen of Puddings

Lemon Meringue Pudding

Tot Fait

Tot Fait au Chocolat

DELECTABLES

Delectables, an old-fashioned word, is often used in the South for sweet dishes that aren't pastries or ice creams. I like the word a lot and have appropriated it here to cover a range of dishes: custards, trifles, Bavarians, curds, jellies, mousses, puddings, and so on. There is a range of ethnicity here, too. The Indian Meal Pudding and Winter's Pudding are from our Indian heritage. Both dishes, and variations on them, are found in the earliest collections of American recipes from New England all down the eastern seaboard. Wine Jelly, and the wonderfully named trifles, curds, bumbles, syllabubs, possets, and nogs come directly from the English. From the French come Bavarians, mousses, and the soufflélike Tot Fait.

SOCIALS

Social events in the South may be intimate such as this wedding tea in
Richmond, Virginia, but most are big, extended gatherings like family reunions.
All center on food. At a "deacon's meeting" in eastern North Carolina, all ages
contribute as young boys churn ice cream while the women finally relax. A
dinner-on-the-grounds is a community project, affirming common values.

A Trifle

A trifle in the South belies its name; it is elegant and fancy and comes to the table at the end of a rather formal dinner (i.e., around 4:00 p.m.) to be served with some ceremony by the hostess or family matriarch. Many homes have special trifle dishes, often heirloom, which are about 12 inches across and 3 or 4 inches deep. These are the traditional dishes from England used for one of that country's finest culinary contributions.

1 recipe Ladyfingers (p. 251)
Raspberry jam
½ c. or more to your taste
   Amontillado sherry
1 recipe Custard Sauce, chilled
   (p. 140)

1½ c. heavy cream
5 Tb. sugar
½ c. toasted whole or slivered
   almonds
Fresh raspberries *or* strawberries

Sandwich the Ladyfingers with the raspberry jam and line the bottom and sides of a clear glass bowl with them. Sprinkle the Ladyfingers with sherry. Pour the Custard Sauce into the bowl. Whip the cream with the sugar and cover the top of the custard with rosettes of cream. Chill well, 4–6 hours. Garnish with the toasted almonds and fruit. ✹ *8 servings*

A Light Pastry Cream

Use the recipe for Custard Sauce (p. 140), but increase the sugar to a total of 1¼ cups. Thoroughly mix the sugar with 4½ table-spoons cornstarch, then beat in the egg yolks and eggs and proceed according to the recipe. Flavor appropriately according to the dish or to your taste, using vanilla, rum, brandy, etc. It is very important to continue stirring the custard until completely cooled. ✹ *4 cups*

Grand Marnier Banana
Pudding

Banana pudding is a much-loved but rather pedestrian dessert of the South. It is a corruption of a classic English trifle and deserves better treatment than commercial vanilla wafers and instant pudding. The following is a delicious and elegant recreation of the original dish.

1 recipe Light Pastry Cream
   (p. 205)
2 tsp. vanilla
1 recipe Ladyfingers (p. 251)
Raspberry jam
3 ripe bananas, about 1 lb.,
   peeled and thinly sliced

Grand Marnier
Whipped cream
Toasted almonds
Shaved chocolate

Flavor the Light Pastry Cream with the vanilla.

Dry the Ladyfingers in a slow oven for 10–15 minutes until crisp. Spread one third of them over the bottom of a dish. Brush lightly with raspberry jam. Cover with one half of the bananas and one third of the pastry cream.

Add a second layer of Ladyfingers. Sprinkle liberally with Grand Marnier. Cover with remaining bananas and another one third of the pastry cream. Spread the remaining Ladyfingers lightly with raspberry jam and place them jam inwards on top of the pudding.

Pour the remaining pastry cream over all. Chill at least 4 hours before serving. Decorate recklessly with whipped cream rosettes, toasted almonds, and shaved chocolate. ✖ *8–10 servings*

BAVARIANS

From Anna Wells Rutledge's Introduction to *The Carolina Housewife* (1847) comes the supplies list for an 1851 ball:

> 🐜 *18 dozen plates — 14 dozen knives — 28 dozen spoons — 6 dozen Wineglasses — As many Chapaigne glasses as could be collected — 4 wild Turkeys — 4 hams 2 for sandwiches & 2 for the supper tables, 8 pates — 60 partridges — 6 pr of Pheasants — 6 pr Canvassback Ducks — 5 pr of our wild ducks — 8 Charlotte Russes — 4 Pyramids 2 of crystalized fruit & 2 of Cocoanut — 4 Orange baskets — 4 Italian Creams — an immense quantity of bonbons — 7 dozn Cocoanut rings — 7 dozn Kiss cakes — 7 dozn Macaroons — 4 moulds of Jelly 4 of Bavarian cream — 3 dollarsworth of Celery & lettuce — 10 quarts of Oysters — 4 cakes of chocolate — coffee — 4 small black cakes —*

Bavarians are usually found in the repertoire of desserts from the grand Southern houses. They have always been and continue to be very much in vogue. Simple ones can be accompanied with fresh fruits or even have the fruits or berries folded into the mixture. Fruit or chocolate sauces may be served with them.

A Charlotte Russe can be made from any Bavarian. Line a cylindrical mold or soufflé dish with Ladyfingers (p. 251). Sprinkle the cakes with fruit juice, wine, or liquor, if appropriate. Pile the Bavarian in the middle. Chill until well set, turn out, and decorate with whipped cream. Another, more humble, Charlotte was popular in the South, France, and England as well. A dish is lined with buttered bread, sometimes toasted or fried, filled with stewed fruit, most commonly apple, covered with more bread and baked. A Charlotte Russe is always the sumptuous Bavarian sort, attributed to the great French chef Carême.

Bavarian Cream

☞ Double boiler

♦ ♦ ♦ ♦ ♦ ♦ ♦ ♦ ♦

1¼ c. milk
4 eggs
¾ c. sugar

Pinch of salt
1½ tsp. vanilla
¼ c. water
1 Tb. gelatin
1½ c. heavy cream

Heat the milk gently to lukewarm. Beat the eggs well and slowly beat in the sugar and salt. Add the milk and cook in a double boiler over simmering water until the custard is hot, thickened, and all raw egg taste is dissipated. Remove and let cool. Add vanilla.

Pour the water over the gelatin in a small dish and let it "sponge." Stir into the custard and continue cooling. For rapid cooling, place the custard in a bowl of ice water. Stir constantly to prevent the gelatin from setting up along the edges or bottom of the bowl.

Whip the cream to good, firm, but not stiff peaks. When the custard is cool to the touch and just starting to set up, fold the cream in gently. Refrigerate at least 4 hours before serving.

Bavarian Cream is most attractive served in small individual dishes. This particular recipe is fragile, but it will stand up if you wish to recreate a faux soufflé. Lightly oil a wide strip of foil and wrap it tightly around a dish — either large or small. Tape securely with masking tape. Just to be sure, lightly crimp the foil in at the top of the dish so no cream can escape. Add the cream and refrigerate about 6 hours before removing the collar. Serve with fruit, or a fruit sauce, or even chocolate sauce. ✖ *6–8 servings*

Orange Bavarian Cream

This is a personal favorite from an excellent Mississippi cook. Use the recipe for Bavarian Cream (above) with the following changes:

Cut the zest of 1 orange in strips, then steep in the milk. Discard the zest. Flavor the custard with 1 tablespoon orange liqueur, 1 tablespoon white rum, ½ teaspoon orange flower water, and a few drops Angostura bitters instead of the vanilla.

Instead of dissolving the gelatin in the ¼ cup water, use ¼ cup fresh orange juice.

Sherried Bavarian Cream

The intense, alcoholic custard base of this Bavarian Cream makes it of the same family of traditional English confections such as syllabubs, possets, and nogs. It is richer, and, seems to me, more old-fashioned than the French-style Bavarian Creams above. Wonderful with raspberries.

☞ Double boiler

• • • • • • • •

1 Tb. gelatin
¼ c. cold water
5 egg yolks

¾ c. dry sherry
½ c. plus ¼ c. sugar
Pinch of salt
2 c. heavy cream
1 tsp. vanilla

Dissolve the gelatin in the cold water. Beat the egg yolks until light. Beat in sherry, ½ cup sugar, and salt, and cook over simmering water, stirring with a whisk, until the custard is very light, thick, and tripled in volume. Gently stir in dissolved gelatin. Cool the custard over ice water, stirring frequently. When the custard is cool, but not yet set, whip the cream with the ¼ cup sugar to firm peaks. Stir in vanilla. Fold one third of the cream into the custard, then fold in the rest. Pour into small dishes, wine glasses, whatever you wish to serve from. ✖ *6 cups*

Lemon Curd

This curd is a custard, and like so many other English curds, chesses, and cheeses again shows the language's ambivalence concerning cooked egg and dairy products. In the South it is also called lemon jelly and is appropriately eaten with toasted bread or cake. Lemon curd is one of the most useful of pantry staples. It sandwiches cookies and ladyfingers, fills little tarts and big cakes, and is the base for mousselike preparations. It keeps 2 or 3 weeks refrigerated, but only if forgotten. Usually it is consumed rapidly.

Most recipes for Lemon Curd call for melting the butter with the egg yolks. Beating the butter in last makes for a more delicate and more suave curd.

☞Double boiler

· · · · · · · · · ·

4 egg yolks
¾ c. sugar

1 Tb. grated lemon zest
⅓ c. lemon juice
Pinch of salt
6 Tb. butter

Beat the egg yolks with the sugar, lemon zest and juice, and salt. Place over simmering water and stir constantly until thickened. Remove from heat and beat in the butter, bit by bit. ✖ *1½ cups*

Lemon Snow

A very light and refreshing dish of great popularity in the past; recipes for it appear in most traditional collections. For ease of preparation, make when the curd is still slightly warm. If the curd was made ahead of time and is quite stiff, thoroughly stir in a bit of the beaten whites to loosen up the base before folding in the rest.

4 egg whites
2 Tb. sugar

1 recipe Lemon Curd (above)

Beat the whites with the sugar until stiff and glossy. Gently and completely fold into the Lemon Curd. Pile into individual dishes and refrigerate. A sprig of mint or lemon balm is a nice garnish. The cream can also be frozen in the freezer compartment of the refrigerator. Again, put into small dishes before chilling. ✖ *6–8 servings*

Lemon Mousse

Richer than Lemon Snow and more appropriately paired with fresh fruit, this is one of the most popular desserts of the South today. It is served with whole or pureed raspberries, but the surest sign of summer is its appearance with fresh blueberries. A little later in the season, a blackberry sauce makes a dramatic contrast.

1 c. heavy cream	2 egg whites
2 Tb. sugar	1 recipe Lemon Curd (opposite)

Whip the cream with the sugar until good peaks form. Beat the egg whites stiffly as well. Fold one quarter of the cream into the curd. Follow with the remaining cream, and then fold in the beaten whites. Put into individual dishes. Serve with fresh fruits or almost any fresh fruit sauce. This can be frozen in small ramekins or cups.

✕ *6–8 servings or enough for 1 Angel Pie (p. 278)*

Lemon-Orange Curd

A curd wholly flavored with orange tastes too cooked; the lemon keeps the flavor sharp. Use the recipe for Lemon Curd (opposite) substituting the following for the lemon zest and juice:

Zest: grate 1 orange and 2 lemons	Juice: squeeze 1 orange and 2 lemons

Peach Curd

A delectable curd can be made from peaches provided they are nothing short of ripe, right down to the pit. It doesn't keep as well as one of lemon, but there is generally a rush to consume peaches in whatever form. Like all curds, it marches well with any sort of toast, from English muffins to Sally Lunn to pound cake.

4 egg yolks
⅔ c. sugar
1 c. fresh peach puree
Lemon juice to taste, about
   1 Tb.

½ tsp. rosewater
6 Tb. butter

Beat the egg yolks with the sugar, peach puree, lemon juice, and rosewater. Place over simmering water and stir constantly until thickened. Remove from heat and beat in butter, bit by bit. Strain well and chill. ✖ *2 cups*

Peach Sponge

The Peach Curd is the basis for an antique form of dessert, the sponge. Reduce the butter and add gelatin for body. A sponge is wonderfully light to tempt hot weather appetites and yet sophisticated enough for fancy dinners. Almost any soft fruit can be used; fresh figs and peaches in combination are memorable.

1 recipe for Peach Curd
   (above), reducing the butter
   to 2 Tb.
1 Tb. gelatin

¼ c. cold water
Dry sherry or white rum to taste
4 egg whites
1 Tb. sugar

Prepare the Peach Curd but add only 2 tablespoons butter. Dissolve the gelatin in the cold water and stir through the warm curd. Strain well and season. Beat the whites with 1 tablespoon sugar and fold into the custard. Chill until serving time. ✖ *4–6 servings*

SYLLABUBS, POSSETS, AND NOGS

Syllabubs, possets, and nogs live in a no-man's-land situated somewhere between dessert and drink. All three are hearty, alcoholic confections rich in cream or eggs, or both. Officially and unofficially, they also exist in the annals of English medicine. Possets, likely the most antique of the three and written of in 1440, were the common remedy for the common cold. James Howell, British author and diplomat, prescribed the syllabub as part of the country cure in 1645: "Leave the smutty Ayr of London, and com hither . . . wher you may pluck a Rose, and drink a Cillibub." Nogs were part of the comforting domestic pharmacopoeia. In 1896, *Harper's Magazine* reassured the invalid: "Mrs. Raker was holding a foaming glass to the sick man's lips. 'There; take another sup of the good nog,' she said." Perhaps Mrs. Raker knew the official pharmacopoeia; in 1872, Dr. Cohen's *Diseases of the Throat* advised, "I would rely chiefly on egg-nog, beef essence, and quinine."

Syllabub crosses the line into desserts more than the other two delectables. Mary Randolph's simple recipe from *The Virginia House-wife* (1824) appears alongside ice cream, floating island, and fools.

🐜 Syllabub. *Season the milk with sugar and white wine, but not enough to curdle it; fill the glasses nearly full, and crown them with whipt cream seasoned.*

Ironically, when André Simon published a recipe for syllabub in *A Concise Encyclopedia of Gastronomy* (1952) it was Mrs. Randolph's recipe word for word. Mr. Simon, though, was duped by Mr. F. P. Streff's use of the recipe in *Eat, Drink and be Merry in Maryland* (1932). Unfortunately, the essential nature of the preparation is omitted by Mrs. Randolph, and that is the shaking or frothing of the milk. Harriott Pinckney Horry's 1770 description in *A Colonial Plantation Cookbook* is explicit:

🐜 To make Solid Syllabub, a nice dessert. *1 pint of cream ½ pint of wine. The juice of one lemon sweetened to your taste. Put it in a wide mouthed bottle — a quart bottle will answer. Shake it for ten minutes. Pour it into your glasses. It must be made the evening before it is to be used.*

Sarah Rutledge in *The Carolina Housewife* (1847) repeats the above, but also gives another, more precise recipe.

🐜 Syllabub. *To one quart of cream put half a pint of sweet wine and half a pint of Madeira, the juice of two lemons, a little finely powdered spice, and sugar to the taste. The peel of the lemons must be steeped in the wine until the flavor is extracted. Whisk all these ingredients together, and as the froth rises take it off with a spoon, lay it upon a fine sieve; what drains from it put into your pan again and whisk it. Put the froth into glasses.*

It is the froth that makes the syllabub, and its inspiration was the milking of the cow. The *Oxford English Dictionary* concurs: "A drink or dish made of milk (freq. as drawn from the cow). . . . " Miss Leslie took a trip to the dairy barn when making syllabub, according to *Miss Leslie's New Cooking Book* (1847).

🐾 *Mix half a pound of white sugar with a pint of fine cider, or of white wine, and grate in a nutmeg. Prepare them in a large bowl, just before milking time. Then let it be taken to the cow, and have about three pints milked into it, stirring it occasionally with a spoon. Let it be eaten before the froth subsides. If you use cider, a little brandy will improve it.*

Karen Hess, in the notes to *The Virginia House-wife,* also notes that lacking a cow on the premises, the cook can turn to a " 'syllabub churn,' an ingenious device that produces a fine long-lasting froth."

The charming name syllabub raises some debate. Some say it is onomatopoeic: the sound made when the drawn milk hits the pail. Having milked under coercion in my youth, I can safely say it is not the sound I heard. Most food writers see the "sylla" derived from Sillery, then "Sille," in the Champagne country, the source of the wine. "Bub" is the bubble, or beverage. The *Oxford English Dictionary,* as often in food name derivation battles, weakly says, "origin obscure." If it weren't for the charm of the name and of the process described by Miss Leslie, syllabub most likely would have disappeared. Certainly our modern dairy products will not yield a dish worthy of such endearment. In the modern South syllabubs are still called for when preparing trifles, but otherwise they don't come to much.

Possets rarely appear in new Southern recipe collections, but occasionally one will pop up, as in the extensive collection *Marion Brown's Southern Cook Book,* originally published in 1951. Mrs. Brown took her recipe from Bernard Chamberlain's 1931 *The Making of Palatable Table Wines.*

🐾 Sir Walter Raleigh's Sack Posset. *(One and one-half quarts) Heat 1 cup of ale and 1 cup of sherry, and add 1 quart of boiling milk; sugar to taste and sprinkle with grated nutmeg; allow this mixture to stand in a warm place for an hour, and just before serving add the yolks of 2 eggs; beat well, and serve hot.*

Possets, though quite popular in the early colonial days, never became Southern in identification and did not endure. Mrs. Randolph, Miss Rutledge, and Mrs. Bryan (in *The Kentucky Housewife,* 1839) all neglect them. When printed, these archaic recipes are still considered thoroughly English, witness "Sir Walter Raleigh" above and "King William's Posset" published in *The Williamsburg Art of Cookery* (1938).

The nog is the talisman drink of the winter holidays. On Christmas mornings, it is considered bad luck to consume anything at all before the first heady glass of eggnog in many Southern households. An English visitor to Baltimore in 1866 wrote: "Christmas is not properly observed unless you brew 'egg nogg' for all comers' everybody calls on everybody else; and each call is celebrated by a solemn egg-nogging." The mixing and serving of the nog was a great ceremony appropriated by the male head of household, and the first drink was accompanied by traditional and grandiloquent toasts. George Washington's unassuming toast underscored his genuine graciousness, "All our friends."

A true eggnog is highly alcoholic and not very sweet. Those accustomed to the unctuous qualities of so-called eggnog mixes from the commercial dairy are usually taken aback at the robust flavors of the true drink. The proper texture is achieved through time; the eggs are set, or cooked gently, by the alcohol of the whiskey. A recipe attributed to George Washington requires several days of setting aside. *The Williamsburg Art of Cookery* advises: "Eggnog is better if it is made some days before it is to be used and is kept in a very cold place. It must be well shaken and mixed before serving." Less alcoholic and sweeter versions of eggnog are very popular in the South today. By the first frost, certainly by Thanksgiving, a host of Bavarian creamlike eggnog pies, eggnog ice creams, and eggnog cheesecakes appear.

Syllabub

Zest of 1 lemon in strips
1½ c. Amontillado sherry
½ c. Madeira
4 c. heavy cream

1 c. sugar
Juice of 1 lemon
Freshly grated nutmeg

Combine the lemon zest and wines; let sit overnight, then strain, discarding the zest. Whip the cream until it begins to form soft peaks. Add the sugar, and then slowly add wine and lemon juice, beating very hard. Serve in tall glasses; sprinkle the confection with fresh nutmeg or use for trifles, for light cake layers, or with fresh fruits. ✁ *8 cups*

Eggnog

6 eggs, separated, at room
   temperature
About ⅓ c. sugar, or to taste
1 c. brandy
1 c. rye whiskey

½ c. dry sherry
½ c. white rum
2 c. milk
2 c. heavy cream
Freshly grated nutmeg

Beat the egg yolks until very light and doubled in volume. Slowly add the sugar, and continue to beat very hard while carefully adding the liquors. Stir in the milk and cream. Beat the egg whites until stiff and fold in. Set aside or refrigerate several hours before serving. Garnish the cups with fresh nutmeg. ✁ *20 servings*

Rum Bumble

The whole family of nogs and all were fortifying warm drinks for winter in their English homeland (the closest thing to them today is the Italian zabaglione). In the southeastern United States, most of these highly alcoholic custards developed into cold punches and desserts. This is the lineage of the Rum Bumble, a winter dessert of the Carolina Low Country. It has been a very popular dessert for the holidays at the restaurant Crook's Corner. Bumble is just a variant of bubble.

The *Oxford English Dictionary* cites from 1630: "Laundreses are testy . . . When they are lathering in their bumble broth."

☞ Double boiler

❖ ❖ ❖ ❖ ❖ ❖ ❖ ❖

4 eggs, separated
1 c. sugar
⅛ tsp. salt
½ c. white or dark rum

½ c. bourbon or brandy
1 Tb. gelatin
¼ c. cold water
2 c. heavy cream
Freshly grated nutmeg

Beat the 4 egg yolks with the sugar, salt, rum, and bourbon over simmering water in the top of a double boiler. Cook until very light, thickened, and the raw taste of the egg is dissipated. Meanwhile, soak the gelatin in the water and add to the custard, off heat, when cooked. Let cool, then beat 2 of the egg whites (save the other 2 for another recipe) until stiff peaks form. Fold into the custard, then beat the cream to stiff peaks and fold in. Put into wine glasses or parfait glasses and chill several hours. To serve, garnish with a little whipped cream and a light sprinkle of freshly grated nutmeg. ✖ *8–10 servings*

Two Whiskey Chocolate Mousse

This richly flavored mousse can be used with a variety of pastries for creating other dishes such as eclairs and angel pies, but it is delicious alone as well. Vary the sugar according to taste and use.

☞ Double boiler

♦ ♦ ♦ ♦ ♦ ♦ ♦

¼ c. boiling water
1 Tb. dark roast, ground coffee
4 oz. unsweetened chocolate
¼ tsp. salt

⅓ c. plus 1 c. heavy cream
2 Tb. butter
8–10 Tb. sugar
1 tsp. vanilla
1 Tb. bourbon
1 Tb. dark rum

Pour the boiling water over the coffee. Let steep a minute or two, strain, then add the flavored water to the chocolate, salt, ⅓ cup cream, and butter. Melt in a double boiler and let cool to lukewarm. Whip the 1 cup cream, adding the sugar slowly, to stiff peaks.

Fold the flavorings into the whipped cream, then fold into the cooled chocolate. ✗ *About 5 cups mousse, plenty for 6 people, or enough for 1 Angel Pie (p. 278)*

Wine Jelly

For second course we had eight pies *down the side of the table, six dishes of glasses of syllabub and as many of jelly, besides one or two 'floating islands,' as they denominate what we called whipped cream, and odd corners filled up by ginger and other preserves.*
— *A travel account by Mrs. Basil Hall,* The Aristocratic Journey, *1827*

Jellies are gelatin desserts, which, before packaged fruit Jell-Os with their artificial flavorings, were considered very elegant dishes indeed. Harriott Pinckney Horry *(A Colonial Plantation Cookbook)* in 1770 made her gelatin by boiling calves feet, hartshorn (deer antler), and isinglass (a gelatin from sturgeon's bladder). In *The Virginia House-wife* of 1824, Mary Randolph directs for Blanc Mange, "Break one ounce of isinglass into very small pieces, wash it well, and pour on a pint of boiling water; next morning add a quart of milk, boil it till the isinglass is dissolved, strain it. . . ." Sarah Rutledge in *The Carolina Housewife* (1847) says, "The Russian {which she is always careful to specify} isinglass is thought preferable, by some persons, to the gelatine," but she gives several recipes for the convenient "three pieces of gelatine, (in summer four)" as alternatives to the laborious and time-consuming traditional ways of congealing dishes.

Wine Jelly is still a winter holiday favorite in the South. At Crook's Corner, we bring back this ancient dessert for Christmas. It is a wonderful combination of intense flavor and refreshing lightness to follow a heavy meal. Serve with a little cream or custard dusted with nutmeg and pound or fruit cake.

2 Tb. gelatin
½ c. cold water
1 c. water
Zest of 2 lemons in strips
Zest of 1 orange in strips
1¼ c. sugar
Juice of 2 lemons and 1 orange,
   about ½ c.

1 c. Amontillado sherry
⅝ c. ruby Port
Whipped cream or Custard Sauce
   (p. 140)
Freshly grated nutmeg

    Dissolve the gelatin in ½ cup cold water. Combine 1 cup water, the citrus zests, and the sugar to make a syrup. Bring to a boil and cook 5 minutes. Remove from heat, strain, and stir in the gelatin. Cool and then add fruit juices, sherry, and Port. Pour into a serving bowl or divide among 8 wine glasses. Chill for 3–6 hours. To serve, top lightly with whipped cream or Custard Sauce and a fine grating of fresh nutmeg. Serve with pound cake or a plain cookie. ✖ *8 servings*

Indian Meal Pudding

The Cameron family of Durham County, North Carolina, assembled a vast collection of manuscript recipes that are in the library of the University of North Carolina at Chapel Hill. These recipes offer rare documented insight into the routine as well as holiday cooking of a great plantation. Most Indian puddings are made from the meager pantry of pioneer cooks. This one, rich in eggs, shows the wealth of the plantation larder.

1 quart of milk and let it boil. Stir in three gills of Indian Meal, beat the yolks of 6 eggs and the whites separate, a gill of molasses and the yolks are poured to the mush and last of all the whites are poured in and then the whole is baked.
— *Cameron Collection, Manuscript Cookbook*

☞Double boiler, top half buttered

½ c. molasses
¼ c. water

1 c. flour
⅓ c. cornmeal
⅛ tsp. salt
½ tsp. baking soda

Stir together the molasses and water. Add the dry ingredients all at once; stir briskly until smooth. Pour into the buttered top half of a double boiler. Place over simmering water, cover, and cook about 2 hours or until middle is set. Let cool slightly, loosen the sides, and turn out. Serve warm with Hard sauce, ice cream, or cream.
6–8 servings

Winter's Pudding

This Winter's Pudding recipe comes from Mississippi. It is an excellent, all-American alternative to the traditional English Plum Pudding, and since it is without suet, a neat solution for vegetarian guests during the holidays. My son Elliott played the young Dylan Thomas in a Carolina Playmakers' production of *A Child's Christmas in Wales*. The blazing pudding that featured in the play's feast scene so captured his imagination that I set this pudding ablaze for him with brandy on Christmas this year and served it with Milk Punch Ice Cream.

Cranberries are thought of as a New England specialty, but they are native to the South as well. Large wild cranberry bogs are common in northeastern North Carolina. Sarah Rutledge, author of *The Carolina Housewife,* knew them in Charleston, and frequent nineteenth-century New Orleans uses of the berry are recorded, as in Winter's Pudding.

☞ Double boiler, top half greased

◆ ◆ ◆ ◆ ◆ ◆ ◆ ◆

¼ c. raisins
¼ c. boiling water
¼ c. bourbon or dark rum
1 c. cranberries
¼ c. chopped, glacéed fruits (orange, citron, pineapple, Pamelas, whatever)
1 recipe Indian Meal Pudding (opposite), omitting the water

Cover the raisins with the boiling water and let steep. Add the whiskey when cooled. Halve the cranberries and, with the glacéed fruits, stir into the raisins. Stir into the Indian Meal Pudding batter until smoothly mixed.

Pour batter into the greased top half of a double boiler. Place over simmering water, cover, and steam for about 2 hours, until the top center is set and reasonably firm to the touch. Let cool slightly, loosen the sides with a knife or small spatula, invert, and turn out. Sprinkle the pudding with whiskey if desired. Serve warm with Hard sauce, whipped cream, or Milk Punch Ice Cream.

To store, let cool thoroughly and wrap well; store in a cool place or refrigerate. A jigger of whiskey added occasionally will improve the pudding as it ages. Will keep a month. ✗ *6–8 servings*

Persimmon Pudding

The natives thought persimmons were delectable and they passed them on to the earliest colonists. John Smith in Virginia described them in the early seventeenth century:

Plums there are of three sorts. The red and white are like our hedge plums. but the other which they call putchamins, grow as high as a palmetto: the fruit is like a medlar; it is first green, then yellow, and red when it is ripe; if it be not ripe, it will draw a man's mouth awry, with much torment, but when it is ripe, it is as delicious as an apricot.

There is a beautiful specimen of the tree on the playground of the Carrboro Elementary School two blocks from my house. It is a sad commentary, but a happy instance for me, that today's children leave the ripened fruit untouched. In October, I send my youngest two out to gather the ignored bounty.

A correspondent for *The Rural Carolinian* sent in the following report in 1871.

This tree (the Diospyrus Virginiana) is found on all variety of soils, but seems to grow best on poor land. It is generally plentiful in old fields and worn out soils, and sometimes becomes a pest in cultivated fields. It is a rapid grower, symmetrical in shape, has beautiful green, glossy leaves, and, I should think, would answer well for shade or ornamental purposes . . . The ripe fruit, after it has been touched by frost, makes nice pudding and custard; and a good beer is sometimes extracted from them . . .

Persimmon Pudding. — Pick all over, rejecting the unripe ones. Force through a sieve in order to separate from the seeds. Add a little sugar, and flavor to your taste. Place in pans, and bake quickly. When done grate some brown bread crust and loaf sugar over them and set back to brown.

Persimmon Pudding was formerly a traditional Thanksgiving dessert in the South. Today it is still made for Christmas giving.

☞ Baking dish approximately 9 × 12 inches, greased

•   •   •   •   •   •   •   •

½ c. plus 2 Tb. butter
1½ c. sugar
3 eggs
2 c. persimmon pulp
1¼ c. all-purpose flour
½ tsp. nutmeg
1 tsp. cinnamon
½ tsp. salt
¾ c. milk
Zest and juice of 1 orange
¼ c. plus 2–4 Tb. dark rum
2 Tb. powdered sugar

Preheat oven to 325° F.

Cream the ½ cup butter and sugar well. Add the eggs, one by one. Stir in the persimmon pulp.

Sift the flour, spices, and salt together. Add to the butter, alternating with the milk. Stir in the orange zest and juice and ¼ cup dark rum. Pour into a greased baking dish and bake for about 1 hour, until lightly browned and set in the middle. Remove from the oven to a cooling rack. Let settle for about 10 minutes.

Meanwhile blend the 2 tablespoons butter, sugar, and the remaining dark rum to taste. Prick the top of the pudding well with a fork. Spread the butter-sugar-rum mixture all about to be absorbed by the warm pudding. This is delicious warm, cut into small squares, with a little Milk Punch Ice Cream. ✗ *16 servings*

Batter Puddings

Batter Puddings are light custards, often combined with fresh or crystallized fruit, nuts, or spices and thickened with flour or breadcrumbs. These simple desserts were enormously popular in the nineteenth century and were often served with a sauce. Sarah Rutledge gives her sauce recipe before those for puddings. I wonder which is the cart and which is the horse? The basic recipe she dubs "A Slight Pudding."

🐾 Pudding Sauce. *Six heaping table-spoonfuls of loaf sugar, half a pound of butter, worked to a cream; then add one egg, one wineglass of white wine, one nutmeg. — When it is all well mixed, set it on the fire until it comes to a boil: it is then fit for use.*
—*Sarah Rutledge, The Carolina Housewife, 1847*

☞ 9-inch cake pan, buttered

Fruit
⅓ c. sugar
2 Tb. water
1¼ lbs. ripe apples, pears, and/or
    peaches, peeled, cored, and
    sliced, about 4 c. in all
Pinch of salt
2 Tb. butter
2 Tb. bourbon, brandy, or rum

Custard
¼ c. all-purpose flour
¼ c. sugar
½ tsp. salt
1½ c. milk
3 eggs

Topping
1 Tb. butter
1 Tb. sugar
Cinnamon to taste

Prepare the fruit. Put the sugar and water in a skillet over moderately high heat and cook to a light caramel. Toss in the sliced fruit and continue cooking until tender. For peaches, only a minute; apples and pears may take up to 10–15 minutes. Add just a few grains of salt, the butter, and the whiskey off the heat.

Prepare the custard by mixing well the flour, sugar, and salt. Beat the milk into the eggs, and stir the liquid into the dry ingredients until smooth. Pour the custard into a buttered 9-inch cake pan. Add the fruit, not stirring. Bake in an oven preheated to 325° F. for about 30 minutes or until set. Remove from the oven and turn the broiler on high.

For the topping, rub the butter over the surface of the pudding with a fork or knife. Mix the sugar and cinnamon and sprinkle over the top, heavily where the fruit peeps through. Run under the broiler to caramelize the sugar topping; watch closely. Serve warm with cream or ice cream. ✘ *6 servings*

Peach Pudding

This version of the batter pudding uses dried fruit. It is a wintertime dish found in the mountain regions of all the Southern states.

Fruit

8 halves dried peaches (or any other dried fruit)

⅓ c. sugar

2 Tb. peach jam *or* orange marmalade

Juice of ½ lemon

2 Tb. dark rum, optional

Custard and Topping

1 recipe Batter Pudding (opposite), using only the custard and the topping, if desired

Cover the dried peaches with water in a saucepan and simmer until very tender. Drain, discard water. Put the peaches, sugar, jam or marmalade, and lemon juice in the processor or blender and puree until smooth. Add the rum if desired, taste for sweetness, stir the puree into the Batter Pudding custard, and bake as directed in the Batter Pudding recipe. Glaze with the topping if you like. ✖ *6 servings*

Crumb Pudding

Crumb Pudding is a rough, country version of Batter Pudding. While batter puddings are rarely made today, Crumb Pudding is still offered by mountain cooks.

Now let me ask you this, did you ever make a crumb pudding? You take your biscuits that you have, your cold bread and you save it. Use biscuits or loaf bread, no cornbread. You take it and work it up with milk, put it in a pan and make it up like you're going to make dough with milk and sugar and eggs. Put it inside the stove and bake it. You got a crumb pudding.
— Levie Ann Bratcher, *Cabbagetown Families, Cabbagetown Food*, 1976

The Queen of Puddings

Recipes for the Queen of Puddings are remarkably consistent all over the South. Even the proportions given are constant. It also pops up under other names; in Maryland it appears rather unregally as Maxwelton Bread Pudding. Here is the formula printed in *The New Dixie Cook-Book* of 1889.

❧ *The Queen of Puddings is a very nice dessert: Mix together pint sifted bread-crumbs, quart milk, cup sugar, yolks of four eggs, butter size of an egg and some add grated rind of lemon; bake until done — but do not allow to become watery — and spread with a layer of jelly. Whip whites of egg to a stiff froth with five tablespoons sugar, and juice of one lemon, spread on top and brown. Serve with Hard Sauce, or it is often eaten without any sauce, and very good cold.*

Baking would be at 350° F. for about 40 minutes. Jellies mentioned are often currant and raspberry. Other recipes direct cook to use stale sponge cake instead of bread crumbs.

Lemon Meringue Pudding

One hundred years since *The New Dixie Cook-Book* came out in 1889, and here we find the same proportions for a pudding as for the Queen. This contemporary recipe comes from Mary Pitts, published in 1984 in *The Foxfire Book of Appalachian Cookery*.

❧ *This is a kind of bread pudding. Use leftover biscuits. You have to put that topping on it to get the kids to eat it. Had to fancy it up a little, but they always went back for seconds.*

2 cups bread crumbs
4 cups milk
½ cup butter
1 cup sugar

4 eggs, separated
Juice and rind of 1 lemon
3 tablespoons confectioners' sugar

Soak bread crumbs in milk. Cream butter and sugar. Add beaten egg yolks, lemon rind, and all but 1 teaspoon of the lemon juice. Mix with bread crumbs. Pour into a baking dish and bake in a 350F degree oven for 45 minutes, or until firm. Cover with a meringue made from the egg whites beaten with the confectioners' sugar and remaining lemon juice. Return to the oven and brown the meringue lightly.

Tot Fait

Tot fait is an old creole dessert from New Orleans, where it is usually prepared in a low baking dish and comes out a lovely, fluffy delicate pudding. It is, to my taste, better prepared as individual soufflés baked in ramekins. I've found this a wonderfully quick and painless, even hardy, alternative to a classic French soufflé. The heavy cooked base is eliminated, and yet almost magically these little puffs can endure even the abuse that children in a kitchen during preparation can inflict. Also miraculously, the mix can be finished off as much as 90 minutes in advance. Spoon the batter into baking dishes and cover with a large bowl inverted to prevent drafts until ready to bake. Ten minutes or so before serving, pop them into the oven. It's the easiest possible way to finish an elegant meal with a little sleight-of-hand.

☞ Six 1-cup ramekins, buttered

6 eggs, separated	3 Tb. milk
6 Tb. sugar	Pinch of salt
¼ c. flour	Zest of 2 lemons
	Juice of 1 lemon
	Powdered sugar

Preheat oven to 425° F.

Beat the yolks until very light. Add the sugar slowly and continue beating until the mixture has tripled in volume. Mix the flour with the milk to a smooth paste and beat into the yolks. Whip the egg whites with a pinch of salt until stiff. Fold into the yolks along with the lemon zest and juice.

Divide the mixture among the 6 ramekins and bake for about 15 minutes or until the soufflés are puffed and browned. Sprinkle with powdered sugar and serve immediately. A few fresh berries on the side are a welcome garnish — perfect small strawberries, fragrant raspberries, or intensely colored blueberries. ✖ *6 servings*

Tot Fait au Chocolat

☞ Double boiler; six 1-cup
    ramekins, buttered

• • • • • • • •

4½ oz. unsweetened chocolate
6 eggs, separated
9 Tb. sugar

3 Tb. flour
3 Tb. milk
Pinch of salt
1½ tsp. vanilla
Angostura bitters
Powdered sugar

Preheat oven to 425° F.

Melt the chocolate in a double boiler.

Beat the egg yolks until very light. Add the sugar slowly and continue beating until the mixture has tripled in volume. Mix the flour with the milk to a smooth paste and beat into the yolks. Fold in the melted chocolate. Whip the egg whites with a pinch of salt until stiff. Fold into the yolk base along with the vanilla and a dash or 2 of bitters.

Divide the mixture among the 6 ramekins and bake for about 15 minutes or until the soufflés are well puffed and browned. Sprinkle with powdered sugar, if desired.

An excellent accompaniment to the chocolate tot fait is Custard Sauce or plain, lightly sweetened whipped cream. ✗ *6 servings*

COOKIES · AND · SMALL · CAKES

Kisses

Kisses and Secrets

Strawberries in Heaven

Brown Sugar Shortbread

Chocolate Glaze

Egg Shortbread

Lemon Squares

Piano Keys

Almond Tarts, Jelly Tots

Basic Brown Sugar
Cookie Dough

Ginger Wafers

Butterscotch Bars

Butterscotch Cookies

Chocolate Chip Cookies

Oatmeal Orange Cookies

Cicada Shells

Turtle Shells

Macaroons

Prune Macaroons

To Do Tarts

Jumbles

Edenton Tea Party Cakes

Racy Gingerbread

Soft Gingerbread

Fruitcake Cookies or Rocks

Ladyfingers

Les Oreilles de Cochon

Brownies

Chevrons

Chocolate Silk Cakes

Fudge Pie

THE TEA TABLE

The tea table is a traditional, important part of Southern social life. It was a well-established function by the mid-eighteenth century and was considered a rather formal entertainment, with one exception. The eccentric Charleston planter John Huger, to defy tradition, set up his tea table on the northeast corner of Broad and Mazyck streets and entertained on the sidewalk. For the most part, though, a tea was and is an elegant occasion when ritual is more important than content. Alcoholic beverages may be served, but no tea is ever faulted for the lack of wines or liquor. The hostess, rather, displays her sensitivity in offering a sophisticated choice of appropriate delicacies, chosen to complement and contrast each with the other. It is more like a painting in miniature than the broad canvas of a meal, and it is one of the South's most gracious moments.

In the late 1860s and 1870s, there was very little to set on the once great Charleston tables. Rose Pringle Ravenel was a debutante in those years. She later recorded her memories, which were published privately along with her distinguished family's heirloom recipes, in a little volume entitled *Rose P. Ravenel's Cookbook* (1893). The great teas, receptions, collations, and balls hardly resembled the splendor of the antebellum entertainments, but the spirit of Southern hospitality endured.

The other afternoon a friend called. She told us she was so busy, that her daughter was going out this winter and she was giving her dinners and dances. There was no trouble in giving a dinner to her friends but to have any kind of entertainment for her daughter and her friends was a labor. It must be new and fashionable. They were severe critics and it was almost impossible to satisfy them. This made me think of the winter I went out. My first St. Cecelia ball was at the South Carolina Hall. There were two long tables at the side of the room covered with fine damask, large dishes of biscuits, silver coffee pots. Biscuits and coffee were handed around. My father was president of the St. Cecelia at that time and Mr. Edward Milliken my father's friend who lived with us, was vice president. We all wore Tarlatan dresses, very pretty and always fresh. They were made at home by our mothers and sisters. We would meet at each other's houses and dance. We had nothing to eat, only water to drink. This went on for years. You never saw young people enjoy themselves more, so happy — they certainly had a good time. How times have changed!

MARKETS

The vitality of Southern markets is often rooted in African traditions. Our food markets also serve as flower markets. There is always a dynamic tension between country and city. And even in the stores a sense of place and history pervades. Note the Robert E. Lee flour in the store-front window of the Golden Rule Store in Mebane, North Carolina.

Kisses

My grandmother loved these old-fashioned meringues, fussed over their preparation endlessly, and presented them as prized heirlooms from her own childhood. We never cared a whit for them and liked them mostly because we could poke our fingers in the crackly shells and wave them about like witches' growths on our stubby hands. Now knowing the difficulty of making a perfect meringue in the humid South, I appreciate her efforts. I keep a humidity gauge in my kitchen, and don't bother with meringues when it goes above 55. Perfectly white meringues from the bakery aren't meant to be made at home. Commercial meringues are usually made from precooked egg whites and taste like beaten paste to me. Homemade meringues are much more delicate in flavor and texture, even if they do color up a bit.

☞ Brown or parchment paper

◆ ◆ ◆ ◆ ◆ ◆ ◆ ◆

4 egg whites, at room temperature

7/8 c. sugar

1 tsp. vanilla, rosewater, orange flower water, or almond extract

Beat the whites slowly at first, then increase the speed as the egg whites foam. Sift in the sugar slowly, gradually increasing the speed of the beating until stiff, glossy peaks form. Add the flavoring. Drop by the tablespoon onto brown or parchment paper leaving a nice peak. Bake in an oven preheated to 250° F. for about 40 minutes or until crisp. Turn off the heat and open the door, leaving the Kisses to cool in the oven. Store airtight when cool.

Kisses may be sandwiched, bottom to bottom, with a little melted chocolate, jam, or buttercream. We always thought this was the kiss.

72 individual cakes

Kisses and Secrets

Mrs. Lettice Bryan in *The Kentucky Housewife* (1839) made a charming fortune cookie from these meringues. She called them Kisses and Secrets:

> *Wrap around each a slip of paper containing a single verse or pun, and envelope them separately in small pieces of fine white paper that is neatly fringed, giving each end a twist.*

Strawberries in Heaven

Madeline and her friend Amanda who lives on the corner are my helpers in making these little tarts. They are a prized celebration of the first strawberries at the Farmers' Market, which appeared on May 7 this year. I know only because I asked. That Saturday I had dawdled over a second cup of coffee, got to the market at 8:15, and missed the last of the watercress as well as the first of the berries. Anyway, the supermarket had fine small North Carolina berries — the large, hollow berries commonly found are too big to bite and usually lack flavor.

Madeline and Amanda both can squeeze out little vacherins from the pastry tube and, from otherwise untapped sources, maintain the patience to fill them up with custard, top them off with a berry, and even spoon a little glaze over each. The meringues go soft quickly; fill them just before serving. Despite the many separate operations, each step is well defined and gives children a very fancy pastry, delightful in its scale, and well within their skills.

☞Brown or parchment paper

1 recipe Kisses (opposite)
About 6 doz. perfect, small
   strawberries

2 c. Light Pastry Cream (p. 205)
   or whipped cream
About ½ c. red currant jelly

Line a baking pan with parchment or brown paper. Prepare the batter for the Kisses and put in a pastry bag fitted with a small plain tip. Pipe small discs about 1¼ inches in diameter for the bottoms. Then build up the outer walls by piping around the circumference to a ¾-inch height, to form small shells. Be sure the shells have a closed bottom and enough of a cavity to hold a little cream. Bake as for Kisses. Clean and cap the strawberries. When ready to serve, fill each meringue shell with a little

pastry cream or whipped cream and top with a whole strawberry, point up. Gently melt the jelly and spoon just a bit over each berry for a glaze. Serve immediately; they will not hold. ✗ 72 *individual tarts*

Brown Sugar Shortbread

This is short'nin' bread.

☞ 9½-inch diameter springform pan

1 c. butter
1 c. light brown sugar

2 c. flour
⅛ tsp. salt
Chocolate Glaze (below), optional

Beat the butter until light. Add the brown sugar and cream well. Mixture should be light and not grainy. Add flour and salt a bit at a time, but quickly. Do not overbeat at this point. As soon as dough is well blended, turn into a 9½-inch diameter springform pan. Spread smoothly and evenly. Prick all over with a three-pronged fork. Bake in an oven preheated to 325° F. for about 35 minutes, until barely brown. Cut into 16 wedges before completely cooled, but allow to age a day stored airtight before serving. ✗ *16 wedges*

Chocolate Glaze

Though purists rail, an unconventional chocolate glaze for the Brown Sugar Shortbread is delicious. Spread evenly over the middle part of the cake leaving a ½-inch margin around the outer edge. Cut into 16 wedges. Top each piece with one perfect toasted pecan half if you're feeling especially reckless. Serve with a small dish of Ruby Red Grapefruit Ice, an exquisite combination and typically Southern in its play on bittersweet flavors.

☞ Double boiler

2 oz. semisweet chocolate
1½ Tb. butter

1 tsp. strong coffee
2 Tb. sieved powdered sugar
Pinch of salt

Combine all ingredients in the top of double boiler. Heat gently until the chocolate is melted and the mixture is smooth upon stirring. ✗ *½ cup*

Egg Shortbread

☞ Cookie sheet with sides about
    9 × 12 inches; baking beans
    or rice

♦   ♦   ♦   ♦   ♦   ♦   ♦   ♦

¾ c. butter

6 Tb. white or light brown sugar
1 egg
2 c. flour
⅛ tsp. salt

Beat the butter well with the sugar, add the egg, and incorporate well. Fold the flour and salt through by hand. Pat out evenly on the cookie sheet, cover with foil, and distribute dried beans or rice over the surface. Bake in an oven preheated to 400° F. for about 10 minutes, reduce heat to 350° F., cooking for 10 more minutes. Remove the foil and beans, reduce heat to 325° F., and bake about 10 more minutes, until well done but not particularly brown. Let cool slightly and cut into 40 thin rectangles. ✖ *40 pieces*

Lemon Squares

It is not surprising that lemon squares are considered the quintessential bar cookie, for historically they are well-tested tarts of the English tradition. Many nineteenth-century recipes direct laying down the lemon curd over a puff paste and baking. Some other recipes call for the traditional shortbread. The Egg Shortbread is really a rich tart dough and its resilience provides a firmer base; the authentic shortbread tends to crumble, puff pastry tends to distract. Some cooks sprinkle the squares with confectioners' sugar when cool.

1 recipe Egg Shortbread (above)
1 recipe Lemon Curd (p. 210)

Confectioners' sugar, optional

Bake the Egg Shortbread as directed. Cover immediately with the Lemon Curd and return to the oven for 5–7 minutes. Let cool on a rack before cutting into small portions. ✖ *48 lemon squares*

Piano Keys

1 recipe Egg Shortbread (p. 237) Apricot jam
Raspberry jam Powdered sugar
2 oz. bittersweet chocolate,
  melted

Prepare the shortbread as directed and when almost cool, cut into rectangles ¾ × 2 inches. Sandwich half with raspberry jam and glaze with chocolate. Sandwich the remaining cookies with apricot jam and sprinkle with powdered sugar put through a sieve. ✖ *36 cookies*

Almond Tarts, Jelly Tots

These are the most irresistible cookies I know of and they come in a great variety in the South. Children love to make them; we produce them in an assembly line. When my elder son Matthew was in school in Vermont, Elliott, Madeline, and I made these cookies for him as a souvenir of the South. They keep well and are good for shipping.

6 Tb. sugar 1 small egg
Pinch of salt 1 Tb. cold water
2 c. flour Blanched whole almonds or tart
½ c. butter jelly and jam

Sift the sugar, salt, and flour together into a bowl. Work the butter in as for pie crust and bind with the egg beaten with water. Beat well; the dough will be very stiff.

Pinch off small amounts weighing ⅓ ounce each, about the size of a large grape, and roll into smooth balls. Place on a greased sheet, press down slightly, and top each with a whole almond. Bake for about 25 minutes in an oven preheated to 300° F. The bottoms of the cookies should brown, but the tops barely color.

These little tarts can be filled with a dab of tart jelly or jam replacing the almond. Currant, plum, apricot, raspberry, blackberry are all good contrasts to the short cookie dough. To fill the cookie make a small X-shaped indentation with the point of a spoon at the top of the dough to hold the jelly as it melts. ✖ *50 cookies*

BROWN SUGAR COOKIES

The Basic Brown Sugar Cookie recipe is delicious by itself, but it can be used as the base for other creations. Five variations follow it, and the possibilities are legion. I find old, thin darkened cookie sheets work best for baking these. If your pans are thick or the cookies tend to stick, use parchment or wax paper to prevent sticking. Let cool a few minutes, then peel off the paper. Store airtight.

Basic Brown Sugar
Cookie Dough

This is an elegant, very crisp wafer for ice cream and sherbets. It can be sandwiched with chocolate or a little butter cream.

☞ Well-seasoned or nonstick pans, lightly buttered or lined with brown paper or parchment paper

· · · · · · · ·

½ c. butter
1¼ c. lightly packed light brown sugar

1 egg
1 egg yolk
1 tsp. vanilla
1 Tb. brandy
¾ c. flour
Scant ½ tsp. salt

Beat the butter until light. Add the brown sugar and cream well. Add the egg, egg yolk, vanilla, and brandy and beat until smooth. Stir in the flour and salt until well blended. Chill well.

Butter lightly well-seasoned or nonstick pans or use paper to line the pans. Pipe out the dough using a pastry bag or form using a spoon into small wafers about 1½ × ⅜ inch. Allow room for spreading.

Bake in an oven preheated to 375° F. for 8–10 minutes or until golden. Let cool on the baking sheet 2 or 3 minutes, then remove to a rack. Store airtight. ✕ *100 wafers*

Ginger Wafers

☞ Well-seasoned or nonstick pans, lightly buttered or lined with brown paper or parchment paper

4–6 Tb. very finely chopped crystallized ginger

1 recipe Basic Brown Sugar Cookie Dough (p. 239)

◆ ◆ ◆ ◆ ◆ ◆ ◆ ◆

Beat the crystallized ginger into the dough. Drop by the spoonful onto lightly buttered well-seasoned or nonstick pans or use paper to line the pans. Bake about 10 minutes in an oven preheated to 375° F. ✕ *100 wafers*

Butterscotch Bars

☞ Baking dish approximately 12½ × 9 inches, buttered and floured

1 c. chopped pecans

1 recipe Basic Brown Sugar Cookie Dough (p. 239)

◆ ◆ ◆ ◆ ◆ ◆ ◆ ◆

Stir the pecans into the dough until well distributed. Turn into a buttered and lightly floured baking dish, smooth out, and cook 35–40 minutes in an oven preheated to 375° F., until golden brown. Let cool to lukewarm in the pan, then cut into 48 squares. Remove with care. ✕ *48 bars*

Butterscotch Cookies

Use the dough for Butterscotch Bars (above), but drop by the tablespoon onto lightly buttered well-seasoned or nonstick pans or use paper to line the pans. Bake at 375° F. for 10–12 minutes, until golden. Let cool 2 or 3 minutes before removing from baking sheet. ✕ *60 cookies*

Chocolate Chip Cookies

This recipe makes a very thin, crisp cookie. Add ½ cup uncooked oatmeal for a more substantial cookie if desired.

☞ Well-seasoned or nonstick pans, lightly buttered or lined with brown paper or parchment paper

• • • • • • • • •

1 recipe Basic Brown Sugar Cookie Dough (p. 239)

1 c. chopped pecans
6 oz. semisweet chocolate cut into chunks (the chocolate will cut much more easily if slightly warm) or chocolate chips

Combine the dough, pecans, and chocolate chunks. Drop by the tablespoon onto lightly buttered well-seasoned or nonstick pans or use paper to line the pans. Bake in an oven preheated to 375° F. for 10–12 minutes, until golden. Let cool 2 or 3 minutes before removing to a rack. ✖ *72 cookies*

Oatmeal Orange Cookies

☞ Well-seasoned or nonstick pans, lightly buttered or lined with brown paper or parchment paper

• • • • • • • • •

1½ c. rolled oatmeal, uncooked

½ tsp. cinnamon
1¼ tsp. very finely chopped orange Pamelas (p. 129)
1 recipe Basic Brown Sugar Cookie Dough (p. 239)

Add the oatmeal, cinnamon, and orange Pamelas to the dough and beat well. Drop by the spoonful onto lightly buttered well-seasoned or nonstick pans or use paper to line the pans. Bake in an oven preheated to 375° F. for 8–10 minutes or until lightly browned. Let cool on the baking sheet 2 or 3 minutes, then remove to a rack. Store airtight. ✖ *72 cookies*

Keep going. By now, you should be able to create your own house specialties based on the basic cookie dough. A few suggestions: try chopped dates with the oatmeal cookies, some cocoa to make chocolate chocolate chips, rum, and coconut; bake any of the drop cookies as for the Butterscotch Bars and you will have chewy, dense squares.

Cicada Shells

The mating song of the cicada is the background music to a night of sitting on the porch. The high-pitched drone is only one of the exotic summer sounds, but one of the most distinctive. The outgrown carapaces that are shed at the bases of oak trees in July and August show the tiny monsters' entire, transparent bodies, frightening in their fragility. All children love to collect them and create little tableaux in sand lots with bits of dried moss and twigs. My daughter Madeline says these cookies are like cicada shells, puffed, brown, and all crackly. They are splendid little confections, too full of nuts and too fragile to be anything other than homemade. Grownups sometimes call these baked pralines or praline cookies.

☞Parchment or wax paper, greased

♦ ♦ ♦ ♦ ♦ ♦ ♦ ♦

1 c. lightly packed light brown
   sugar
2 Tb. flour

¼ tsp. salt
2 c. chopped pecans
1 tsp. vanilla
3 egg whites, stiffly beaten

Mix thoroughly the brown sugar, flour, salt, and pecans. Sprinkle the vanilla over and work into the mix. Fold in the beaten egg whites until well incorporated. Drop by the scant tablespoon onto greased parchment or wax paper on a baking sheet. Cook for about 30 minutes in an oven preheated to 275° F., until puffed, browned, and crisp. Let cool a few minutes and peel off the paper. Store airtight. ✖ *30 cookies*

Turtle Shells

Even tastier, though not as euphonious as cicadas, turtle shells are my son Elliott's inspiration.

1 recipe Cicada Shells
   (above)

2 recipes Chocolate Glaze
   (p. 236)

Spread the tops of the cooled cicadas with the warm chocolate. Let cool before serving. ✖ *30 shells*

MACAROONS

One pound of sweet almonds, and half a pound of bitter, blanched and pounded until fine in a marble mortar, with half a glass of rose-water; then add one and a half pounds of powdered loaf sugar, and the whites of four eggs whipped to a stiff froth; beat all well together, and drop a dessert-spoonful of the mixture at a time upon a grated paper or upon tin sheets; bake in a slow oven.
—Sarah Rutledge, <u>The Carolina Housewife</u>, 1847

The old recipes for macaroons call for part bitter almonds (*Prunus amygdalus*); the sweet (*Prunus amygdalus dulcis*) is the only type available in our markets. Save the inner kernels of the pits of fresh peaches, apricots, plums; several of these added to this and other almond recipes will intensify the . flavor. I keep the kernels in brandy, which makes the old-fashioned cordial noyaux, a nice doubled-edged way around the bitter almond's exile from our kitchens. Noyaux also happily replaces the strident almond extract in baking.

Parchment or greased brown
   paper
• • • • • • • •
6 oz. (about 1½ c.) unblanched
   almonds preferably with added
   fruit kernels (see above)

¾ c. sugar
3½ tsp. orange flower water
4 egg whites

Toss the unblanched almonds into a saucepan of boiling water, let the water return to the boil, drain, and refresh under cold water. The almonds should slip easily out of their skins.

Refrigerate the almonds until perfectly cool, about 15 minutes to be sure. Then combine all the ingredients in the bowl of a food processor. Run continuously until the batter is smooth and thick. Drop by small spoonfuls onto an ungreased baking sheet lined with parchment or greased brown paper. Bake in an oven preheated to 300° F. for about 10 minutes or until lightly browned. Let cool on the paper a few minutes before removing. ✖ *24 small macaroons*

Prune Macaroons

If we didn't have such negative associations with the word prune (prune faced, for instance) perhaps we could hear music in the phrase prune macaroon. Alas, English does not encourage such tuneful talk, but I'm sure the palate will appreciate this old-fashioned confection. Many steps exist between this page and the little cake, but the whole procedure is almost foolproof, and it takes little more than time to produce a confection that will be as sophisticated as the finest French sweet.

☞ Parchment or greased brown paper

1 recipe Macaroons (p. 243)

1 recipe Almond Stuffed Prunes (p. 152)

Powdered sugar scented by a vanilla bean

Drop a small dollop of macaroon batter onto the baking paper. Dip your finger into cold water and spread the batter about ¼-inch thick to the shape of a prune. Place 1 prune on the batter and cover it thinly but completely with macaroon dough. Bake in an oven preheated to 325° F. for about 30 minutes or until lightly browned. Let rest a minute or 2 before removing to a dish of powdered sugar. Roll well in the sugar. Remove to a rack. Serve before completely cooled.

✗ *18 prune macaroons*

To Do Tarts

To Do Tarts are a kind of Southern macaroon, using pecans instead of almonds. In addition to their fine flavor, they are easy to prepare thanks to the appliance world. The mortar and pestle of the original recipe would put this cookie beyond the scope of most people's time and patience. With a food processor or blender, the preparation time is about 10 minutes. The cookie, rich but not too sweet, is excellent with strong coffee.

3 oz. pecans, about ¾ c.
2 Tb. sugar
Grated zest of 1 orange

1 slice stale loaf bread, about 1 oz.
1 egg white, stiffly beaten

Combine the pecans, sugar, zest, and stale bread in the container of a food processor or blender and spin until very fine. Be cautious about overheating the nuts or they will be greasy. Gently fold the stiff egg white into the nut dough to lighten it. Shape into small balls (about ¼ ounce or the size of a cherry tomato) and bake on a buttered sheet in an oven preheated to 325° F. for about 12 minutes or until lightly browned. The cookies can be flattened with the tines of a fork before baking, if desired. A pinch of plain or cinnamon sugar can be dropped over each cookie before baking as well, but do not make too sweet.

✄ *18 cookies*

Jumbles

The word jumbles goes all the way back to the Latin *geminus,* or twin. The shape of these little spice cookies earned the name, for they are like the gemmel, an eighteenth-century goldsmith's trick of intertwined hoops forming a finger ring. Their popularity was as great in the antebellum South as in their English home. To form, a piece of dough is broken off, rolled out quickly into a thin round bat, and joined up end to end to make two circles. Toward the end of the nineteenth century, such shaping niceties were lost. *The New Dixie Cook-Book* (1889) says, "mix rather stiff, roll, and cut with cake cutter." By the twentieth century the jumbles disappeared as an active teacake.

Take 4 eggs leaving out 2 of the whites, half pound Butter, 1 lb. Sugar beat them up together as for pound cake, then thicken it with flour till it comes like thin paste which will take about 2 lb. of flour which must be well dried. Sprinkle in some carraway seeds, a glass of Brandy, and a tea cup of rose water; role them out with the hand and make them into small circles, then dip them into pounded sugar and put them on tin sheets and bake them.
— Harriott Pinckney Horry, A Colonial Plantation Cookbook, *1770*

Some Advice: 1 pound of sugar 1 pound of butter two eggs and a gill of rose water 1 pound and ½ of flour. and now let me give you a piece of advice yes I must use that word although I know it is <u>peculiarly obnoxious</u> to the ears of <u>young</u> people like yourself always give out sufficient <u>materials</u> and if your cook happens not to make them to suit exactly don't say "I think you are the most provoking negro I ever laid my eyes upon."
— A sister to sister letter, Cameron Collection, May 18th, 1884

1 c. butter	1½ tsp. cinnamon
1 c. plus 2 Tb. sugar	1 tsp. freshly grated nutmeg
3 egg whites, beaten to a froth	1 tsp. caraway seeds, crushed
2 c. flour	3 Tb. rosewater
Pinch of salt	

Beat the butter until very light and add the sugar. Beat well, add the egg whites, and continue beating until smooth. Add the flour and seasonings, and beat until smooth. Refrigerate until firm.

Then shape as directed in *Miss Leslie's New Cooking Book* (1857):

Flour your hands and your pasteboard, and lay the dough upon it. Take off equal portions from the lump, and with your hands form them into round rolls, and make them into rings by joining together the two ends of each. Place the jumbles (not so near as to touch,) in tin pans slightly buttered, and bake them in a very brisk oven little more than five or six minutes, or enough to color them a light brown. If the oven is too cool, the jumbles will spread and run into each other. When cold, sift sugar over them.

Baking is at 375° F.; time depends on the thickness of the cookie, but more like 8–10 minutes or until lightly browned. ✗ *50 jumbles*

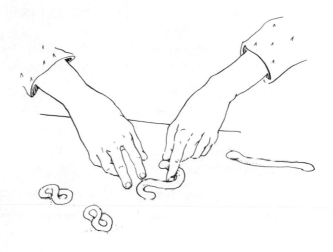

Edenton Tea Party Cakes

On October 17, 1774, the following notice appeared in the South Carolina *Gazette*: "AN ASSOCIATION OF PROTESTANT SCHOOLBOYS . . . have resolved not to Use any India Teas after the 1st Day of November." Revolutionary fever was running high in the Southern colonies.

A week later, the first known organized political action by women in the American colonies took place in the lovely port of Edenton, North Carolina, on October 25, 1774. Women from five counties met under the leadership of Penelope Barker to respond to the actions of the British Parliament by issuing resolutions of protest. The resolutions rest in the British Museum, but the recipe for the cakes served at the party is a traditional favorite in the state. All published recipes are almost identical, evidence of the cook's respect for the historical associations.

3 eggs	1 tsp. vanilla
2 c. lightly packed dark brown sugar	6 Tb. butter
1 tsp. baking soda	6 Tb. lard
1 Tb. warm water	4 c. all-purpose flour

Beat the eggs well, then beat in the brown sugar. Dissolve the baking soda in the warm water; stir into the eggs along with the vanilla. Work the butter and lard into the flour, then stir in the egg mixture. Chill, then roll out thinly. Cut into shapes (rounds, squares, diamonds) and bake on lightly buttered baking sheets in an oven preheated to 400° F. for about 10 minutes or until lightly browned. Cool on a rack. ✷ *100 cookies*

Racy Gingerbread

This recipe is derived from a nineteenth-century Virginia source. The original calls for six races of ginger, a race being a corruption of the Middle French *rais* from the Latin *radix,* all meaning a root. In truth, the ginger race is not a root at all, but a specialized underground stem with the capacities of food reserve and nodular growth. Such growths are called rhizomes from the Greek *rhiza,* root again.

The use of fresh ginger for cakes, or for any cooking in the South, is rare, surprising, too, considering its liberal use in savoury and sweet cooking in the islands of the Caribbean so near by. Its inclusion in this Virginia recipe may harken to a traditional Scotch cake of oatmeal, treacle, and green ginger. Its presence is immediately announced and prolonged, a delight for those who like their ginger direct and unadulterated.

This batter is better behaved than that of most gingerbreads, which tend to fall in the middle. It can also be baked in three round 9-inch tins, iced with whipped cream when cooled, and decorated with crystallized ginger. It keeps well when frozen.

☞ Baking dish approximately 9 × 11 inches, greased

- - - - - - - -

8 oz. fresh ginger
½ c. butter
1 c. sugar
3 eggs
1 c. molasses
3 c. all-purpose flour
¾ tsp. baking soda
½ tsp. salt

Peel or scrape the ginger and chop. Process in a blender or processor until very fine and rub through a fine sieve with some force. You should have about ⅓ cup of the ginger essence.

Cream the butter and sugar. Add the ginger, and, one by one, the eggs. Incorporate the molasses.

Sift the dry ingredients together and combine all until the batter is smooth. Turn into a greased dish and bake in an oven preheated to 350° F. for 20 minutes. Reduce the heat to 325° F. and cook about 20 more minutes. ✗ *36 squares*

Soft Gingerbread

Cake-style gingerbread is usually designated "soft" or "loaf" in nineteenth-century cookbooks to distinguish it from the crisp cookie gingerbread. This is the traditional cake, slightly spongy with a chewy top, found from Louisiana to Maryland. Old recipes specify New Orleans or "Porto Rico" molasses, and warn, "never syrups." Like the Racy Gingerbread this freezes well.

☞ Baking dish approximately 9 × 11 inches, greased

• • • • • • • • •

½ c. butter
½ c. lard
1 c. sugar
1 c. molasses
½ c. water
1 Tb. powdered ginger
1½ tsp. cinnamon
2½ c. all-purpose flour
2½ tsp. baking soda
1 tsp. salt
2 eggs

Put the butter, lard, sugar, molasses, and water in a saucepan with the spices and bring to the boil: remove from the heat and allow to cool.

Sift the flour, soda, and salt into a large bowl. Stir the cooled liquid quickly through. Beat the eggs well and stir them into the batter. Pour the batter into a greased baking dish and bake in an oven preheated to 350° F. for about 35 minutes or until the top is well browned and the sides pull away slightly. ✂ *36 pieces*

Fruitcake Cookies or Rocks

Fruitcake cookies are made from the Cherokee Fruitcake batter (p. 294), but the amount of fruits and nuts is cut by half. Drop by the tablespoon on parchment or lightly greased brown paper. Put in a cold oven and turn to 350° F. Bake about 20 minutes or until the cookies are lightly browned. Let cool slightly, then remove from the paper.

Fruitcake cookies come in handy when you're too impatient to wait for the whole cakes to ripen, or when the holidays arrive and your pantry is bare. Again, as with all fruitcakes, if you don't like one kind of fruit, omit it, and put in an equal amount of one you do like.

Ladyfingers

Children, at least the ones in my neighborhood, love to shape these little cakes and then to fill them after baking. Their efforts are usually slightly erratic and we end up with fatty fingers as well as ladyfingers. Then I put out the pantry's store of jam and jellies. Mixing and matching flavors to their own code, the children sandwich the cakes and envelop them in a small dust storm of powdered sugar.

Prepare ½ the batter for Lemon Sponge Cake (p. 305). You can omit lemon and flavor with vanilla, if desired. Line baking sheets with parchment or brown paper. Spread the batter in long thin strips, about 3-inches long and ½-inch wide, using a spoon or a pastry bag. Bake in an oven preheated to 350° F. for about 10–12 minutes, until just very lightly browned. Let cool a minute, then remove from the paper and cool on a rack. ✖ *30 individual Ladyfingers*

Les Oreilles de Cochon

Les Oreilles de Cochon are pigs' ears translated but a deep-fried pastry in the kitchen. They are a speciality of southwest Louisiana where the Cajuns prepare cane syrup to drizzle over the ears. If you can find good cane syrup use it in place of the corn syrup below.

☞ Thermometer for frying

	2 eggs
✦ ✦ ✦ ✦ ✦ ✦ ✦ ✦	1 Tb. water
2 c. all-purpose flour	1 tsp. apple cider vinegar
¼ tsp. salt	Shortening and/or lard for frying
1 tsp. sugar	1 c. cane or corn syrup
4 Tb. butter	½ c. sugar

Sift the flour, salt, and sugar together. Rub in the butter with the fingertips as for pie dough. Beat the eggs with the water and vinegar, then pour over the flour mixture and beat well. Turn the dough out on a lightly floured surface and knead it 2–3 minutes until smooth. Chill for 30 minutes; divide into 12 pieces.

Roll out very thin, like pasta dough, into rough 5-inch squares. Cut each square in half on the diagonal. Fry the pieces in single layers in about ½ inch of hot fat at 360° F.; lard is traditional, but you may use shortening. Turn once when golden brown. In the meanwhile, combine the syrup and ½ cup sugar in a saucepan. Cook to the soft crack stage, about 270° F. Drain the fried pastries on brown paper and drizzle about 1 tablespoon of the syrup over each. Eat at once. ✖ *24 cookies*

Brownies

Brownies are a favorite in the South as they are all over the United States and, in general, are not improved upon by increasing chocolate to truffle proportions or by any other of today's excesses. Nor are they indulgently consumed in quantity. Rather, brownies are usually part of a selection of cakes and cookies presented more or less at tea time. They are often cut quite small, 1¼-inch squares, topped with a pecan half or dusted with powdered sugar to be consumed in contrast to jelly tarts, shortbread, lemon squares, and so forth. Restraint produces desire; three or four such petits fours are more enticing than any number of chocolate slabs on a baking sheet.

☞ Double boiler; 9 × 11-inch baking dish, greased

◆ ◆ ◆ ◆ ◆ ◆ ◆ ◆

4 oz. unsweetened chocolate
½ c. butter, at room temperature
2 c. sugar
4 eggs
1 c. all-purpose flour
½ tsp. salt
1 c. chopped pecans
1½ tsp. vanilla

Melt the chocolate in a double boiler. Beat the butter lightly and add the sugar. Beat briefly. Add the eggs, one by one, but quickly, while beating. Add the melted chocolate, beat quickly; then add flour, salt, nuts, and vanilla. Incorporate all ingredients but do not overwork. Pour the batter into the greased pan and bake in an oven preheated to 350° F. for 25–30 minutes. The top should be crisp and the center set. Cut into squares when cool. *24–36 brownies*

Chevrons

Chevrons ornamentally are continuous zigzags, a unit of which is often heraldic. The shape is typically French when applied to cooking, and in baking has the advantage of producing more edge and sharper angles for crisp cookies than right angles would produce for the same area.

The preceding brownie dough spread very thinly and baked long becomes a rarity — an excellent, rich, chocolatey, and crisp wafer. The ordinary powdery quality of cocoa cookies is deliciously absent. Alter the brownie recipe only by grinding the pecans very fine. When the cookies are done, work very quickly — cut into chevrons and gently remove to a cooling rack while the pan is still warm. The chevrons can be stored airtight or frozen. Plain, they are an excellent ice cream wafer. Sandwich them with jam or buttercream, dust one half with powdered sugar and dip the other into a Chocolate Glaze for their most elaborate incarnation. Plain or fancy, these easily made Chevrons extend the general range of homemade cookies into a sophisticated realm of tea-time pastries.

☞ Pan approximately 17 × 12½ inches or several smaller baking sheets, greased

• • • • • • • •

2 oz. unsweetened chocolate
4 Tb. butter
1 c. sugar

2 eggs
½ c. all-purpose flour
¼ tsp. salt
½ c. very finely chopped pecans
¾ tsp. vanilla
1¼ tsp. rosewater, optional

Prepare the batter according to the Brownies (opposite) recipe. Spread thinly on a greased baking sheet and bake about 20 minutes in an oven preheated to 375° F. until lightly browned. Do not overcook or wafers will be bitter. The dough can be spread quite thinly and with practice you will produce paper-thin wafers, if desired. To begin, a jelly-roll pan approximately 17 × 12½ inches will bake a crisp thin cookie that will also be easy to handle.

When done, cut the sheet into Chevrons, working quickly but patiently. Remove the cookies to a rack. When cool, either eat or store. Or proceed as described on page 254.

✗ 48 cookies

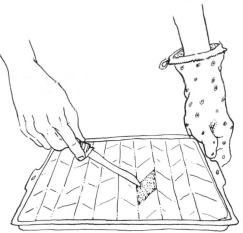

....*Gilding the Chevrons*. Much as I usually like simplicity, I cannot resist elaborating upon the foil these Chevrons provide for other flavors. Sieved raspberry jam spread thinly and sandwiched is a favorite combination; apricot jam and orange marmalade are equally tart and delicious. A little coffee buttercream is divine. This is when you can really congratulate yourself on all those little dabs of this and that sweet in the refrigerator you couldn't bear to throw away. A few spoonfuls of glacéed fruit or a bit of preserves will lead to a frenzy of cookie creating. You can, of course, go on and on.

Chocolate Silk Cakes

☞ Double boiler; baking pan, approximately 9 × 11 inches, greased

♦　♦　♦　♦　♦　♦　♦

8 oz. unsweetened chocolate
½ c. butter, at room temperature

1¼ c. sugar
4 eggs
¾ c. all-purpose flour
1 c. chopped pecans
½ tsp. salt
1 tsp. vanilla

Melt the chocolate in a double boiler. Beat the butter well and slowly add the sugar until the mixture is light. Beat the eggs vigorously. Add the melted chocolate to the butter mixture and fold in the eggs. Lightly scatter the flour, nuts, and salt over the surface and fold in thoroughly but gently. Add the vanilla.

Turn into a greased pan and bake in an oven preheated to 350° F. for 25–30 minutes, until set in the middle and the sides pull away slightly. Cut into 1½-inch squares when cool. Ice if desired.
✗ *24 squares*

Fudge Pie

Fudge Pie is not a pie, but more of a big, very delicate yet intense brownie. It has been around Southern kitchens for years, and preceded the chocolate craze of the 1970s and 80s. The minimal amount of flour and intense chocolate presages the order of fallen soufflé chocolate cakes that are the trademarks of many renowned restaurants today.

☞ Double boiler; 9-inch pie plate, buttered

• • • • • • • •

2 oz. unsweetened chocolate
½ c. butter
2 eggs
⅞ c. sugar

¼ c. all-purpose flour
¼ tsp. salt
1 tsp. vanilla
1 Tb. dark rum, brandy, or bourbon
½ c. chopped pecans or black walnuts, optional

Melt the chocolate and butter in a double boiler. Beat the eggs until foamy. Slowly add the sugar and beat well. Sift the flour and salt together. Stir into the batter gently. Add the melted chocolate, the vanilla, liquor, and nuts if desired. Stir just until smooth and pour into a well-buttered 9-inch pie plate. Bake in an oven preheated to 350° F. for 30 minutes, until the top is puffed and the center is just set. Serve with Soured Cream or ice cream. ✵ *8 servings*

PIES · TARTS · AND · SWEET · DUMPLINGS

Pie Dough

Lemon Chess Pie

Chocolate Chess Pie

Brown Sugar Pie

Pecan Pie

Cheesecake

Ginger Pear Pie

Three Seasons Pie

Sweet Potato Pie

Apple Pie

Coconut Pie

Japanese Coconut Pie

Pumpkin Ginger Pie

Vanity Pie

Osgood Pie

Rhubarb Pie

Pear, Peach, and
Apple Pie

Lemon Meringue Pie

Black Bottom Pie

Key Lime Pie

Angel Pies:
Lemon Curd and
Two Whiskey Chocolate Mousse

Apple Dumplings

Cherry Dumplings

ROLLING OUT
PIE DOUGH

Rolling out chilled pie dough requires a light and fast touch, which no one is born with but luckily is easily learned. For a 9-inch pie plate, you need 9 ounces of dough rolled evenly out to a circle with a diameter of 13½ inches. Sprinkle the rolling surface lightly with flour. If the dough is very cold, knead the edges lightly; the dough will spread evenly at the edge of the circle and not crack or tear raggedly during rolling.

Start from the center of the dough and roll out in one direction and then another to keep the circular shape. Always think: roll out, not press down. This prevents stretching the dough (which will inevitably draw up if stretched) and also avoids surface sticking. Sprinkle lightly with flour. You can pick up the dough, turn it over once or twice during rolling, always sprinkling it very lightly and evenly with flour. At no point add so much flour that the surface seems dry or caked.

When you have an even circle with a 13½-inch diameter, lightly fold the dough in half, and then again to form a quarter circle. Put the point at the midpoint of the pie plate and gently unfold. Keep the edges loose and gently work the dough into the bottom edge of the plate. Do not pull or tear the dough to work it into a close fit, or slide it over the plate's surface. Lift the dough up to get the slack required.

To crimp properly, for either a single or double pie crust, the bottom pastry should extend beyond the lip a good ½ inch all around. Trim away excess with sharp scissors, but save scraps in case you need them to repair tears.

For a single crust pie, you are ready to crimp. Brush the overhang lightly with water. Place the second knuckle of the right hand's forefinger on the plate's edge. Lift up the pastry to the left with the left hand's forefinger and press it at a 45-degree angle, turning slightly against the right forefinger. Lift up the right hand forefinger, move to the left of the crimp and repeat all around the edge. You can go back and exaggerate the folds for decoration but remember: Crimping is a purely functional, geometric exercise to reduce the greater circumference of the outer pie pastry to fit back inside the smaller pie plate so as to anchor the shell and prevent its slipping down the walls of the plate. Crimping incrementally absorbs the difference in the outer and the inner shell and prevents big lumps of dough accumulating on the outer crust. It is not magical as some would have you believe, but simply mathematical.

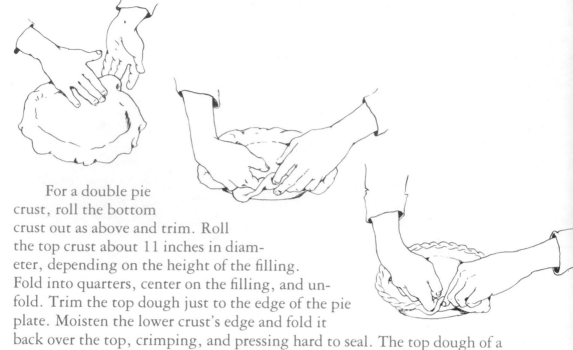

For a double pie crust, roll the bottom crust out as above and trim. Roll the top crust about 11 inches in diameter, depending on the height of the filling. Fold into quarters, center on the filling, and unfold. Trim the top dough just to the edge of the pie plate. Moisten the lower crust's edge and fold it back over the top, crimping, and pressing hard to seal. The top dough of a double crust pie will need steam vents during baking. Cut about six or eight around and a good one in the middle. Be sure these are open when you put the pie in the oven or they will immediately reseal in the oven. If the top crust is to be glazed, glaze it before cutting the vents.

Prebaking shells

The major fault with most pies is a doughy, steamed bottom crust. Prebaking the shell eliminates the problem for single crust pies. (For double crust pies, prebaking is impossible, but here is some remedy. First, use a clear glass baking dish if possible. Second, lightly, *very* lightly, butter the pie plate. Third, bake the pie in the lower third of the oven.) For prebaking single crust pies, preheat the oven to 450° F. Lightly press a piece of foil into the pie shell. Pour about 10 ounces or 1½ cups dried beans or rice into the foil to weight it down. Bake 8 minutes. Remove the foil; save the beans for another pie. Prick the bottom all over thoroughly with a fork and the sides sparingly. Return to the oven and bake 8 more minutes for a partially baked shell. Check occasionally. If the crust is puffing enthusiastically, gently prick it again and very gently press out the bubble with a clean kitchen towel. Cook about 8 additional minutes for a completely baked shell.

Examine your pie shells carefully before filling. If there are any holes or cracks through which liquid might escape, patch them with any leftover pastry trimmings. If you have no trimmings, make a thick paste of flour and water and dab on sparingly. For either repair job, return the patched pie shells to the oven for a few moments to set the paste.

Carol Dare is the Betty Crocker of North Carolina. Under this pseud-onym, a cooking column with many traditional and local recipes was pub-lished in *The State Magazine* from 1936 on. These were compiled into *The Carol Dare Cookbook* published in 1971. From it I learned the neatest dodge on pie pastry in a recipe from The Seafare restaurant in Nags Head, North Carolina. The results are not as good as with the prebaking procedure, but, if you're weekend baking away from home and you are without your stash of dried beans and rice, it works: "run this unbaked shell under the red-hot broiler for 60 seconds. This will do wonders for the crust . . ."

Pie Dough

2 c. all-purpose flour

¾ tsp. salt

6 Tb. butter, chilled

4 Tb. lard, chilled

7 Tb. cold water

Sift the flour and salt into a bowl. Cut the fats into small pieces. Rub quickly through flour, using the thumb to press the fat and flour across the fingertips with some degree of certainty. Don't dally or the fat will warm and make a greasy crust. When the mixture is fairly homogeneous, quickly work the water in using a fork or a flat wooden spoon.

Turn the dough onto a lightly floured surface and knead lightly about 3 strokes. Divide into 2 pieces, wrap, refrigerate. Chill for at least 20 minutes before rolling out. ✗ *Dough for 2 bottom crust pies or 1 double crust pie*

. . . . *Benne Seed Pie Dough or Wafers.* This is of the African heritage in Low Country and Louisiana cooking. Add hulled benne seeds to your taste— 1 to 4 tablespoons to the recipe for Pie Dough. Roll out as desired; or add a dash of cayenne, roll thinly, sprinkle with coarse salt, cut into strips, and bake as for wafers.

Lemon Chess Pie

Chess pie is the classic Southern pastry, rich, sweet, and intense. The name is a corruption of cheese, for in the British culinary tradition eggs and cheese share the same terminology — witness curd for a lemon custard. The *Oxford English Dictionary* says a cheesecake is "a cake or tort of light pastry, originally containing cheese; now filled with a yellow butterlike compound of milk-curds, sugar, and butter, or a preparation of whipped egg and sugar." The Southern version is the latter. But perhaps the occasional inclusion of a bit of buttermilk is a vestige of the former with its milk-curds. The recipe is so simple and reliable I suspect it has always been either and both in the same kitchen with the same cook, the variable being the pantry. At any rate, the buttermilk and cornmeal make this pie distinctly Southern. Many Southern cooks insist it is not chess pie at all without the cornmeal.

The custards are generally flavored three ways. The classic chess pie is pointed up with vanilla and/or nutmeg. Lemon chess, perhaps the favorite, receives just enough citrus flavor to name, but not dominate, the custard. Chocolate chess is the rich choice. Any of these custards are often used for small tarts. Variations on the chess theme are Brown Sugar Pie, and with nuts, Pecan Pie.

4 eggs	Zest of 1 lemon
1⅓ c. sugar	3 Tb. lemon juice
Pinch of salt	Not enough nutmeg to measure
4 Tb. buttermilk	1 partially baked 9-inch pie shell
2 Tb. cornmeal	(p. 260)
½ c. melted butter	

Beat the eggs lightly, beating in the sugar. Stir in the salt, buttermilk, cornmeal, and melted butter until smooth. Flavor with lemon zest and juice, and nutmeg.

Pour the custard into the partially baked pie shell. Place in a 450° F. preheated oven, immediately reduce the temperature to 325° F., and bake until the custard is just set, but not puffed — about 35 minutes. ✗ *6–8 pieces*

Chocolate Chess Pie

Chocolate Chess Pie is a variation on the basic custard chess with one or two slight changes. It never has the cornmeal that is found in regular chess and lemon chess pies; neither is it as frequently produced, though it is known throughout the region. When my children have bake sales, this is the first item to go. Serve cold with unsweetened Soured Cream.

☞ Double boiler

· · · · · · · ·

2 oz. unsweetened chocolate
½ c. butter
4 eggs
1¼ c. sugar
¼ tsp. salt

2 Tb. all-purpose flour
2 Tb. heavy cream
1½ tsp. vanilla
1 Tb. bourbon or rum
1 partially baked 9-inch pie shell
    (p. 260)

Melt the chocolate and butter together in a double boiler. Beat the eggs lightly. Toss the sugar, salt, and flour together and stir into the eggs. Add the cream and the melted butter and chocolate. Flavor with vanilla and whiskey.

Pour into the partially baked pie shell and bake in an oven preheated to 325° F. for about 35 minutes, until the custard is set in the middle and has a slightly crusty top without excessive puffing.

✖ 6–8 pieces

Brown Sugar Pie

½ c. butter
1¼ c. lightly packed light brown
   sugar
3 eggs, beaten
1 c. buttermilk
½ tsp. salt

½ tsp. freshly grated nutmeg
Grated zest of an orange, lemon,
   or tangerine
1 partially baked 9-inch pie shell
   (p. 260)

Cream the butter, add the sugar, beat well. Combine the eggs, buttermilk, and seasonings and stir into the butter. Do not overwork. Pour into the partially baked pie shell and bake in an oven preheated to 325° F. for about 1 hour, until the custard is set. ✗ *6–8 slices*

Pecan Pie

Brown sugar and pecans are the classic Southern dessert combination; it shows up in cakes, ice creams, sauces, pralines, and most often as a pie.

☞ 9-inch glass pie pan, lightly
   buttered

♦   ♦   ♦   ♦   ♦   ♦   ♦

5 Tb. butter
1 c. lightly packed light brown
   sugar
½ c. white sugar
2 Tb. all-purpose flour

⅔ tsp. salt
4 eggs
1¼ c. pecan halves
1 tsp. vanilla
1 Tb. dark rum
Pie dough for a 9-inch single
   crust pie (p. 261)

Beat the butter until light and add the sugars slowly. Beat in flour and salt. Beat the eggs separately, just enough to make them smooth. Stir into the butter mixture, add pecan halves, vanilla, and rum. Roll out 1 piece of dough to fit into the bottom of the pie pan. Pour the filling into the pie and place in the lower part of an oven preheated to 450° F. Immediately reduce the heat to 325° F. and bake 40 minutes, until set in the middle. ✗ *8 servings*

Cheesecake

Cheesecakes of this sort are pies, belonging directly to the English tradition, and are found in the South in the areas of greatest British influence — the coastal, plantation country of Maryland, Virginia, the Carolinas, Georgia. This pie has a distinctly eighteenth-century flavor, not very sweet, just aromatic and rich. Glacéed fruits or citrus zest may be added at the cook's discretion. This is not a "New York"–style cheesecake.

¼ c. currants
¼ c. sherry
3 eggs
½ c. sugar
¼ tsp. salt
1 c. cottage cheese

½ c. heavy cream
⅓ tsp. freshly grated nutmeg
¼ tsp. cinnamon
1 c. stale bread crumbs
1 partially baked 9-inch pie shell
   (p. 260)

Put the currants with the sherry in a saucepan and warm gently. Remove from heat and let cool.

Beat the eggs lightly with the sugar and salt. Rub the cheese through a fine sieve and add to the eggs along with the cream, spices, and bread crumbs. Stir in the sherry and currants. Pour into the partially baked pie shell.

Place in an oven preheated to 450° F. and immediately reduce the temperature to 325° F. Bake about 30 minutes or until the custard is set, lightly browned, but not puffed. This pie is better served at room temperature or slightly chilled than warm. ✘ *6–8 pieces*

Ginger Pear Pie

Ginger and pears meet up a lot in Southern cooking, mostly in chutneys, pickles, and preserves. Their partnership is equally assured in this pie, and the relatively light-handed approach produces a fruit pie that, when following a heavy holiday meal, doesn't stifle or stuff. The tangerine, much neglected in most American and European kitchens, provides a traditional tone for the winter holidays and an exotic one for those who visualize North African shores on a whiff of the tangerine's aromatic oils.

☞ 9-inch glass pie pan, lightly buttered

• • • • • • • •

6 c. sliced pears, about 2¼ lbs. whole
½ c. plus 1 tsp. sugar
1¾ Tb. cornstarch
⅛ tsp. salt
2 Tb. finely chopped crystallized ginger

Juice of ½ lemon
1 tsp. tangerine zest
Pie Dough for a 9-inch double crust pie (p. 261)
3 Tb. butter
1 egg
1 Tb. water

Put the sliced pears in a bowl. Combine the ½ cup sugar, cornstarch, and salt and sprinkle over the pears. Toss well and season with ginger, lemon, and tangerine zest. Set aside for 15 minutes while you roll out 1 piece of dough to fit into the bottom of a pie pan. Roll out the second piece.

Fill the pie with the fruit, dot all over with bits of the butter, and moisten the edges of the bottom crust with water. Cover with a top layer of dough, crimping or pinching to seal.

Glaze the pastry, if you like, with the egg well-beaten with water and brushed on evenly and lightly. Sprinkle the teaspoon sugar over all, again if you like. Cut steam vents in the top crust. Bake in the lower third of an oven preheated to 350° F. for about 45 minutes or until the top crust is golden. ✕ *6–8 servings*

Three Seasons Pie

The seasons of the South blend almost imperceptibly. Summer is tenacious and often its warmth persists until and beyond Thanksgiving. By holiday time, when we're thinking mostly about cranberries, farms will still be bringing out the last of the hard green tomatoes that Southern cooks only, it seems, appreciate. This pie combines them with the fall's pears and the winter holidays' cranberries for a confection that looks both forward and back.

Southerners embrace condiments of every sort and a delicious one can be made from this recipe. Use 1½ tablespoons cornstarch instead of flour. Add good, hot curry powder and a little salt to taste during the last few minutes of cooking. Serve as a cold chutney, or, traditionally, as a hot chutney. An excellent choice (and good alternative to the ubiquitous cranberry sauces) for Thanksgiving and Christmas boards.

1½ lbs. green tomatoes
1½ c. sugar
1¼ Tb. minced chopped fresh
   ginger
3 good strips orange zest
2 whole cloves
2 c. peeled, roughly cut pears
   (about 4 whole pears)

2 Tb. all-purpose flour
2½ Tb. cold water
⅔ c. raw cranberries
1 partially baked 9-inch pie shell
   (p. 260)
3 Tb. plain cookie crumbs

Pare the green tomatoes with a swivel-handled vegetable peeler. Chop coarsely and, in a heavy-bottomed saucepan, combine with the sugar and ginger. Stud one piece of orange zest with the 2 cloves (for easy removal) and toss into the pot with the rest of the zest. Bring to a boil, reduce heat, and simmer, stirring occasionally for 30 minutes. Add the pears and cook a little more briskly 10 more minutes.

Dissolve the flour in the cold water. Slowly stir in about 1½ cups of the hot fruit liquid, then whisk the binder back into the cooking pot. Bring up to the boil and simmer until thickened. Add the cranberries. Cook 2 or 3 minutes and remove from the heat.

Pour the hot fruit into the partially baked pie shell. Bake in an oven preheated to 400° F. for 10 minutes. Sprinkle the cookie crumbs over the top of the pie. Bake 10 more minutes or until fruit is bubbling and crust is brown. Cool on a rack for 15–20 minutes before serving or serve chilled. ✖ *6–8 pieces*

Sweet Potato Pie

Sweet potatoes (*Ipomoea batatas*) were enormously popular in sixteenth-century Europe, especially England. Sir Francis Drake wrote: "These potatoes be the most delicate rootes that may be eaten, and doe farre exeed our passeneps or carets. Their pines be of the bignes of two fists, the outside whereof is of the making of a pine-apple, but it is soft like the rinde of a cocomber, and the inside eateth like an apple but it is more delicious than any sweet apple sugred." An apocryphal belief in the sweet potato's aphrodisiacal gifts did not hinder its consumption.

Africans in the South knew the yam (*Dioscorea alata*) from their homeland and the two tubers have become virtually interchangeable in Southern cooking. Most Southern sweet potato recipes have been developed by blacks from their traditional cuisine, but this pie with its spices and sherry would have been at home on Henry VIII's royal board.

¾ c. lightly packed light brown sugar
½ tsp. salt
1 tsp. cinnamon
½ tsp. freshly grated nutmeg
2 Tb. molasses
1½ c. mashed, cooked sweet potatoes

⅔ c. half-and-half
2 eggs, separated
6 Tb. dry sherry
1 partially baked 9-inch pie shell (p. 260)

Mix sugar, salt, cinnamon, and nutmeg. Add molasses and sweet potatoes; beat well. Stir in half-and-half, egg yolks, and sherry. Beat the whites until stiff, fold in, and pour into the partially baked pie shell. Put in an oven preheated to 425° F. Immediately reduce heat to 375° F. and bake about 35 minutes, until the pie is nicely browned and set in the middle. Serve warm or cold with whipped or Soured Cream. ✕ *6–8 slices*

Apple Pie

This pie is aromatic in the old English tradition with spices, brandy, and rosewater.

☞ 9-inch glass pie pan, lightly
    buttered

♦ ♦ ♦ ♦ ♦ ♦ ♦

6 c. peeled, cored apples
About 1 c. plus 1 Tb. sugar
Pinch of salt
¼ c. all-purpose flour
1 tsp. cinnamon

¼ tsp. freshly grated nutmeg
2 tsp. brandy
¾ tsp. rosewater
Pie Dough for a 9-inch double
    crust pie (p. 261)
2 Tb. butter
1 egg
1 Tb. milk

Very thinly slice the apples into a large bowl. Sift about ¾ cup sugar (adjust the amount to your taste), salt, flour, and spices over the fruit and stir it well. Add the brandy and rosewater. Roll out 1 piece of dough to fit into the pie pan. Roll out the second piece.

Fill the pie with the fruit, then shave the butter over the top of the fruit. Moisten the edges of the bottom crust with water. Cover with the top dough, trim it to the edge of the pan's rim, and crimp or pinch the lower dough over the edge of the top crust to seal. Beat the egg with the milk and brush it over the top of the pie. Sprinkle with the remaining tablespoon of sugar and cut vents for steam. Bake in the lower third of an oven preheated to 425° F. for 10 minutes, reduce the heat to 350° F., and continue baking about 40 more minutes, until the top is quite brown and the fruit is bubbling inside the pastry, but not overflowing. ✖ *6–8 pieces*

Coconut Pie

There's much of the West Indies in this very old recipe for Coconut Pie. Like many early Southern pies, this one has only a very thin filling. Later this recipe was enriched with cream and butter, but the delicacy of flavor in the original is lost. If you want to try the more modern version, add about 2 tablespoons softened butter and ½ cup heavy cream to the ingredients below.

3 eggs
1 c. sugar
¼ tsp. salt
1 c. fresh, grated coconut

1 tsp. orange flower water
2 Tb. white rum
1 partially baked 9-inch pie shell
 (p. 260)

Combine all the ingredients for the filling and beat well by hand. Pour into the partially baked pie shell and bake in an oven preheated to 325° F. for 25–30 minutes or until the center is just set and the top is lightly browned. Do not overcook or let puff up. ✗ *6–8 pieces*

Japanese Coconut Pie

This is no more Japanese than the fruitcake of that name, but is simply the cake's coconut filling turned into a custard pie. It is very rich; serve in small slices with strawberries or raspberries and Soured Cream.

1 recipe Coconut Filling (for
 Japanese Fruitcake, p. 295)
3 eggs

1 partially baked 9-inch pie shell
 (p. 260)

Beat the eggs into the coconut filling. Pour into the partially baked pie shell and bake in an oven preheated to 325° F. for about 40 minutes, until the top is slightly brown but not puffed up. ✗ *6–8 pieces*

Pumpkin Ginger Pie

2 c. cooked, strained pumpkin
1¼ c. lightly packed light brown
   sugar
½ tsp. salt
1½ tsp. cinnamon
¼ tsp. freshly grated nutmeg
2 Tb. finely chopped crystallized
   ginger, plus extra for garnish

Grated zest of 1 lemon, orange,
   or tangerine
2 eggs, well-beaten
2 Tb. brandy
1 Tb. bourbon
1 partially baked 9-inch pie shell
   (p. 260)

Combine all the ingredients for the filling and beat well. Pour into the partially baked pie shell and bake in an oven preheated to 325° F. for about 50 minutes or until the center of the pie is set. Serve with lightly sweetened Soured Cream and garnish with a little crystallized ginger. ✖ *6–8 pieces*

. . . . *Variations.* Sweet potatoes or any of the meaty winter squashes can be used in place of the pumpkin. One fourth cup raisins plumped in the liquors also can be added. One cup milk or half-and-half can also be added to the filling.

Vanity Pie

A contrasting fruit sauce such as raspberry or blackberry sets off this aromatic pie. In the fall, good firm cooking pears can be used in combination with the apples.

3 eggs
1¼ c. sugar
⅓ c. stale cake or bread crumbs
2½ c. grated apple, about 3 large
   cooking apples
Juice and grated zest of 1 orange

½ tsp. orange flower water
1 Tb. orange liqueur or white
   rum
2 Tb. melted butter
1 partially baked 9-inch pie shell
   (p. 260)

Beat the eggs lightly and add the other ingredients, stirring until smooth. Pour into the partially baked pie shell and bake at 325° F. in a preheated oven about 40 minutes, until lightly browned, set, and slightly puffed. Best warm with a slightly acid fruit sauce or Soured Cream. ✖ *6–8 servings*

Osgood Pie

I wish I could tell you where the name for this deliciously rich pie comes from, but I can't. It rarely appears in cookbooks other than local collections of the lower South. Its name, its chess-type base, and its fruit and nut content all put it squarely in the English tradition. Elizabeth Sparks, who knows as much if not more than anyone about Southern cooking, says in *North Carolina and Old Salem Cookery* (1955) that this is sometimes called Osogood Pie, but I suspect that is a corruption.

⅓ c. raisins, chopped
⅓ c. currants
2 Tb. brandy
4 Tb. butter
¾ c. sugar
2 eggs, separated

1 c. pecans, chopped
1 c. grated apple, about 1 large
   cooking apple
1 prebaked 9-inch pie shell
   (p. 260)

Put the raisins, currants, and brandy in a small saucepan over low heat, cover, and let plump for about 5 minutes.

Cream the butter, add the sugar, then the egg yolks. Stir in the pecans, grated apple, and plumped fruits. Fold in the 2 egg whites, stiffly beaten. Pour into a prebaked pie shell and bake in an oven preheated to 300° F. for about 35 minutes or until the pie is set in the middle, lightly browned, and just slightly puffed. ✖ *6–8 slices*

Rhubarb Pie

My grandmother grew pie plant in her garden next to the sage. I did not know rhubarb by any other name for years. Many nineteenth-century recipes call for the pie plant as well. Most people know it combined with strawberries but that is a rather unhappy marriage to my taste. Orange and pecan set it off better.

☞ 9-inch glass pie pan, lightly buttered

• • • • • • • •

1 orange
½ c. pecans, chopped
1½ c. sugar
½ tsp. salt
¼ c. flour
1 lb. rhubarb—the red stalks only, *no* leaves
1 Tb. butter
Juice of ½ lemon
Pie Dough for a 9-inch double crust pie (p. 261)

Halve the orange, seed and chop finely, flesh and peel. Combine with the pecans, sugar, salt, and flour in a heavy-bottomed saucepan. Cook over low heat, stirring, until the orange peel is tender, about 45 minutes. Be on guard for scorching.

Wash the rhubarb stalks well and slice thinly on the diagonal. You should have about 4 cups. Add to the orange mixture, raise the heat, and cook about 5 minutes. Remove from heat, stir in butter and lemon juice, and let cool a little.

Roll out 1 piece of dough to fit into the bottom of the pie pan. Roll out the second piece. Then fill the pie with fruit, moisten the edges of the bottom crust with water, and apply the top crust, crimping or pinching to seal. If desired, glaze the top crust with an egg beaten with a little water, then sprinkle with a teaspoon of sugar. Cut steam vents in the top crust. Bake in the lower third of a preheated oven at 350° F. for 45 minutes, until the top crust is golden. ✕ *6–8 slices*

Pear, Peach, and Apple Pie

This is a winter farm pie; it ought to be served in a warm kitchen to good friends or relatives, near an open fire or wood stove, with hot coffee and Soured Cream.

☞ 9-inch glass pie pan, lightly buttered

• • • • • • •

½ c. stewed dried pears (p. 171)
1 c. stewed dried apples (p. 171)

1 c. stewed dried peaches (p. 171)
Pie Dough for a 9-inch double crust pie (p. 261)

Prepare the dried fruits and season well to your taste. Combine all three together. Roll out 1 piece of dough to fit into the bottom of the pie pan. Roll out the second piece.

Fill the pie with the fruits. Smooth out the filling, moisten the edges of the crust with water, and cover with top dough, crimping or pinching to seal. Cut steam vents in the top crust. Place the pie in the bottom third of an oven preheated to 450° F. Immediately reduce the heat to 325° F. and bake about 1 hour or until the crust is golden brown. Because dried fruits are intensely flavored, cut this pie into smaller wedges than you might ordinarily. Soured Cream is a good old-fashioned partner for this old-fashioned pie. ✗ *8 servings*

Lemon Meringue Pie

Lemon Meringue Pie has been around a long time in the South and most likely grew out of the vast repertoire of puddings, whose popularity pies eclipsed in the late nineteenth century. It is remarkably similar to the Queen of Puddings.

Lemon Pies — Take two lemons, grate away the yellow rind and chop the rest very fine. Into two teacupsful of hot water, stir well two tablespoonsful of corn-starch, and boil; add two teacupsful of white sugar; when cool, the beaten yolks of four eggs; then add the chopped lemons with their juice, stirring well together. Line two plates, pour in the material and bake until the crust is done. Beat the whites of the four eggs to a froth, adding five tablespoonsful of white sugar, pour on the pies while hot and return to the oven and bake to a delicate brown. We have never eaten any pie superior to this preparation.
— The Rural Carolinian, March 1871

3 or 4 lemons	3 eggs, separated
1⅓ c. plus 6 Tb. sugar	1¼ c. boiling water
4½ Tb. cornstarch	4 Tb. butter
¼ tsp. salt	1 prebaked 9-inch pie shell
½ c. cold water	(p. 260)

The number of lemons depends on their size. Grate enough zest to make a teaspoon. Squeeze enough juice out to measure just under ½ cup. Remove the peel and membrane from 1 whole lemon. Cut each segment of pulp from the membrane (as described for the grapefruit in Ruby Red Grapefruit Ice, p. 178) and chop the fruit, discarding the peel, seeds, and membrane. Reserve all, zest, juice, and pulp.

Sift the 1⅓ cups sugar, cornstarch, and salt together. Slowly work in the cold water, stirring constantly to dissolve the cornstarch. Add the egg yolks, lemon zest, juice, and pulp. Stirring, pour in the boiling water, and cook over low heat about 4 or 5 minutes after the boiling point is reached. Stir constantly or it will scorch. The filling should be quite thick; all taste of raw cornstarch should be gone. Beat in the butter. Set aside to cool some, stirring occasionally to let the steam escape.

Beat the egg whites to good, firm peaks with 6 tablespoons sugar. Pour the lemon filling into the prebaked pie shell. Top with the meringue, pulling it to small peaks all over the top. Brown in a preheated oven at 350° F. for about 10–15 minutes. Cool the pie on a rack. At room temperature or chilled, the pie will set up and slice neatly. While warm, it is delicious but runny. ✹ *6–8 slices*

Black Bottom Pie

Marjorie Kinnan Rawlings, author of *The Yearling*, declared Black Bottom Pie "the most delicious pie I have ever eaten." My daughter Madeline agrees. Most recipes call for a cookie crumb crust but this version uses a traditional pastry.

☞ Double boiler

• • • • • • • •

1 Tb. gelatin
¼ c. cold water
9 Tb. plus 8 Tb., plus 1 scant Tb. sugar
1½ Tb. cornstarch
⅛ tsp. salt
3 eggs, separated

1 egg
1½ c. milk
½ c. plus ½ c. heavy cream
1 tsp. vanilla
2 oz. unsweetened chocolate
2 Tb. rum
1 prebaked 9-inch pie shell (p. 260)
Semisweet chocolate

Soften the gelatin in the cold water. Mix the 9 tablespoons sugar, cornstarch, and salt well. Beat in the 3 egg yolks and 1 whole egg. Heat the milk and ½ cup cream; beat into the egg mixture and cook in a double boiler until thickened and the taste of raw cornstarch is dissipated. Off heat, add vanilla and the gelatin. Stir the custard until smooth. Melt the chocolate and add 1 cup of the custard to it. Let the remaining custard cool to room temperature. Beat 3 egg whites to a froth, slowly beat in 8 tablespoons sugar, and beat to stiff peaks. Fold into the cooled custard with the rum.

Spread the chocolate custard over the bottom of the prebaked pie shell. Pour the rum custard over and chill well, at least 6 hours, preferably more. To serve, whip the remaining ½ cup cream with the scant tablespoon of sugar to stiff peaks. Pipe 8 rosettes around the edge of the pie and shave semisweet chocolate over the cream. ✖ *8 servings*

Key Lime Pie

Key limes came from Southeast Asia and traveled through Europe to the West Indies where they were well established by 1520. The British sailors took their nickname "limeys" from the fruit. Originally, rum was believed to prevent scurvy and it was issued in staggering rations to the Royal Navy, half a British pint daily, often taken on an empty stomach. The Scottish Naval Surgeon Lind in 1752 disproved rum's efficacy and convincingly showed that citrus juice was effective in warding off the naval scourge. It was too late to retract the rum, but lemon or lime juice became the regular addition to the sailor's ration.

Lime juice, on average, contains 1½ times more citric acid than lemon juice, and the Key limes of the Florida Keys are much more tart than the hybrid Tahiti or Persian limes found in the supermarket. Most of the Key lime crop is processed for juice at harvest and it is rarely seen on the mainland United States. Unfortunately, the bottled juice always tastes stale. As to the pie's crust, it authentically is made from the traditional pie pastry, not from cracker or cookie crumbs. Though the pie enjoys current vogue, it has been a part of Conch cuisine for about one hundred years.

4 egg yolks
One 14-oz. can sweetened
   condensed milk
¾ c. fresh lime juice, preferably
   from Key limes
1½ tsp. plus 1 tsp. grated
   lime zest

1 Tb. white rum
1 prebaked 9-inch pie shell
   (p. 260)
1 c. heavy cream
4 Tb. sugar

Beat the egg yolks well. Add the condensed milk, lime juice, 1½ teaspoons lime zest, and rum. Let stand a few minutes, then pour into the prebaked pie shell. Bake in an oven preheated to 350° F. for 10 minutes. Cool to room temperature, then refrigerate.

Whip the cream with the sugar to soft peaks. Garnish the pie with the cream when serving and sprinkle a teaspoon lime zest on top for color. ✖ *6–8 slices*

Angel Pies: Lemon Curd and Two Whiskey Chocolate Mousse

Angel Pies aren't traditional pies but are meringues baked in a pie plate and filled. Southerners who are very fond of soft meringues atop their pastries sometimes call these upside-down pies. Vacherins are the more elegant versions of these desserts, but an angel pie holds up much better in our climate than the free-form vacherin. Almost any filling from Fools to ice cream to mousses shows up in these shells. They are always considered a very fancy dessert, and most hostesses have perfected a signature version of their own creation for special parties.

☞ 9-inch pie pan, well buttered

· · · · · · · ·

3 egg whites, at room
   temperature
Pinch of salt

¾ c. powdered sugar
1 tsp. vanilla extract
1 recipe filling (below)
½–¾ c. finely chopped almonds
   or pecans, optional

Beat the whites slowly at first, then increase the speed as they foam. Add the salt. Sift in the sugar slowly, gradually increasing the speed of the beating until stiff, glossy peaks form. Add the vanilla. Spread the meringue in the well-buttered pie pan, building up the sides above the edge of the plate. Bake in an oven preheated to 250° F. for about 1 hour, 10 minutes, or until crisp. Turn off the heat, leave the door ajar, and cool in the oven. ✗ *Baked shell yielding 8 slices when filled*

. . . . *Lemon Filling.* Fill the baked shell with the Lemon Mousse (p. 211) made from the Lemon Curd (p. 210). If desired, put a layer of blueberries or raspberries in the shell and cover with the mousse. Chill for at least 2 hours. Decorate the top with whipped cream rosettes, a few berries, or toasted almonds. Or serve with a fruit sauce (p. 141).

. . . . *Chocolate Mousse Filling.* This was a favorite dessert I often made at my first cooking job, preparing desserts at Chapel Hill Country Club. Fill the angel shell with the Two Whiskey Chocolate Mousse (p. 218). Chill for at least 2 hours. Decorate with whipped cream and toasted almonds or pecans.

Apple Dumplings

Baked dumplings are most often filled with apples in the South, but many other fruits can be used. Cut a blanched, peeled peach in half, stuff the cavity as below, reform, wrap, and bake in the same manner, but raise the heat to 400° F. and bake about 25 minutes. Cherries, plums, and all berries are used. The dish itself is associated with the German community of the South. The Moravian restaurant at Old Salem, North Carolina, used to offer it daily.

½ recipe Pie Dough (p. 261)

Syrup
¼ c. water
¼ c. sugar
¼ c. butter
2 cinnamon sticks

Fruit
4 small baking apples
6 Tb. lightly packed light brown sugar
6 Tb. butter
¼ tsp. cinnamon

Divide the Pie Dough into 4 pieces, wrap, and refrigerate.

For the syrup, boil the ingredients together for 5 minutes. Set aside to cool.

To prepare the fruit, peel and core the apples. Beat the sugar, butter, and cinnamon together. Pack into the apples' cavities.

To assemble the dumplings, thinly roll each piece of the pie dough to a 7-inch square. Put a stuffed apple in the middle of each. Pull each corner of the square up to the top of the apple, pressing the overlapping edges together to seal. Place in a buttered baking dish. Pour over the syrup. Bake in an oven preheated to 350° F. for about 45 minutes, until the pastry is golden brown and the syrup in the pan is lightly caramelized. If the sauce has caramelized completely, dissolve it with a little water. Serve warm with whipped cream and a little of the sauce spooned over the dumplings. ✖ *4 dumplings*

Cherry Dumplings

1 recipe Pie Dough (p. 261)

Syrup

1 c. sugar
1 c. water
1 cinnamon stick
½ c. butter
Pits from the cherries

Fruit

1½ c. sugar
5 tsp. cornstarch
1½ c. pitted cherries
4 drops almond extract
4 Tb. butter, softened

Divide the Pie Dough into 8 pieces, wrap, and chill well.

For the syrup, boil together the sugar, water, cinnamon, butter, and cherry pits for 5 minutes. Strain and let cool.

Mix sugar and cornstarch well. Stir in the cherries, the almond extract, and the softened butter. Reserve.

Roll each piece of dough to a 6 × 4-inch rectangle. Put about 2 tablespoons of the fruit filling in the center of the dough. Wet the edges of the pastry with water, fold over, and press with the tines of a fork to seal. Put in a buttered baking pan. Pour the syrup over the dumplings. Bake in an oven preheated to 375° F. for about 25 minutes, until the pastry is golden brown and the syrup in the pan is lightly caramelized. If the sauce has caramelized completely, dissolve it with a little water. Serve warm with whipped cream and a little of the sauce spooned over the dumplings. ✕ *8 dumplings — 4 or 8 servings*

HOME-BAKED· CAKES

Strawberry Shortcake

Pinto Bean Cake

Oat Cake

Pineapple Filling

Jim Steele's Sausage Bread

Rosewater Pound Cake

Indian Meal Pound Cake

Mississippi Praline
Pound Cake

White Fruitcake

Cherokee Fruitcake

Japanese Fruitcake

Pecan Torte

1-2-3-4 Cake

Vanity Cake

Fresh Coconut Cake

Fluffy Icing

Pecan Cake with
Caramel Icing

Plum Upside Down

Moss Rose Cake

Lane Cake

Sunday Night
Chocolate Cake

Chocolate Icing

Lemon Sponge Cake

Robert E. Lee Cake

Coconut Cream

Mt. Airy Chocolate
Soufflé Cake

Angel Food Cake

Snowballs

Chocolate Angel
Food Cake

Angel Cake Fantasies

SOUTHERN CAKES

One can't find much trace of native cookery in the traditional Southern cakes. There is a Pinto Bean Cake in both Afro-American and Indian kitchens and it is probably a hybrid of those two cultures. This cake also shows a good deal of the English influence in its wine and spices. The result is a prime example of what Southern cooking really is — a blend of Native American, African, and European ingredients and techniques adapted to a new, and often pioneer, setting.

I have included a little Oat Cake, most likely a bannock originally, which is a product of the settlers from Scotland throughout the Piedmont and mountain regions (kilts are still seen on Sundays outside Charleston's Scots' Presbyterian church). The sausage bread cake — Jim Steele's Sausage Bread — is a Tennessee and Kentucky specialty. It is the pioneer adaptation of traditional English suet and fruit cakes, using what the settlers had: pork sausage. Strawberry Shortcake starts with a rich buttery biscuit and should not be confused with the sugary spongecakes that go under its name today.

The traditional English pound cake was the heart of Southern desserts for hundreds of years. Extended, sweetened, brandied, it became fruitcake, white and dark, and developed into specifically Southern types such as the Mississippi Praline Pound Cake, rich in the classic Southern combination of brown sugar, bourbon, and pecans. Pecans also replaced the usual almond in tortes to create a creole cake — a Pecan Torte — rich and mysteriously light at the same time like its European counterparts.

Baking powder was the agent that revolutionized Southern cake making. Once it became reliable, cooks experimented widely and, around the turn of the century, created a number of extravagant cakes — Japanese Fruitcake, Lane Cake, Lady Baltimore, Moss Rose Cake. Cooks were smitten with the airy and fine crumbed qualities of the baking powder layers but did not want to lose the richness of the old English-style cakes. The fruits and nuts went into dense fillings between the layers instead of into the batter. The whole cake was usually enveloped in some very light and white icing. Cakes of this sort are still coming out of Southern kitchens. German chocolate cake is a twentieth-century version.

The egg-leavened cakes are, to my taste, the best. The Robert E. Lee Cake has been around for ages, but in the South it took the General's name when his fancy for it became well known. It has that widespread but still curious British/West Indies blend of a traditional Lemon Curd and tropical components; like all the best of Southern cooking, it is the meeting ground of experimentation between centuries-old traditions and New World discoveries.

A letter on cake making.

My dear Beck: I was afraid you would not understand about the cakes. Your mother sent word by Jesse. you must send the materials for the plum-cake *over to Aunt Kate's, and let Aunt Betsey go over there and make it under Aunt Kates supervision.*

The citron cake, of course cannot be made before tomorrow but you must have the materials for it prepared today — the almonds blanched and dried, the citron half of it sliced thin, and the other chopped fine. Be sure to remember to send to the Depot at 11 oclock in the morning for the cocoanuts. The lemon cake, sister Annie said she would have made when she got back and send you the receipt. Goodby, am up to my eyebrows in icing — so no wonder if my letter sound uncommon sweet — Yours always — Katey K———, The Cameron Collection, University of North Carolina

Strawberry Shortcake

🐚 *Have your berries culled and quite ready for serving, and as cool and fresh as possible. Bake two shortcakes the size of a breakfast plate, and half an inch thick: mix as you would for pie crust. The moment they are cooked, split them open, butter on both sides of each half cake, spread the berries generously and sugar them plentifully, until you have three layers of berries alternating with the shortcake. On the top half-cake put no berries, put only butter and sugar. Pour a cup of rich cream over the top, and eat immediately, cutting the cake as you would a pie. If you cannot procure cream, do not attempt milk as a substitute; be content with butter and sugar. This should be prepared in as rapid a manner as possible.*
— *The Rural Carolinian*, May 1873

This is the classic Strawberry Shortcake as it used to be practiced in the South, and it is superior to any of the extravagant, overly sweetened and enriched versions of today.

☞ Baking sheet, about 11 × 17 inches, lightly buttered

• • • • • • • •

1 egg
¾ c. milk
½ c. heavy cream

For the Shortcake

3 c. all-purpose flour
3 Tb. sugar
4 tsp. baking powder
¾ tsp. salt
¾ c. butter

To Assemble

Unsalted butter
4 c. sliced strawberries
1 c. heavy cream
Sugar, to taste

Sift flour, sugar, baking powder, and salt together. Work the butter through with the fingertips. Beat the egg, milk, and cream together and stir into the dough. Turn out on a lightly floured surface and give the dough a very light kneading, 8–10 quick strokes. Divide into 2 portions. Shape into 8-inch rounds about ⅔-inch thick. Transfer gently to the lightly buttered baking sheet. Prick about 8 times with a fork. Bake about 18 minutes in an oven preheated to 450° F., until light brown.

The shortcake is only a rich butter biscuit. It must be warm when served, though it is easier to bake the biscuit and let it cool on a rack before splitting. Slice, add sugar to, and stand the strawberries at room temperature for about 30 minutes before assembling.

When cooled, split each biscuit and spread each layer with unsalted butter. Return the biscuits to a 250° F. oven and heat gently. The butter should not melt to the point of greasiness but should remain warm, soft, and creamy. Assemble the shortcake by generously spreading strawberries over each split layer as you stack them. Top with the last layer of biscuit. Then whip 1 cup cream lightly with about 1½ tablespoons of sugar and get a child to pour it over. He or she will delight in the luxurious fall of cream over the precipitous cliffs of cake and berries. ✗ *8–10 servings*

Pinto Bean Cake

This recipe is an adaptation of Mrs. Selena Robinson's cake. She was a famous cook from Brevard, North Carolina, and said this was a cake to make from leftovers. It is a prime example of the creativity of black cooks who often worked with a limited pantry. There are many Afro-American pinto bean–based desserts, other cakes, many pies, but this is one of the very best of the lot. Mashed sweet potatoes or pumpkin can replace the beans — both of which would make a cake more nutritious than is usually found at dessert time.

☞ 9-inch diameter tube pan, greased and floured

• • • • • • • •

2 c. raisins
2 c. finely chopped raw apple
¼ c. dry sherry, scuppernong wine, or bourbon
½ c. butter, at room temperature
⅞ c. sugar
1 egg

1½ c. drained, pureed pinto beans
1½ c. flour
¾ tsp. salt
1 tsp. baking soda
1 tsp. cinnamon
1 tsp. powdered allspice
½ c. chopped pecans
2 tsp. vanilla

Toss the raisins and apple together with the sherry and set aside.

Cream the butter well and add the sugar slowly. Beat in the egg until quite light and add the bean puree slowly. Sift the flour, salt, soda, and spices together. Lightly fold into the batter. Stir in the pecans, then the fruit with its liquor and the vanilla extract.

Pour into the tube pan and bake about 1 hour in an oven preheated to 350° F., until golden and the sides pull away. Cool 15 minutes on a wire rack, then invert to turn out. ✗ *16 slices*

Oat Cake

German and Scotch Irish settlers of the Piedmont Carolinas and Virginia added oats to the Southern pantry of cereals. This simple old-fashioned cake refers readily to its highland homeland. In the winter it is welcome simply toasted and served with butter. In summer, serve it just warm with fresh raspberries and whipped cream. As a child, my favorite way to eat such a cake was to split a piece and layer it well with mashed ripe bananas, then refrigerate it for 3 or 4 hours until the cake mellowed. It was, of course, topped with cream. The whole preparation was one of those innocent rituals of childhood, curiously performed only on Sunday afternoons. Another variation for weekend dress for this basic torte is the pineapple filling that follows the recipe. Split the cake and fill it a day before serving.

☞ 9½-inch springform pan, greased

• • • • • • • •

4 Tb. butter, at room temperature
1 c. sugar
3 eggs, separated

½ c. buttermilk
2 c. uncooked oatmeal
1 c. all-purpose flour
⅛ tsp. salt
1½ tsp. vanilla
1½ tsp. orange flower water

Cream the butter and sugar until very light. Add the egg yolks, one by one, beating well. Add the buttermilk and beat until smooth. Fold in the oatmeal, flour, and salt. Beat the egg whites until stiff. Fold into the batter in thirds. Stir in the flavorings. Pour into the greased springform pan and bake 1 hour, until golden brown, in an oven preheated to 325° F. Cool on a rack. ✗ *6–8 slices*

Pineapple Filling

1 lb. fresh pineapple (peeled and cored)
¾ c. lightly packed light brown sugar
¾ c. water

2 tsp. diced orange Pamelas (p. 129) or glacéed orange peel
1 Tb. apricot preserves
1 Tb. currants
2 Tb. finely chopped pecans

Finely chop the pineapple removing any fibrous brown bits. Put into a saucepan with all the other ingredients. Bring to a boil, reduce heat, and simmer slowly for about 1 hour or until thickened. Add more water if necessary to prevent sticking. ✗ *1½ cups*

Jim Steele's Sausage Bread

Jim Steele, a friend through food, from Winston-Salem, North Carolina, sent me a recipe a few years back noting: "This 'bread' really ends up like a sort of fruitcake. I got this recipe from a friend and modified it to my liking. It may not sound too tasty, but I think it's absolutely delicious. I have served it to friends at work. Very few people could taste the sausage. For some reason I think the flavour is quite distinct. I have never made a bad loaf of this." This is his recipe verbatim. It works and smacks curiously of the old style of recipe writing.

½ cup currants (you may use raisins, but these plump better)
1 pound Neese's red hot sausage (I like this brand best)
1½ cups brown sugar
1½ cups white sugar
2 eggs
1 cup chopped walnuts (you may use pecans, I never have)
3 cups flour
1 teaspoon spice blend*
1 teaspoon baking powder
1 cup cold coffee (for goodness sakes, don't consider instant!)
1 teaspoon baking soda
½ cup chopped fruit (I almost forgot this)

Simmer the fruit — all of it, currants, too — in enough water to cover for five minutes to plump it up. Five minutes should do. Drain it. Mix up the sausage, sugars, and eggs. Stir in the nuts and fruits. Mix up the flour, spices, and baking powder. Stir the baking soda into the coffee. Blend the coffee and flour mixture into the sausage mixture. Pour all of this into a greased, floured nine inch tube pan. (I always use a bundt pan.) Bake this at 350 degrees for an hour and a half. Oh, yes, I forgot one thing, add a good shot of Jack Daniels or bourbon if you prefer. This goes in with the fruit right after you drain it.

* Spice blend consists of cinnamon, coriander, nutmeg, allspice, powdered cloves, ginger and mace in decreasing quantities. Mix this up to your pleasure.

Rosewater Pound Cake

Rosewater is an ancient flavoring and perhaps the most delicate in baking. Today when we bring roses inside, we put them in a vase, but in times past the flowers, leaves, and hips were all considered essential to good health.

Culpeper's Complet Herbal of the mid-seventeenth century has five-and-a-half pages of rose concoctions to cover almost any ailment from headaches to backaches. A rose hip conserve "mixed with *aromaticum rosarum,* is a remedy for those who faint, swoon, or are troubled with weakness and tremblings of the heart, it strengthens both it and a weak stomach, helps digestion, stays casting, and is a preservative in the time of infection" and so on. For a modern learned discussion of the rose, see *Rose Recipes* by Eleanor Sinclair Rohde (1939).

Children love the rose and are enchanted by cooking with rosewater, especially in winter. Little girls can splash some on their wrists for perfume while adding it to the batter of a pound cake. Since pound cake is such a valuable staple and so easily committed to memory, I think it a good idea that the young get it down early on. Children can measure much more accurately (as can we all) by weight rather than volume; mine go wild with the opportunity to play mad scientist; it takes only a set of scales to turn the kitchen into their laboratory.

This is really a half pound cake, and if you have kitchen scales, weigh out the sugar, butter, flour, and eggs (without shells) to ½ pound each. Have all ingredients at room temperature.

☞ Loaf pan of 7 cups volume, buttered and lightly floured

• • • • • • • •

1 c. butter, at room temperature (½ lb.)
1 c. sugar (½ lb.)
4 egg yolks, at room temperature

⅜ tsp. salt
1⅔ c. all-purpose flour (½ lb.)
2 Tb. rosewater
2 Tb. brandy
5 egg whites, at room temperature

Beat the butter until very light, then add the sugar slowly. Beat in the egg yolks one by one, beating very well after each addition, until the whole mixture is fluffy. Beat in the salt, then lightly but thoroughly stir in the flour. Add the flavorings, then beat the egg whites until stiff. Fold one third of the whites into the batter thoroughly to lighten the whole, then carefully and lightly fold in the remaining whites. Pour into the buttered and lightly floured loaf pan and bake in an oven preheated to 325° F. for 90 minutes or until a straw inserted in the middle comes out clean. ✖ *12 servings*

Indian Meal Pound Cake

This American adaptation of the classic English cake was baked all over the South, judging from the published recipes. It has nice old-fashioned flavors, a distinctive crumb, and an enticing aroma.

☞ Loaf pan of 7 cups volume, approximately 9 × 5 × 3 inches, buttered and floured

♦   ♦   ♦   ♦   ♦   ♦   ♦   ♦

1 c. butter, at room temperature
1 c. sugar
Grated zest of 1 orange
6 eggs, separated, at room temperature

¾ tsp. whole coriander seeds
½ tsp. freshly grated nutmeg
½ tsp. salt
¾ c. flour
1 c. cornmeal
1 Tb. sherry
1 Tb. bourbon
1 Tb. brandy

Beat the butter until very light, then add the sugar slowly with the grated zest. Beat in the egg yolks one by one, beating well after each addition until the whole mixture is fluffy.

Grind the coriander seeds in a mortar and pestle. Sift together with the nutmeg, salt, flour, and cornmeal. Stir into the butter and eggs. Flavor with the sherry, bourbon, and brandy. Beat the egg whites until stiff. Fold one third into the batter thoroughly to lighten, then carefully and lightly fold in the remaining whites.

Pour into the buttered floured loaf pan and bake in an oven preheated to 325° F. for 90 minutes or until a clean straw inserted in the middle of the cake comes out clean. ✖ *12 servings*

Mississippi Praline
Pound Cake

☞ 9-inch diameter tube pan,
    buttered and floured

• • • • • • • • •

1½ c. butter, at room
    temperature
1¾ c. lightly packed light
    brown sugar
6 eggs, separated, at room
    temperature
½ tsp. salt
½ tsp. baking powder
½ tsp. baking soda

3 c. flour
⅞ c. buttermilk
1 tsp. vanilla
1 Tb. bourbon
1 c. chopped pecans
½ c. white sugar

Bourbon Glaze
½ c. light brown sugar
¼ c. butter
2 Tb. water
¼ c. bourbon

Beat the butter until very light and gradually beat in the brown sugar. Add the egg yolks one by one. Sift salt, baking powder, soda, and flour together. Add to the butter mixture in 3 parts, alternating with the buttermilk. Stir in vanilla, bourbon, and pecans. Beat the egg whites until frothy and slowly add the white sugar. Beat until stiff peaks form. Fold into the batter, turn into the greased and floured tube pan. Bake in an oven preheated to 325° F. for about 1 hour, 15 minutes, or until a clean straw inserted in the middle of the cake comes out clean. Let cool 15–20 minutes then invert to turn out.

For the glaze, melt the brown sugar, butter, and water together and bring to the boil. Remove from heat. When lukewarm, stir in the bourbon. Spoon the bourbon glaze slowly over the cake while it is still warm. ✖ *12–15 servings*

White Fruitcake

Hundreds of White Fruitcake recipes were passed around and printed in the nineteenth century, and they are — almost all of them — restrained and elegant. Some combination of citron, almonds, and coconut figures in them, and only once in a while, a few currants. Most of these cakes are no longer in our repertoire. The few recipes that resemble the originals, often in name only, are found in community cookbooks and may call for pecans, cherries, dates, and so forth; they look more like the dark or black fruit-cakes that are still baked for the winter holidays. Or they used to be. In as conservative a Southern city as Savannah, the 1980 *Savannah Style, A Cookbook* offers recipes for Black Forest Cherry Cake, Italian Cream Cake, and Crème de Menthe Brownies, but none for fruitcakes.

Most White Fruitcakes omit the yolks of the eggs, but I like very much an old Virginia recipe using both whites and yellows. If you compare it to the Rosewater Pound Cake, this recipe is clearly only a gussied up pantry staple. If you want to omit the yolks, use about 16 egg whites total. Either way, the cake keeps well wrapped in cheesecloth or foil and stored airtight in a cool place. It should age at least 3 days before serving.

☞ 2 loaf pans of 7 cups volume, approximately 9 × 5 × 3 inches, buttered and lightly floured

• • • • • • • •

2 c. butter, at room temperature
2 c. plus 2 Tb. sugar
8 egg yolks, at room temperature
¾ tsp. salt
3 c. flour

1 c. blanched almonds, ground
1 c. finely chopped citron
1 fresh coconut, grated, about 3 c.
¼ c. rosewater
¼ c. brandy
½ c. coconut liquid
10 egg whites, at room temperature

Beat the butter until very light and add the 2 cups sugar slowly. Beat in the egg yolks one by one, beating very well after each addition until the whole mixture is fluffy. Add the salt, and stir in the flour lightly. Add ground almonds, citron, and grated coconut. Pour the liquids over all and stir through. Beat the egg whites with the 2 tablespoons sugar until stiff. Fold one third of the whites into the batter thoroughly to lighten the whole, then carefully and gently fold in the remaining whites.

Divide the batter between the 2 buttered and lightly floured loaf pans. Bake in an oven preheated to 300° F. for 1 hour, 50 minutes, until the tops are nicely browned and a clean straw inserted into the middle of the cake comes out clean. ✖ *30–40 servings*

Cherokee Fruitcake

☞ 2 buttered loaf pans of 7 cups
  volume, approximately 9 × 5
  × 3 inches, bottoms lined with
  parchment or brown paper

◆ ◆ ◆ ◆ ◆ ◆ ◆ ◆

2 c. pecans
1 c. chopped glacéed cherries
1 c. chopped glacéed orange
1 c. chopped glacéed pineapple
1 c. chopped glacéed citron

1 c. chopped glacéed pear
1 c. currants
½ c. plus 1½ c. all-purpose flour
1 c. butter, at room temperature
1 c. sugar
4 eggs, at room temperature
⅛ tsp. salt
1 tsp. baking powder
¼ c. plus ½ c. brandy
1½ Tb. rosewater

Combine pecans and all the fruits in a large bowl and toss with
½ cup flour.

Beat the butter until it is very light and fluffy and slowly add
the sugar. Beat well, then add the eggs, one by one, again beating
well after each addition until the whole mixture is fluffy. Sift the
1½ cups flour, salt, and baking powder together and stir into
the butter mixture. Add the brandy and rosewater and pour over
the fruits and nuts. Fold together thoroughly. Turn into the 2 loaf
pans, well buttered and lined with parchment or brown paper in
the bottom. Bake in an oven preheated to 300° F. for about 1 hour,
40 minutes, until the tops are quite brown and the edges pull
slightly away from the pan.

Cool for 20 minutes, invert, and turn out. Discard the baking
paper. When the cakes are quite cool, sprinkle the tops and bottoms
well with brandy, about ¼ cup or more for each cake. Wrap in
cheesecloth and store in an airtight tin or box in a cool place. The
cakes can be eaten after a few days, but are much better left to cure
for a month. Sprinkle with brandy each week if desired.

To serve, slice very thinly. Fruitcake is a delicious accompaniment to the elegant, subtle Charlottes, Bavarian Creams, and
Milk Punch Ice Cream, but it should always be served as very small,
thin slices to entice, not overwhelm, the eater. ✖ *30–40 servings*

Japanese Fruitcake

Japanese Fruitcake is an exotically named, typically Southern dessert cake, especially popular in the twentieth century. This same cake was once called Oriental cake, but there is nothing of the Far East about it, except the spices, none of which is Japanese in origin. Like Lane Cake and Lady Baltimore, Japanese Fruitcake is one of the Edwardian dessert extravaganzas with its rich fruit and nut fillings hidden under mounds of fluffy white icing.

☞ Four 9-inch cake pans, greased and floured

• • • • • • • •

The Cake Layers
1 recipe 1-2-3-4 Cake (p. 297)
  with the additions noted below
¼ c. brandy
1 tsp. cinnamon
½ tsp. powdered cloves
1 tsp. powdered allspice
½ c. chopped raisins
½ c. chopped pecans

Coconut Filling
1 medium coconut
1½ c. sugar
2 Tb. cornstarch
Pinch of salt
2 lemons, grated zest and juice

• • • • • • • •

Whipped cream *or* Fluffy Icing
  (p. 299)

Prepare the 1-2-3-4 Cake batter. Stir in the brandy. Divide the batter into two batches. Fill 2 greased and floured 9-inch cake pans with one batch. To the other batch add the spices, raisins, and nuts. Pour into the other 2 pans and bake all for 30 minutes in an oven preheated to 350° F., until the tops are just golden brown and the edges pull slightly from the sides of the pan. Cool on a rack and turn out.

For the filling, drain the juice from the coconut and reserve. Crack the coconut, discard the outer shell, and pare away the brown skin. Grate the meat and add to a saucepan with 1½ cups sugar. Measure the liquid from the coconut. If necessary, add water to make up ¾ cup liquid and stir into the saucepan. Bring to boil and cook about 5 minutes. Dissolve the cornstarch in 2 tablespoons of coconut liquid if you have it, or water. Add some of the hot liquid to the cornstarch slurry slowly, stir about, and stir back into the pot, stirring. Continue to cook at the simmer 3 or 4 more minutes. Season up with a few grains of salt and lemon zest and juice. Set aside to cool, stirring occasionally.

To assemble, start with a dark layer. Spread with one third of the coconut filling. Alternate light with dark. Ice the outside of the cake with whipped cream or Fluffy Icing. The finished cake is sometimes sprinkled with more coconut. ✖ *16 servings*

Pecan Torte

This old creole recipe is a superb blend of European technique and new world ingredients; the rich pecan layers end up amazingly light. Usually this cake is served stacked, with whipped cream between the layers and on the outside. Fresh fruits, lightly sweetened, can be placed between the layers. An extra surprise is two fruits, one for each layer of filling. Strawberries, raspberries, blueberries, peaches, figs are our usual progression of summer fruits, and it's fun to use them for this cake as their seasons overlap.

Sometimes the layers aren't assembled or iced at all, but simply cut into six pieces each, eighteen in all, and the wedges are served with cream, custard, and/or fruit. Another way is to spread each layer with melted semisweet chocolate, then ice with whipped cream. The torte batter can also be cooked in a jelly-roll pan on parchment paper. Cook at 400° F. for about 12 minutes or until the center of the cake springs back under a light touch. When baked, turn the cake out onto a sugared towel and roll up. Let cool, unroll, discard the paper, and spread with melted chocolate, whipped cream, and peaches, or lemon mousse and blueberries. Reroll and slice; it will make 12–15 servings.

☞ Three 9-inch cake pans, buttered, bottoms lined with buttered parchment or brown paper

3 c. finely ground pecans
2½ Tb. flour
1 tsp. baking powder
Pinch of salt

6 eggs, separated, at room temperature
1 c. plus ½ c. sugar

1 tsp. vanilla
Whipped cream, barely sweetened

Beat the egg yolks until very light and doubled in volume. Add 1 cup sugar and continue beating until almost tripled in volume.

Toss the ground pecans with the flour, baking powder, and salt. Fold the beaten yolks in the nut mixture. Beat the egg whites until frothy. Slowly add the ½ cup sugar and beat to stiff, glossy peaks. Fold into the batter along with the vanilla.

Pour the batter into the 3 buttered and lined pans and bake in an oven preheated to 350° F. for about 20 minutes, until brown and set in the middle. Remove to a rack to cool and turn out. Discard the paper. When completely cooled, ice between the layers with barely sweetened whipped cream. ✕ *16 servings*

1-2-3-4 Cake

1-2-3-4 Cake is the warhorse of layer cakes. A velvety crumb and excellent keeping qualities are matched to a variety of icings and fillings. Caramel and chocolate icings are favorites. Its most elegant appearance is as Vanity Cake (p. 298), with a simple lemon-apple curd filling and a dusting of powdered sugar over the top.

In theory 1-2-3-4 — 1 cup of butter, 2 cups of sugar, 3 cups of flour, 4 eggs — is a great mnemonic device but most Southern cooks have their own formulas in practice. Witness the following.

☞ Three 9-inch cake tins, buttered and floured

• • • • • • • •

1 c. butter, at room temperature
1⅞ c. sugar
4 eggs, separated, at room temperature

2⅔ c. all-purpose flour
2 tsp. baking powder
⅔ tsp. salt
1 c. milk
2 tsp. vanilla

Beat the butter until light and add the sugar slowly. Beat in the egg yolks one at a time, beating very well after each addition. This is the key to success: Beat butter, sugar, egg yolks very well until the mixture is very fluffy.

Sift flour, baking powder, and salt together. Add to the above mixture in thirds with ½ cup milk added after the first part and another ½ cup milk added again after the second. Stir in the vanilla.

Beat the egg whites until stiff and fold into the batter. Divide among the 3 buttered and floured pans and bake in an oven preheated to 350° F. for approximately 30 minutes, until the tops are just golden brown and the edges pull slightly from the sides of the pans. Let cool about 5 minutes on a rack, then invert, and turn out. Let cool completely before assembling. ✄ *Three 9-inch layers*

Vanity Cake

Vanity Cake is a refined, elegant, and understated confection. Like many Mississippi delectables, it is often and better presented at tea time rather than at the end of a meal. It needs no gilding, yet a little Custard Sauce is rarely refused. The filling itself is a lemon-apple curd which can find many other spots to fill in the kitchen. A variation on it (refer to p. 271) makes an aromatic pie. Or spread the curd over sweet cookie dough, as for Lemon Squares, to make wonderful cookies.

☞Double boiler

2 eggs
1 c. sugar
2¼ c. grated apple (about
   2 large apples)

Juice and grated zest of 1 lemon
Pinch of salt
2 Tb. butter
1 recipe 1-2-3-4 Cake (p. 297)
Powdered sugar

Combine all the ingredients in a double boiler and cook slowly, stirring constantly until the mixture is hot, thickened, and all raw egg taste is dissipated. Cool. Spread between 2 of the 3 layers of a rich, butter cake such as the 1-2-3-4 Cake or a split pound cake. Dust the top of the cake with powdered sugar put through a fine sieve. Serve with sherry or tea. ✗ *12–15 servings*

Fresh Coconut Cake

1 fresh coconut
1 recipe 1-2-3-4 Cake (p. 297),
   with changes noted below

1 recipe Fluffy Icing (below)

    Pierce 2 of the 3 eyes of the coconut and collect the liquid in a cup. Replace up to ½ cup milk in the 1-2-3-4 Cake with up to ½ cup coconut liquid. Otherwise, follow the recipe. If there is any more coconut liquid, use it in place of the water in the Fluffy Icing recipe.

    Crack the coconut, remove the dark skin and grate it.

    Assemble the cooled layers with a layer of icing and fresh coconut between. Ice the top and sides of the cake and cover heavily with coconut. ✕ *12–15 servings*

Fluffy Icing

    Fluffy Icing is classically known as an Italian meringue. It is perfectly easy to execute as long as one understands that the syrup must be hot enough to cook the egg whites as it is added. It can be flavored in a variety of ways according to one's taste or the nature of the cake. Raisins, currants, nuts, and coconut can be stirred in at the last minute.

1 c. sugar
⅓ c. water
¼ tsp. cream of tartar
Pinch of salt
2 egg whites

1 tsp. lemon juice, 1 tsp. vanilla,
   or ½ tsp. almond extract,
   brandy, rum, bourbon,
   whatever is appropriate to
   the cake
½ c. chopped raisins, currants,
   or pecans, optional

    Combine sugar, water, cream of tartar, and salt in a saucepan; bring to a boil and cook 5 minutes. Beat the egg whites until frothy. Continue to beat and slowly pour the very hot syrup over the whites. Continue beating at high speed to form stiff, glossy peaks. Flavor according to the cake. Add fruit or nuts if desired. ✕ *Enough to frost top and sides of three 9-inch layers*

Pecan Cake with
Caramel Icing

These very light layers are topped with what is probably the South's most beloved icing, caramel. Caramel-covered cakes are strictly special-event desserts — for Sundays, holidays, birthdays. A friend told me of a dowager in Charlotte, North Carolina, who threw her own birthday party every year. It was the same party she had as a child, when she decided it was perfect, so she repeated it for more than eighty years with pony rides, balloons, and a promenade of all the guests. Her cake, for eighty years, was iced with caramel.

☞ Three 9-inch cake pans, bottoms lined with parchment paper, buttered and floured; candy thermometer

⁜ ⁜ ⁜ ⁜ ⁜ ⁜ ⁜ ⁜ ⁜ ⁜

Layers

4 eggs, separated, at room temperature
1 c. lightly packed light brown sugar
½ c. half-and-half cream
2 c. all-purpose flour
1½ tsp. baking powder
⅔ tsp. salt
1½ c. ground pecans
1 tsp. vanilla

Syrup
½ c. sugar
½ c. water
¼ c. bourbon

Caramel Icing
2 c. brown sugar
1 c. heavy cream
Pinch of salt
3 Tb. light corn syrup
6 Tb. butter

Beat the egg yolks until very light. Slowly beat in the brown sugar, then the half-and-half. Sift the flour, baking powder, and salt together. Toss with the nuts and fold into the yolk-sugar mixture. Beat the whites until stiff peaks form and fold into the batter along with the vanilla.

Divide the batter among the 3 pans lined with parchment paper, buttered, and floured. Bake in an oven preheated to 350° F. for about 20 minutes, until the sides pull away and the center is set. Cool on a rack 5 minutes, turn out, remove paper, and cool to room temperature.

Make a syrup by boiling sugar and water together 5 minutes. Cool, add bourbon, and pour over the 3 layers.

To make the icing, put the brown sugar, cream, salt, and syrup in a heavy-bottomed saucepan and bring to the boil over high heat. Cook to 240° F., the far edge of the soft ball stage. Remove from heat and cool to 110° F. without stirring or agitating the pan. Then beat vigorously, adding the butter, bit by bit, until the icing is just about at room temperature.

Place the bottom layer of the cake on a plate and cover with caramel icing. Cover with the second layer, ice, and repeat for the third. Cover the cake with the rest of the caramel icing. ✂ *12–16 servings*

Plum Upside Down

Plum Upside Down is a beautiful dessert or coffee cake, richly colored by fresh fruits. My daughter Madeline says it looks like a stained-glass window. Almost any plum will do—even the common Santa Rosas are especially pretty; do not peel them. The outer skin has the color and the slightly bitter taste that gives depth to the flavor.

☞ 9-inch cake pan

◆ ◆ ◆ ◆ ◆ ◆ ◆ ◆

3 good-sized fresh plums
3 fresh apricots
½ c. fresh blueberries
½ c. butter, at room temperature
½ c. lightly packed light brown sugar
¼ c. water
¾ c. white sugar
1 egg
Milk, a good ¾ c.
1½ c. all-purpose flour
2 tsp. baking powder
¼ tsp. salt
½ tsp. almond extract, if desired

Wash the plums and apricots, halve them, remove the pits. Do not peel either fruit. Rinse the berries and drain them well.

Melt 2 tablespoons of the butter in a 9-inch cake pan over medium heat. Add the brown sugar and the water to the pan and bring to a boil. Remove from the heat and place the plum and apricot halves around the pan, skin side down. Scatter the blueberries in the spaces between the fruits.

Cream the remaining butter and slowly beat in the white sugar. Beat the egg in a measuring cup and add enough milk to make 1 cup total liquid. Sift flour, baking powder, and salt. Add the flour to the butter and sugar mixture, alternating with the liquid. Stir in the almond extract if desired. Pour the batter over the fruit and smooth out. Bake in an oven preheated to 350° F. for about 30 minutes or until the top is brown and well set. Cool on a rack for a few minutes, then turn out onto a plate. Pour any sauce left within the bottom of the pan over the cake, cut into 8 pieces, and serve warm. ✂ *8 servings*

. . . . *Variation.* Fresh peaches can be used in place of the plums, but skin them first by dropping into boiling water for a minute, refreshing under cold water, and rubbing gently.

Moss Rose Cake

Around the beginning of the eighteenth century descriptions of a new rose began to appear in Europe. Its sepals bore soft, downy whiskers, resembling moss. Intense hybridization began early in the nineteenth century, and the moss rose became a Victorian specialty with a catalogue of romantic French names: "Celine," "Félicité Bohain," "Marie de Blois." Moss roses are no longer widely grown, though I have the charming "Alfred de Dalmas" in my garden. A Victorian cake with its almost fuzzy outer layer of coconut was named after the moss rose; like the plant its popularity has waned, though its charm is considerable.

☞ Three 8-inch cake pans, buttered with bottoms lined with parchment or brown paper

♦ ♦ ♦ ♦ ♦ ♦ ♦ ♦

For the Layers
4 eggs, at room temperature
2 c. sugar
1 c. milk
2 c. all-purpose flour
1½ tsp. baking powder
½ tsp. salt
¼ tsp. almond extract

For the Frosting
1 recipe Fluffy Icing (p. 299)
1 orange
3 c. freshly grated coconut
2 Tb. sugar

Beat the eggs until very light and doubled in volume. Slowly beat in the sugar and continue to beat well.

Heat the milk to a little more than lukewarm. Sift together flour, baking powder, and salt. Fold the flour into the eggs in 3 parts, alternating with the warm milk in 2 parts. Add the almond extract.

Divide the batter evenly between the 3 buttered and lined pans and bake in an oven preheated to 350° F. for 20 minutes or until the tops are lightly browned and edges just pull away. Let cool a few minutes, turn out, discard paper, and cool completely on a rack.

For the frosting, prepare the Fluffy Icing and set aside. Grate the zest from the orange and add to the coconut. Peel the orange completely, cut the pulp away from the membrane, and chop it finely. Add to coconut along with the sugar.

To assemble, spread icing on each layer and sprinkle about ⅔ cup of the orange-coconut mixture over the icing. Repeat for the next layer, then ice the outside of the cake. Pat the orange-coconut mixture over the sides and top of the layers. ✖ *12–15 servings*

Lane Cake

☞ Three 9-inch cake pans, greased,
with bottoms lined with paper;
double boiler

◆ ◆ ◆ ◆ ◆ ◆ ◆ ◆

Cake Layers
1 c. butter, at room temperature
2 c. sugar
3¼ c. flour
2 tsp. baking powder
⅛ tsp. salt
1 c. milk, at room temperature
1½ tsp. vanilla
8 egg whites, at room
temperature

The Filling
8 egg yolks
¾ c. sugar
½ c. butter
1 c. chopped pecans
¾ c. chopped raisins
¾ c. grated coconut
½ c. chopped glacéed cherries
¾ c. bourbon

◆ ◆ ◆ ◆ ◆ ◆ ◆ ◆

Fluffy Icing (p. 299)

Cream the butter well and beat in the sugar. Sift the flour, baking powder, and salt 3 times. Add the flour to the butter in 3 parts, alternating with the milk added in 2 parts. Stir in vanilla. Beat the egg whites until stiff, fold into the batter. Turn into the greased 9-inch pans with bottoms lined with paper. Bake at 350° F. for about 25 minutes or until the cake's center is just set. Cool on a rack 5 minutes then turn out, remove paper, and cool completely.

For the filling, combine the yolks, sugar, and butter in the top of a double boiler and cook over simmering water until thickened and hot to the touch. Off heat stir in the nuts, fruit, and bourbon. Spread evenly between the cake layers. Cover the outside of the cake with Fluffy Icing. ✖ *A large rich cake serving 16 easily*

Sunday Night Chocolate Cake

In the South, a chocolate cake is made from white or yellow cake layers and iced with chocolate. A cake with chocolate layers usually has its own specific name, such as Devil's Food. This particular cake is a good example of the sort of dessert that shows up at church suppers where cooks are often highly competitive. It is judged by its fine and tender crumb and the smoothness of the icing. Woe be to any child who chooses a cake other than his mother's! These same layers are also covered with caramel icing and topped with toasted pecans.

☞ Three 9-inch pans, greased and
   floured

• • • • • • • •

1½ c. butter, at room
   temperature
1⅓ c. sugar
3 eggs, at room temperature
2 c. plus 2 Tb. White Lily* or
   cake flour

2 tsp. baking powder
½ tsp. salt
¾ cup milk
1 tsp. vanilla

• • • • • • • •

Chocolate Icing (opposite)

Cream the butter until light and add the sugar slowly. One by one, add the eggs, beating well after each addition, until the whole mixture is fluffy.

Sift the dry ingredients together and add to the batter in 3 parts alternating with the milk added in 2 parts. Stir in the vanilla extract and turn into the prepared pans. Bake in a 350° F. oven for 25 minutes, until the layers are golden and pull away from the edges of the pans. Let cool about 10 minutes before turning out onto a rack.

To ice, place a cooled layer on a serving plate. Cover with about one fifth of the Chocolate Icing. Place the second layer on top and spread it with another one fifth of the icing. Top with the third layer and use the remaining icing to cover the top and sides. If the icing does not spread evenly or smoothly, dip the blade of the icing knife in warm water as you ice the cake. ✄ *12–15 servings*

* *See discussion of White Lily flour (p. 42).*

Chocolate Icing

☞ Thermometer

• • • • • • • •

1¾ c. plus 2 Tb. sugar
½ c. cocoa
¼ tsp. salt
½ c. milk

½ c. butter
1 oz. unsweetened chocolate
1 tsp. vanilla
2 tsp. heavy cream

Bring the sugar, cocoa, salt, milk, and butter to full boil. Add the chocolate, broken up, and continue boiling for about 3 minutes. Let the burner cool off to 110° F. Do not stir, shake, or jostle until cooled. Beat in the vanilla and the cream. Continue beating hard for a fudgelike icing, or stop if you want a glaze. ✄ *Enough for three 9-inch layers*

Lemon Sponge Cake

Use this batter for Ladyfingers and jelly rolls and the Robert E. Lee Cake that follows.

☞ Two 9-inch cake pans, buttered
and floured

• • • • • • • •

8 eggs, separated, at room
temperature

2 c. sugar
2 tsp. grated lemon zest
2 Tb. lemon juice
2 c. flour
½ tsp. salt

Beat the egg yolks until they are very light and lemon colored. Slowly add the sugar while continuing to beat until the yolks are quite thick and tripled in volume. Beat in the lemon zest and juice. Sift the flour and salt together. Sprinkle the flour over the egg yolks and fold lightly until smooth. Beat the egg whites until stiff and fold in. Divide the batter between the 2 buttered and floured cake pans. Bake in an oven preheated to 325° F. for 25–30 minutes, until the layers are golden brown and just pull slightly away from the sides. Remove to a rack and cool about 10 minutes before turning out. ✄ *Two 9-inch layers*

Robert E. Lee Cake

Many Southern cakes and pies that carry the names of military and political heroes were not created to honor those men. Most of these confections were traditional dishes that were renamed to denote an individual's favorite. What we now call Jeff Davis pie is an old custard pie flavored with nutmeg. General Robert E. Lee was particularly fond of this cake and by the end of the nineteenth century it carried his name, though the cake itself was well known in the South long before the Civil War.

1 recipe Lemon Sponge Cake (p. 305)
1 recipe Lemon-Orange Curd (p. 211)

1 recipe Coconut Cream (below)

Split the sponge layers and stack with the curd between. Spread the top with Coconut Cream, letting it drip down the sides.
✘ *12 servings*

Coconut Cream

☞ Double boiler

Pinch of salt
¾ tsp. gelatin
1 Tb. buttermilk
Orange flower water or rosewater, optional

1 c. heavy or Soured Cream (p. 144)
¼ c. grated fresh coconut
1 Tb. plus 2 tsp. sugar

Stir the cream, coconut, sugar, and salt together in the top of a double boiler and heat gently over simmering water about 20 minutes. Dissolve the gelatin in the buttermilk. Stir into the cream and cool over ice water. Stir at first as the mixture thickens, beat more vigorously until it forms small peaks and is quite cold.

Flavor with orange flower or rosewater before cooling if desired or appropriate. ✘ *2 cups*

Mt. Airy Chocolate
Soufflé Cake

This cake, created at the restaurant Crook's Corner, takes a little from Fudge Pie, and a lot from Tot Fait. Of all the sort of fallen soufflé cakes popular now, this is lightest — not a speck of flour goes into it — and the chocolate never weighs down the batter. Mt. Airy is a North Carolina town (Mt. Pilot to television fans) famous for its traditional music and musicians. I named it for the play-on-words: air, as in music — airy — soufflé, French for a puff of wind.

☞ 9-inch springform pan;
    parchment paper; double boiler

• • • • • • • •

1 lb. semisweet chocolate
1 c. butter
6 Tb. brandy

9 eggs, separated
1 c. plus ¼ c. sugar
1 tsp. salt
1 tsp. cream of tartar
1 Tb. vanilla

Butter the springform pan. Line the bottom with parchment paper. Cut a strip of parchment paper about 30 × 5 inches and line the sides of the pan forming a collar.

Melt the chocolate and butter in the top of a double boiler. Add brandy off heat.

Beat the egg yolks until very light and lemon colored. Gradually beat in the 1 cup sugar. Fold into the chocolate mixture. Beat the egg whites with the ¼ cup sugar, salt, and cream of tartar until stiff peaks form. Fold all together with the vanilla extract.

Pour into the prepared springform pan. Bake in an oven preheated to 350° F. for 55 minutes, until the center is just set. Let cool on a rack 20 minutes. Remove the pan's walls and the paper collar. Continue to cool at room temperature; cut into 12 pieces with a knife blade dipped in warm water. Serve at room temperature with cold Soured Cream.

✖ *12 servings*

Angel Food Cake

Angel Food Cake is truly American in origin, perhaps from the Pennsylvania Dutch, and almost inexplicably popular. A readers' survey in *The New York Times* in 1988 reported Angel Food Cake as one of the most beloved and comforting foods known in this country. It is best with fresh fruit, absolutely saturated in strawberry or peach juices, and accompanied by whipped cream.

☞ 9-inch tube pan

1 c. flour
⅓ c. sugar
¼ tsp. salt
1½ c. egg whites (about 10), at
   room temperature
1 tsp. cream of tartar

1 c. sugar
Flavorings: 1 tsp. vanilla and
   ½ tsp. almond extract, *or*
   rosewater, orange flower water,
   white rum, bourbon *or*
   whatever is appropriate to the
   cake

Sift the flour, sugar, and salt together 3 times. Beat the egg whites with the cream of tartar, slowly at first, then increasing the speed. When the whites are quite frothy, slowly sift in the sugar, beating hard, until firm peaks form. Slowly sift the flour over the whites, folding constantly and gently until it is all smooth. Flavor as desired.

Turn into the ungreased tube pan and bake in an oven preheated to 325° F. for about 50 minutes, until the cake browns well and is slightly resistant to the touch. Cool inverted over a rack. Loosen sides and bottom, if necessary, with a thin knife or spatula to free the cake. Serve at room temperature. ✕ *12–15 servings*

Snowballs

Tear an Angel Food Cake (above) into balls about the size of an egg using 2 forks. Coat each ball with whipped cream and roll in freshly grated coconut. Chill well before serving. This very old and clever use of leftover or slightly stale cake is generally adored by children, especially in the heat of summer. Often it is served at birthday parties with a candle in each serving, a play on fire and ice.

Chocolate Angel Food Cake

Make the Angel Food Cake (opposite) recipe, but in place of 1 cup flour, use:

¾ c. flour   ⅓ c. cocoa

Sift flour and cocoa together 3 times. Proceed as for regular Angel Food Cake. When cool and turned out, split twice for 3 layers. Ice between layers and over outside with Two Whiskey Chocolate Mousse (p. 218). ✕ *15–18 servings*

Angel Cake Fantasies

All sorts of variations are performed on the basic Angel Food Cake, many of which resemble a trifle. The most common practice is splitting the cake horizontally and spreading the bottom with Custard Sauce, usually flavored with orange zest and/or whiskey. The top layer is replaced and the whole is iced with whipped cream and decorated with citron and almonds.

A similar "Cream Cake" is a Southern country club favorite. This is somewhere between a trifle and a Charlotte Russe.

☞ 9-inch tube pan   1 recipe Sherried Bavarian Cream
                                                  (p. 209)
½ recipe Angel Food Cake   Whipped cream, fresh fruit,
   (opposite)   almonds, optional

Tear the cake into 1-inch square chunks using 2 forks. You should have 6–7 cups. Prepare the Sherried Bavarian Cream. Just before it sets up, pour part of the cream into a clean tube pan. Layer with the chunks of cake, finishing with the cream. Refrigerate until firm, about 6 hours. To turn out, dip a long thin knife in hot water and run around the edges. Invert onto a platter. It is easier than you may anticipate. Slice and serve.

Cream cake can be iced with whipped cream; it often is and then studded with whole toasted almonds and whole strawberries or raspberries for serving. One cup of cream whipped should be enough to lightly cover the cake. I usually omit the outer icing, but layer in some fresh fruit — strawberries, peaches, figs, thinly sliced and lightly sweetened, blueberries or plain whole raspberries — with the cake. Any of the fruit sauces can be served with it as well. ✕ *15 servings*

SELECT
BIBLIOGRAPHY

Aykroyd, W. R. *Sweet Malefactor.* London: Heineman, 1967.

Bass, Tommie. *Plain Southern Eating.* Durham, N.C.: Duke University Press, 1988.

Bowes, Frederick P. *The Culture of Early Charleston.* Chapel Hill: The University of North Carolina Press, 1942.

Brown, Marion. *Marion Brown's Southern Cook Book.* Chapel Hill: The University of North Carolina Press, 1951.

Bryan, Mrs. Lettice. *The Kentucky Housewife.* Cincinnati: Shepard & Stearns, 1839.

Bullock, Helen. *The Williamsburg Art of Cookery.* Richmond, Va.: Dietz Press, 1938.

The Carol Dare Cookbook. Raleigh, N.C.: *The State* magazine, 1972.

Carson, Jane. *Colonial Virginia Cookery.* Williamsburg, Va.: The Colonial Williamsburg Foundation, 1985.

David, Elizabeth. *English Bread and Yeast Cookery.* New York: Viking, 1980.

Doar, David. *Rice and Rice Planting in the South Carolina Low Country.* Charleston, S.C.: The Charleston Museum, 1936.

Four Great Southern Cooks. Atlanta: Dubose Publishing, 1969.

Grimé, William (ed.). *Ethno-Botany of the Black Americans.* Algonac, Mich.: Reference Publications, 1979.

Grosvenor, Vertamae. *Vibration Cooking.* Garden City, N.Y.: Doubleday & Co., 1970.

Hall, Margaret Hunter. *The Aristocratic Journey.* Edited Pope-Hennessey. New York, London: G. P. Putnam's Sons, 1931.

Hardeman, Nicholas P. *Shucks, Shocks, and Hominy Blocks.* Baton Rouge: Louisiana State University Press, 1981.

Hess, Karen (ed.). *Martha Washington's Booke of Cookery.* New York: Columbia University Press, 1981.

Heyward, D. C. *Seed from Madagascar.* Chapel Hill: The University of North Carolina Press, 1937.

Hilliard, Sam Bowers. *Hog Meat and Hoecake.* Carbondale: Southern Illinois University Press, 1972.

Holmes, Francis S. (ed.). *The Southern Farmer and Market Gardener.* Charleston, S.C.: N.p., 1852.

Hooker, Richard J. (ed.). *A Colonial Plantation Cookbook: The Receipt Book of Harriott Pinckney Horry, 1770.* Columbia: The University of South Carolina Press, 1984.

Huguenin, Mary V. and Stoney, Anne M. (ed.). *Charleston Receipts.* Charleston, S.C.: Walker, Evans, & Cogswell Co., 1950.

Hammond-Harwood House Association. *Maryland's Way.* N.p. Judd & Detweiler, 1966.

Junior League of Savannah, Inc. *Savannah Style.* Kingsport, Tenn.: Kingsport Press, 1981.

Leslie, Eliza. *Directions for Cookery in its Various Branches.* Philadelphia: Carey & Hart, 1837.

Lewis, Oscar. *Life in a Mexican Village: Tepoztlán Restudied.* Urbana: University of Illinois Press, 1951.

McGee, Harold. *On Food and Cooking.* New York: Charles Scribner's Sons, 1984.

Mariani, John F. *The Dictionary of American Food and Drink.* New Haven, Conn.: Ticknor and Fields, 1983.

Marszalek, John F. (ed.). *The Diary of Miss Emma Holmes 1861–1866.* Baton Rouge: Louisiana State University Press, 1979.

Page, L. G. and Wiginton, E. (ed.). *The Foxfire Book of Appalachian Cookery.* New York: E. P. Dutton, Inc., 1984.

Parker, Cherry and Bradsher, Frances. *The Hand-Me-Down Cookbook.* Durham, N.C.: Moore Publishing, 1969.

Parris, John. *Mountain Cooking.* Asheville, N.C.: Asheville Citizen-Times Publishing Co., 1978.

The Picayune Creole Cook Book. New Orleans: The Picayune Publishing Co., 1901.

Porter, Pam Durban (ed.). *Cabbagetown Families, Cabbagetown Food.* Atlanta: Patch Publications, 1976.

Randolph, Mary. *The Virginia House-wife.* Washington: Davis and Force, 1824.

Recipe Book of Eliza Lucas Pinckney 1756. Charleston, S.C.: Charleston Lithographing Co., 1936.

Rose P. Ravenel's Cookbook. N.p. Lellyett and Rogers, 1983.

Rhett, Blanche S. *Two Hundred Years of Charleston Cooking.* Columbia: The University of South Carolina Press, 1930.

Rutledge, Sarah. *The Carolina Housewife.* Charleston, S.C.: W. R. Babcock & Co., 1847.

Service League of Lafayette, Inc. *Talk about Good, Volumes I and II.* Austin, Texas: Hart Graphics, Inc. Volume I, copyright 1979. Volume II, copyright 1969.

Simmons, Amelia. *American Cookery.* Hartford, Conn.: Hudson & Goodwin, 1796.

Simon, André L. *A Concise Encyclopedia of Gastronomy.* Woodstock, N.Y.: The Overlook Press, 1981.

Sparks, Elizabeth H. *North Carolina and Old Salem Cookery.* Kernersville, N.C.: N.p., 1955.

Tyree, Marion Cabell (ed.). *Housekeeping in Old Virginia.* Louisville, Ky.: John P. Morton Co., 1879.

Walden, Howard T. *Native Inheritance.* New York: Harper and Row, 1966.

Weatherwax, Paul. *Indian Corn in Old America.* New York: MacMillan, 1954.

Welty, Eudora. *The Golden Apples.* New York: Harcourt, Brace, 1949.

Wilcox, Estelle Woods. *The New Dixie Cook-Book.* Atlanta: L. A. Clarkson & Co., 1889.

Woman's Club Cook-Book of Southern Recipes. Charlotte, N.C.: Ray Printing Co., 1908.

Woodmason, Charles. *The Carolina Back Country on the Eve of the Revolution.* Chapel Hill: The University of North Carolina Press, 1953.

Wright, Louise W. *A Southern Girl in '61.* New York: Doubleday, Page, and Company, 1905.

INDEX

TEXTUAL ACKNOWLEDGMENTS

Grateful acknowledgment is made to the following for permission to reprint previously published material:

E. P. Dutton: Recipe from *The Foxfire Book of Appalachian Cookery.* Copyright © 1984 by The Foxfire Fund. Reprinted by permission of E. P. Dutton, an imprint of Penguin Books USA Inc.

Hammond-Harwood House Association, Inc.: Excerpts from *Maryland's Way,* The Cookbook of The Hammond-Harwood House Association, Annapolis, Maryland. Reprinted by permission.

Harcourt Brace Jovanovich, Inc.: Excerpt from "The Wanderers" in *The Golden Apples* by Eudora Welty. Copyright 1949 and renewed 1977 by Eudora Welty. Reprinted by permission of Harcourt Brace Jovanovich, Inc.

Louisiana State University Press: Excerpts from *The Diary of Miss Emma Holmes 1861–1866,* edited by John F. Marszalek. Copyright © 1979 by Louisiana State University Press. Reprinted by permission.

The Overlook Press: Excerpt from *A Concise Encyclopedia of Gastronomy* by André L. Simon. Copyright 1952 by André L. Simon. Published by The Overlook Press, Lewis Hollow Road, Woodstock, NY. Reprinted by permission.

The University of North Carolina at Chapel Hill: Selected passages from the Cameron Family Papers and selected photographs from the Odum Papers from the Southern Historical Collection, Library of the University of North Carolina at Chapel Hill. Reprinted by permission.

The University of North Carolina Press: Excerpt from *Seed from Madagascar* by Duncan Clinch Heyward. Copyright 1937 by The University of North Carolina Press. Excerpt from *Marion Brown's Southern Cook Book,* edited by Marion Brown. Copyright © 1951 by The University of North Carolina Press. Reprinted by permission.

University of South Carolina Press: Excerpts from *A Colonial Plantation Cookbook,* edited by Richard J. Hooker. Copyright © 1984 by University of South Carolina Press. Excerpts from *The Carolina Housewife* by Sarah Rutledge. Copyright © 1979 by Anna Wells Rutledge. Excerpts from *Two Hundred Years of Charleston Cooking,* gathered by Blanche S. Rhett. Copyright © 1976 by University of South Carolina Press. Reprinted by permission.

Viking Penguin: Excerpts from *English Bread and Yeast Cookery* by Elizabeth David. Copyright © 1977 by Elizabeth David. Published by Allen Lane in London. Rights in Canada administered by Penguin Books Ltd., London. Reprinted by permission of Viking Penguin, a division of Penguin Books USA Inc. and Penguin Books Ltd., London.

PHOTOGRAPHIC
ACKNOWLEDGMENTS

Photographs reproduced in this book were provided with the cooperation and kind permission of the following:

North Carolina Collection, University of North Carolina Library at Chapel Hill, Wootten-Moulton Collection: 8 (all), 9, 96 (bottom), 112 (top), 113 (both), 149 (both), 150, 202 (bottom), 232 (top)

Southern Historical Collection, Wilson Library of the University of North Carolina at Chapel Hill: 35 (both), 36 (both), 37 (both), 38 (both), 75, 76 (both), 94 (both), 95 (both), 96 (top), 203 (both), 232 (bottom), 233 (center and bottom)

North Carolina Department of Archives and History: 112 (bottom), 202 (top), 204, 232 (top)

A NOTE ABOUT
THE AUTHOR

Bill Neal was born and grew up in South Carolina. He graduated from Duke University and did graduate work at the University of North Carolina at Chapel Hill. Since 1976 he has been a restaurateur in Chapel Hill, North Carolina, cooking at La Residence from 1976 to 1981, and at Crook's Corner from 1981 to the present. His first book, Bill Neal's Southern Cooking, *was published in 1985; the revised edition, in 1989. He also edited the work of Elizabeth Lawrence in* Through the Garden Gate, *published in early 1990 by the University of North Carolina Press. He lives in Carrboro, North Carolina, and has three children.*

A NOTE ON
THE TYPE

The text of this book was set in Garamond No. 3, a modern rendering of the type first cut by Claude Garamond (c. 1480–1561). Garamond was a pupil of Geoffroy Tory and is believed to have based his letters on the Venetian models, although he introduced a number of important differences, and it is to him we owe the letter which we know as "old style." He gave to his letters a certain elegance and a feeling of movement that won for their creator an immediate reputation and the patronage of Francis I of France.

Composed by Dix Type, Inc., Syracuse, New York
Printed and bound by Kingsport Press, Kingsport, Tennessee
Designed by Stephanie Tevonian
Part title and binding illustrations by John O'Leary
Spot illustrations by Denise Dodge

KNOPF COOKS AMERICAN

The series of cookbooks that celebrates the culinary heritage of America, telling different aspects of our story through recipes interspersed with historical lore, personal reflections, and the recollections of old-timers.

"Our food tells us where we came from and who we are..."